STAFF MANAGEMENT
IN
HUMAN SERVICES

STAFF MANAGEMENT
IN
HUMAN SERVICES

Behavioral Research and Application

By

DENNIS H. REID, MARSHA B. PARSONS
& CAROLYN W. GREEN

Habilitative Management Consultants, Inc.
and
Western Carolina Center
Morganton, North Carolina

CHARLES C THOMAS • PUBLISHER
Springfield • Illinois • U.S.A.

Published and Distributed Throughout the World by

CHARLES C THOMAS • PUBLISHER
2600 South First Street
Springfield, Illinois 62794-9265

© *1989 by* CHARLES C THOMAS • PUBLISHER

ISBN 0-398-05547-5

Library of Congress Catalog Card Number: 88-29498

With THOMAS BOOKS *careful attention is given to all details of manufacturing
and design. It is the Publisher's desire to present books that are satisfactory as to their
physical qualities and artistic possibilities and appropriate for their particular use.*
THOMAS BOOKS *will be true to those laws of quality that assure a good name
and good will.*

Printed in the United States of America
SC-R-3

Library of Congress Cataloging-in-Publication Data

Reid, Dennis H.
    Staff management in human services.
    Includes bibliographies and index.
    1. Human services personnel—United States—
Supervision of.   2. Supervision of social workers—
United States.   I. Parsons, Marsha B.   II. Green,
Carolyn W.   III. Title.   [DNLM: 1. Personnel Management
—methods.   HF 5549   R354s]
HN40.54.R45   1989   361.3'068'3   88-29498
ISBN 0-398-05547-5

To our children:
Cason and Nate,
Stephen and Anna,
Joshua and Jennifer

PREFACE

A critical component in the provision of human services is the effective supervision of staff performance. In essence, supervisors in human service agencies are responsible for the work performance of the staff they supervise, with subsequent responsibility for the services staff provide to clients. Unfortunately, however, supervision is often a difficult process within human service operations. The difficulty is due in large part to the fact that many persons who work as supervisors were not formally trained to function in that capacity—most human service supervisors are former teachers, nurses, psychologists, etc. Relatedly, even in those situations where individuals have received training in supervisory practices, it is not clear that such training has provided the supervisors with strategies that are truly effective and/or realistic for managing the work activities of human service staff on a day-to-day basis.

In the early 1970s a rather unique approach to supervision began to be applied in human service settings: *organizational behavior management.* An ongoing purpose of organizational behavior management has been to develop supervisory procedures that can indeed be used to effectively manage the daily work activities of human service staff. This approach to management or supervision is best characterized by its focus on clearly articulated procedures for managing staff performance, as well as its reliance on applied research conducted in typical human service agencies to demonstrate the efficacy of the procedures. It is the purpose of this text to describe and critically review organizational behavior management research and application as it pertains to the supervision of staff performance in human service settings. Over 120 applied research investigations are discussed that have evaluated methods of improving staff work performance in a variety of human service agencies, including, for example, institutions for mentally retarded and mentally ill persons, schools, nursing homes, preschools, and mental health centers.

An important outcome of the investigations in organizational behavior management has been the gradual development of a working technology of staff management. Although the technology is by no means complete at this point, sufficient progress has occurred such that a relatively broad repertoire of strategies for effectively managing staff work performance is available for supervisory personnel. We will discuss the (developing) technology, with special emphasis on those supervisory procedures that have been successfully used to resolve noted problems with staff performance as well as on current shortcomings of existing procedures.

In light of the focus of organizational behavior management on developing supervisory strategies for improving staff work performance, and on applied research to demonstrate the effectiveness of the procedures, the information to be discussed in this text should be of particular relevance for two major audiences. One primary audience is supervisors (and aspiring supervisors) in the human services. The second audience is current and future researchers in the management field.

A portion of the research to be discussed in the following chapters is based on our own investigations in the management area and those of our colleagues. In this regard, we are sincerely appreciative of the managers with whom we have worked who have been willing to attempt new supervisory strategies by collaborating on applied research endeavors. The number of current and past colleagues is far too large to permit individual recognition here. However, many of their contributions are exemplified in the references in this text to their published works. In addition, special appreciation is expressed to Ms. Carole Daves for her patience, diligence, and competence in assisting with the preparation of the text.

Dennis H. Reid
Marsha B. Parsons
Carolyn W. Green

CONTENTS

STAFF MANAGEMENT
IN
HUMAN SERVICES

Chapter 1

STAFF MANAGEMENT AND
HUMAN SERVICE PROVISION:
AN OVERVIEW

Human service delivery represents one of the largest and most pervasive organizational systems in our society. Essentially every individual in the civilized world has been and/or will be a recipient of a human service program. Ranging from preschool programs for infants and toddlers to nursing homes for senior citizens, human service operations impact all age groups. Human service programs also affect basically all handicapped and nonhandicapped populations ranging from profoundly mentally retarded and chronically mentally ill persons in state institutions to gifted and talented youth in special school classes.

One of the most important determinants of how well human service programs fulfill their designated mission of providing helpful services to people in need is the proficiency with which human service staff perform their work. The degree to which students in a second grade classroom acquire basic academic skills is, for example, in large part dependent on how effectively the second grade teacher actually teaches his/her class. Similarly, how much habilitation a severely physically and mentally handicapped resident receives in a state institution is a direct result of the amount and quality of treatment activities provided by the institutional caregivers. The importance of staff performance in this regard has been well recognized in the professional literature (Gardner, 1973; Greene, Willis, Levy, & Bailey, 1978; Kunz et al., 1982). However, it has also been frequently noted that staff performance in human service systems often has been, at best, less than competent and, at worst, very problematic. Serious problems with staff work behavior have been highlighted in essentially every type of human service setting, including nursing homes (Sperbeck & Whitbourne, 1981), schools (Gross & Ekstrand, 1983), mental health clinics (Lovett, Bosmajian, Frederiksen, & Elder, 1983), psychiatric hospitals (Prue, Krapfl, Noah, Cannon, & Maley, 1980),

3

institutions for the mentally retarded (Realon, Wheeler, Spring, & Springer, 1986), and preschools (Kunz et al., 1982). Problematic areas of staff performance in these settings have been numerous and varied, involving such diverse topics as poor health care of dependent, institutionalized clients (Iwata, Bailey, Brown, Foshee, & Alpern, 1976), ineffective classroom teaching and management practices (Jones & Eimers, 1975), inadequate administrative performances (Repp & Deitz, 1979), excessive absenteeism (Shoemaker & Reid, 1980) and physical abuse of clients (Blatt, 1976), to name just a few of the reported problem areas.

The problems with staff performance in the human services should not be overemphasized to the point that the accomplishments in human service provision resulting from *competent* staff performance are not recognized. Clearly, many people in need have been significantly helped by the sincere and proficient efforts of staff in human service agencies. Undoubtedly, for every human service setting in which a problematic area of staff performance has been highlighted, and for every specific work problem noted, there have also been countless cases of exemplary staff performance. Nevertheless, the numerous examples of laudable staff performance notwithstanding, problematic areas that continue to exist should not be ignored — at least if human service agencies are to thoroughly fulfill their specified purpose of helping people in need.

In attempting to understand the reasons for the problems with staff performance in the human services, a misconception that often arises is a devaluation of the personnel who work in human service agencies (Reid & Whitman, 1983). That is, problematic situations in service provision are, in essence, mistakenly viewed as a function of the (poor) quality of the type of person who works as a staff member in a human service setting. Such a view not only is an insult to most human service personnel, it really represents a serious misunderstanding of the factors associated with the reported problems in human service provision. As will be discussed throughout this text, a more accurate view is that *where pervasive problems in staff performance exist, the primary cause is ineffective supervision and management.* In short, if problems in staff work activities occur in human service systems, then management personnel must be held accountable for those problems. Unfortunately, in this regard, the history of staff supervision and management practices in the human services has not been very laudable and often has set the occasion for poor work performances of human service staff.

The Development and Existence of Ineffective
Staff Management Practices

The reasons why staff management practices in human service settings have often been ineffective are varied and, at least in part, somewhat complex. However, one rather apparent reason is that usually there is not a clear and visible index of the varying degrees of effectiveness with which human service staff are expected to perform their jobs (and, consequently, how effectively managers are managing). To illustrate, in nonhuman service business and industry, there is always a bottom-line index of how well staff are performing: the profit margin. Although many variables can obviously affect whether or not a business enterprise makes a profit, in many cases serious fluctuations in a business's profit margin nevertheless can serve as a good indicator as to whether a manager should alter what he/she is doing with staff in order to change or maintain current staff performance. In contrast, in most human service agencies, there is no bottom-line profit figure with which to measure the effectiveness of an agency's management practices.

In one sense, an index within human service agencies that is somewhat analogous to the profit margin in nonhuman service businesses is *client welfare.* Typically, a human service program exists to ensure and/or improve some aspect of the welfare of the program's clients. In schools, for example, client welfare is reflected in academic learning and progress. In psychiatric hospitals, client welfare generally refers to the development of mentally healthy functioning and the remission of mental illness. In essence, any given human service can be described in terms of its goal of sustaining and/or improving client welfare, be it skill development, maintenance of good physical health, reduction of maladaptive behavior or any number of beneficial outcomes for people. However, rarely does a human service agency really *specify* what it means by client welfare to the point that a clear and visible index exists (such as a profit margin figure) of how well or poorly that welfare is being attended to by an agency's staff. Consequently, there is really no accurate and sensitive measure by which the effectiveness of staff performance can be evaluated unless an overt crisis develops such as some of the more serious problems within human service systems as exemplified earlier (at which point it becomes very obvious that there are problems with staff performance). A supervisor in a human service setting is basically left to his/her own judgment regarding whether or not staff are performing proficiently—a judgment that, because of its idiosyncratic and subjective nature, is readily susceptible to disagreement among the supervisor's peers, staff, and superiors in the organization.

In many cases, even if attempts are made to carefully delineate aspects of client welfare for which staff are responsible, a clear index of client service provision to use in evaluating staff performance still does not exist. The reason that such an index is frequently lacking is that there is not always a readily apparent outcome of staff work behavior in regard to client welfare. For example, for many seriously handicapped clients, staff must conduct therapy regimes for a number of weeks before any improvement in client functioning will be observable. Hence, on a day-to-day basis, there is no noticeable outcome to staff work performance (i.e. conducting therapy programs) to indicate how well staff perform, or even to indicate if staff did indeed complete their (therapy) assignments. In contrast, in many non-human service businesses, it is quite apparent on a daily basis whether or not staff have fulfilled respective work assignments (products, for example, either are or are not constructed, changes in physical environments either are or are not completed through staff labor, etc.).

A second reason why management practices in the human services are frequently ineffective is that it is very uncommon for a human service manager to have any preparation for functioning as a manager. Typically what occurs in human service professions is that an individual is trained to provide some type of direct service to clients and then that individual is hired, or promoted, at some time in his/her career into a managerial position. Unfortunately, the skills that are relevant for providing direct service to clients are not the same skills that are needed to supervise other human service providers. To illustrate, an individual who displays good skills in teaching physical education to elementary school students may or may not have the skills to supervise classroom teachers when the former physical education teacher is promoted to school principal. Relatedly, a psychologist who demonstrates proficiency as a clinician in treating clients at a community mental health clinic may or may not exhibit competence if he/she is employed by another clinic and charged with directing the performance of other psychologists (and social workers, psychiatric nurses, etc.). In short, supervising staff performance is a different task than providing direct client services, and most human service managers have been trained only in fulfilling the latter type of task.

A third reason for the prevalence of ineffective management practices in the human services is related to the lack of preparation of managers, as just noted. Most individuals who become managers, and who were not previously trained to function as managers, soon realize that they were not well prepared for a managerial role. As a result, many human service managers are quite receptive to learning about approaches to management that are popularly publicized. Indeed, during the 1970s and 1980s numerous human service agencies inserviced their supervisors regarding a variety of models and theories of management. Noted examples of management models that have been popularized since the 1970s and have formed the content of staff training programs include managerial grid theory (Kast & Rosenzweig, 1974, p. 323), interaction management (Developmental Dimensions, 1974), and leadership traits (Stogdill, 1974). At first glance it would seem that the availability of different approaches to staff management would be advantageous to human service managers, particularly when considering that most managers have not received formal training in supervisory practices. Unfortunately, however, there are some very significant shortcomings to the management theories and models that have been presented to human service managers since the 1970s.

The first major problem with most management models is that they do not *specify* what a manager should actually *do*. Managerial models frequently espouse a particular theory about, for example, personality styles of supervisors or human motivation. Although such psychologically oriented theories often are appealing to managers in terms of generally explaining certain phenomena that occur in the work place, they do not assist a manager in determining what supervisory *action* should be taken during day-to-day work routines. To be of optimal benefit to a manager, a model or approach to supervision should provide the manager with a technology of practical working strategies. Such a technology should assist a supervisor in knowing what *action steps* to implement in order to resolve identified problems with staff performance, be they excessive absenteeism, insufficient staff work effort, interpersonal bickering among staff—basically any undesirable area of staff performance that may arise.

A second major problem with many approaches to staff management in the human services is that there is no real documentation that the various approaches are actually *effective*. As just mentioned, most of the popularized management models have their foundation in a psychologically oriented theory. It is not clear whether a given theory is truly accurate and, more importantly, which theory (when applied) has demonstrated utility for improving staff performance in typical human service agencies. In actuality, for most management models there is no hard data or documentation based on supervisory application in human service agencies to demonstrate that the models are useful. Even though many managerial models seem to have intuitive appeal for supervisory personnel, if the models are not actually effective in helping such personnel to work with their staff, then the models are of limited value at best and, at worst, counterproductive to effectively managing staff performance.

An Alternative Approach to Management: A Procedurally Specific and Effective Supervisory Strategy

Due in large part to the noted problems with staff performance in human service settings and the recognition that existing approaches to staff management suffered serious shortcomings, in the 1970s applied researchers began taking a new direction to determine effective supervisory strategies. Investigations began to be conducted to develop and describe *specific actions* for supervisors to take with staff performance and to *demonstrate* through applied research that the actions are effective in improving staff work behavior in typical human service agencies. This approach to staff management, with its focus on specific, action-oriented supervisory procedures with empirically documented effectiveness, generally is best described as *organizational behavior management* (see *Journal of Organizational Behavior Management*, Vols. 1–9). Organizational behavior management is not really a management model per se but, rather, a continuously expanding set of supervisory strategies that have been developed and validated through applied research in typical organizational settings. A basic link among the strategies and corresponding evaluative research of organizational behavior management is that the primary focus is changing (inadequate) and maintaining (desirable) staff performance in the work place.

The purpose of this text is to discuss organizational behavior management in regard to managing staff performance in human service settings. A key focus of the text is the applied research through which supervisory procedures have been developed, evaluated and demonstrated as effective. Emphasis will also be directed to specific areas of staff performance that have been traditionally problematic for managers and how organizational behavioral management can be (and has been) used to resolve such problems. An attempt will be made to demonstrate that effective management of staff work performance in human service agencies is built on the application of a growing technology of empirically derived behavior change procedures—procedures that can be used to alter staff perormance when such performance is less than adequate *and* to maintain and improve performance that is adequate.

Overview of Organizational Behavior Management

Because organizational behavior management basically consists of a continuously expanding set of specified supervisory procedures in contrast to a more traditional, static model or theory of supervision, some discussion is warranted to help delineate exactly what types of supervisory strategies are considered to fall within the realm of organizational behavior management. For purposes of this text, two primary criteria will be used to identify the domain of organizational behavior management. First, only those supervisory strategies that focus on *staff behavior* will be addressed. Because it is what staff *do* in the work place that determines the degree of effectiveness of client services, it is essential that supervisory procedures actually impact the day-to-day working performance of staff. Approaches to human service management that focus on variables in the job environment other than staff performance (cf. Foxx et al., 1986, for exemplification) will not be addressed in this text.

The second criterion for identifying the domain of organizational behavior management pertains to the research that is used to develop and evaluate given supervisory strategies. Specifically, emphasis will be on those supervisory procedures that have been targeted through *applied behavioral research.* It is beyond the scope of this text to discuss in depth the merits of applied behavioral research relative to other research methods and the reader is referred to other sources for elaboration (Barlow & Hersen, 1984; Baer, Wolf, & Risley, 1968). Suffice it to say here that applied behavioral research is especially well suited for evaluating behavior change procedures (in this case, behavior change involving staff performance) in natural, nonlaboratory environments (i.e. human service agencies) in terms of its purpose and experimental methodology (see Reid, 1987, chap. 5, for discussion). Additional information pertaining to the advantages of applied behavioral research for developing effective management procedures will be provided in subsequent chapters.

By focusing on what staff do in the work setting along with the applied research that has demonstrated methods of changing staff behavior, this text describes practical procedures that managers can use to effectively improve staff performance. In essence, a working technology for managing staff job behavior will be presented. The management technology to be discussed is by no means complete; as just noted, organizational behavior management is continuously being refined and expanded as applied research demonstrates new and better ways of managing staff performance. Nevertheless, a very substantial amount of applied research has been conducted such that management procedures are available that can be used to improve important areas of staff performance in human service agencies. Management procedures will be discussed that can be used to effectively resolve rather pervasive and notorius problems in typical human service agencies, including, for example, lack of therapeutic staff interactions and service provision in congregate living situations such as state institutions for seriously handicapped clients (Chapter 5), inadequate staff proficiency in conducting client therapy and training regimes (Chapter 6), excessive staff absenteeism (Chapter 7), problematic administrative staff performances ranging from insufficient record keeping to lack of punctuality in performing assigned work tasks (Chapter 8), and ineffective classroom teaching and student management practices (Chapter 9). Remedying staff performance problems that affect a wide variety of human service practices due to lack of adequate work skills among staff will also be addressed through a description of a well-documented technology of staff training (Chapter 3).

In order to resolve the types of staff performance problems just noted, organizational behavior management research has developed a wide variety of supervisory strategies. Such variety is due in part to the rather general criteria summarized previously regarding what procedures constitute organizational behavior management applications: essentially any supervisory actions that have been demonstrated through applied behavioral research to change staff work performance. Relatedly, not being restricted to procedures derived from a given theory of human work performance allows flexibility in the types of management approaches that can be developed and evaluated. However, based on results of investigations on changing staff work behavior, some general guidelines have also evolved that form the basis of a number of the more frequently used organizational behavior management procedures.

The guidelines that affect the development and (proficient) application of behavioral supervisory procedures are derived from well-established principles of human behavior (e.g. Skinner, 1969). Such principles will be referred to intermittently throughout this text and have been validated through applied research with adult behavior across a variety of situations (see, for example, Willis & Giles, 1976, for summaries of behavior change research with adults). Of particular concern here is the application of principles of human behavior to staff performance in the work place (i.e. human service settings).

Generally, translating what is understood about the principles of behavior into workable supervisory strategies involves conceptualizing factors that affect human performance into two categories: *antecedents* and *consequences.* Antecedents involve those actions that a supervisor can take prior to staff members engaging in certain work behaviors to increase the likelihood that the staff persons do indeed complete the respective job tasks and do so appropriately. Chapter 2, and to a lesser degree Chapters 3 and 4, provide an in-depth discussion about antecedent management procedures. Consequences, on the other hand, refer to what a supervisor can do after staff have engaged in a given work activity to affect the future (non)occurrence of such work performance. Chapter 4 elaborates on the use of consequence management procedures.

The conceptualization of management activities that affect staff performance in terms of antecedent and consequence supervisory actions will be reflected throughout the discussion of organizational behavior management procedures. In addition, various relationships between staff behaviors of concern and antecedent/consequence actions will be addressed. Temporal relationships, for example, between the occurrence of a staff work behavior and a supervisor's delivery of a consequence for the behavior will be discussed. Similarly, attention will be given to the relationship between the frequency of occurrence of targeted work behaviors and the relative proportion of those behaviors that are followed by supervisory-presented consequences. These types of relationships, which represent an integral part of organizational behavior management, are as important in managing staff performance as the particular antecedent and consequence components themselves.

General Format of Text

The format for the remainder of the text consists of two main sections. In the first section, Chapters 2 to 4, the basic procedures that constitute the core of organizational behavior management are described. The next section, Chapters 5 to 10, discusses how the procedures described in the preceding section have been used to improve specific areas of staff performance in human service settings.

Earlier in this chapter it was noted that a shortcoming with most popularized models of human service staff management is that there generally has been no documentation that the models actually work when applied in typical human service agencies. It was also stressed that one of the identifying features of organizational behavior management is its emphasis on documentation of the effectiveness of supervisory procedures through applied research. In order to thoroughly understand the degree of demonstrated efficacy of respective supervisory procedures for improving designated areas of staff performance, as well as existing limitations of the procedures with certain performance areas, the research that evaluated the supervisory strategies must be studied. Consequently, in each chapter that discusses the use of organizational behavior management procedures to improve specific performances of staff (second section of text), a critique of the available research regarding that particular area of staff performance will be provided.

Criteria for Critiquing Staff Management Research

In order to evaluate whether the research on organizational behavior management practices has been appropriately conducted and, consequently, whether valid and definitive conclusions can be formed regarding the efficacy of given supervisory procedures, a number of criteria for conducting and reporting applied research must be adhered to. Necessary criteria in this regard generally are considered integral to applied behavior analysis as an experimental and epistemological process (Baer et al., 1968; Whitman, Scibak, & Reid, 1983, chap. 3), as well as fundamental to applied research specifically involving staff performance in human service settings (Reid & Whitman, 1983). It is beyond the purpose of this text to discuss each of these criteria in depth. However, a brief summary of the most important criteria and their relevance for staff management will be provided to help the reader evaluate the research through which the relative merits of different organizational behavior management procedures have been denoted. References to more elaborate discussions of the research criteria will also be provided for the interested reader.

Social Significance of Target Behaviors

The first criterion for evaluating the adequacy of staff management research is the degree of *social significance* of the behaviors that are targeted for change or improvement by the research. That is, a determination must be made as to whether the staff performance area that is addressed in respective investigations is really important or relevant in terms of a human service agency's service provision. In this regard, research in human services has often been plagued by an emphasis on what is of interest to theoreticaly oriented researchers and what is easy to measure and/or manipulate experimentally in contrast to an emphasis on what is truly important in respect to routine staff performance in the work place (Reid, 1987, chap. 1). Of particular concern here is whether the targeted area of staff performance addressed in the research significantly impacted services to clients and, subsequently, client welfare. In essence, useful staff management research must often not only identify relevant staff behaviors warranting change but also clearly *identify indices of client performance or welfare* that are improved when staff performances are altered (Greene et al., 1978). For example, if respective supervisory strategies are implemented to improve the personal care provided to dependent senior citizens in nursing home settings, then the effectiveness of those strategies cannot be convincingly demonstrated unless it is documented that staff behavior was improved *and* that the senior citizens' personal care was actually enhanced. In short, in many cases it is at best difficult, and at worst impossible, to adequately evaluate the effectiveness of staff management practices on staff performance if related measures of client welfare are not provided (Reid & Whitman, 1983).

Thoroughness and Reliability of Measurement Systems

The second criterion for judging research adequacy pertains to the measurement of the indices of staff performance and/or client welfare that are targeted to be changed within applied investigations. Basically, monitoring systems must be used that objectively and sensitively measure the staff and/or client dependent entities in order to ensure that such entities improve as a result of the application of a respective supervisory approach (Reid & Shoemaker, 1984). Further, observation systems must be reliable, in that they consistently measure the same entity or representation of staff/client activity across time and when the measurement systems are implemented by different people (Kazdin, 1977).

An additional measurement concern that will be discussed in subsequent chapters that warrants special attention in staff management research is the *thoroughness* of the measurement or observation system. Investigations that lack thorough observation systems because, for example, they monitor only a very small representation or sample of relevant staff and/or client behavior, render conclusions about the efficacy of whatever staff management practice was evaluated tentative at best. That is, it is one thing to improve staff performance during a 20-minute experimental demonstration period and quite another to improve staff performance for eight hours per day across the work day, week, and year. For maximum utility for human service managers, the latter time span is the more relevant concern.

Validity of Experimental Methodology

A third criterion of considerable importance relates to the degree of validity with which conclusions can be drawn about the effectiveness of management practices that are evaluated based on the experimental designs used in respective investigations (Whitman et al., 1983, chap. 3). Attention in this text will be given to *internal validity* within research studies in terms of whether the specific experimental designs employed allow conclusions as to whether or not it was the management interventions per se that were responsible for the staff and/or client behavior change observed in contrast to some incidentally related event. *External validity* will also be addressed in regard to the degree of confidence with which certain experimental findings can be extended to management situations beyond a single investigation or two. Management interventions are more likely to be successful in a given situation if those interventions have previously been shown to be effective in a wide variety of work settings with different staff members than if the interventions have been effectively applied in only one specific work situation.

Effectiveness of Management Intervention

If the experimental criteria just noted are fulfilled in respective investigations, then the occasion is set for evaluating the primary criterion of concern in this text: *the effectiveness of the staff management procedure.* Once the relevance and adequacy of the experimental question and methodology in an applied research study have been ensured, then the focus can shift to the main issue of whether the management strategy employed fulfilled its intended purpose of actually improving staff performance and client welfare. The effectiveness of a management intervention will be judged in terms of the degree of socially significant or relevant change in targeted staff and/or client behavior on both an immediate *short-term* basis as well as on an extended *long-term* basis (Reid & Whitman, 1983). As alluded to earlier, to maximize the benefit of a staff management procedure, it is necessary to ensure that the procedure can be effective across an extended time period (i.e. at least across a number of months) and not just a brief experimental demonstration period (Parsons, Schepis, Reid, McCarn, & Green, 1987).

Acceptability of Management Practice

The final criterion for judging the value of applied research studies in organizational behavior management is the acceptability of the staff management procedures that have been investigated (Kazdin, 1980). The issue here is that even if various management practices are effective in enhancing staff performance and/or client welfare, the practices will be of limited value if they are not well accepted, and subsequently adopted, by supervisory personnel in typical human service settings. For example, if a given management procedure can effectively improve staff work performance but the strategy is not well accepted by managers because it is very effortful to apply, then the management procedure will not be of much use to anyone because most managers will not routinely use the procedure. Relatedly, if the staff recipients of the management practice seriously dislike the supervisory approach, then the technique is not likely to be used very often in many human service agencies. Hence, the degree to which staff management researchers evaluated staff acceptance of management interventions (and the outcome of such evaluations) will be scrutinized in forthcoming chapters.

Staff acceptance of management practices represents a crucial, yet often overlooked variable that affects the utility of such practices. Lack of staff acceptance of a respective management procedure can literally destroy the effectiveness of the procedure. Staff can overtly refuse to comply with supervisory directives and related practices or subtly sabotage a management program (Reid & Whitman, 1983). Relatedly, in many cases staff nonacceptance of management practices can result in serious conflict between an agency's management personnel and union representation of the agency's staff—conflict that can seriously impede an agency's provision of services to its clients (Greene et al., 1978). One of the advantages of an organizational behavior management format is that the approach lends itself nicely to *positive* procedures for managing staff performance; methods of supervising staff behavior that focus on reinforcing or rewarding staff work activity relative to punishing staff behavior in the work place (Reid & Shoemaker, 1984). A central theme throughout this text will be the application of effective management procedures wherever possible that involve a positive format and, consequently, have a strong likelihood of being well accepted by staff members.

Specific Chapter Format

The criteria just noted for evaluating the adequacy of applied research will be referred to in each chapter in the second section of this text (i.e. the chapters that discuss methods of resolving specific problems with staff performance) subsequent to a description of the applied research that exists. Following the critique of the research for each problem area will be a summary of what can be legitimately concluded from the existing research. Within the latter summary special attention will be directed to describing what appears to be the management procedure with the greatest likelihood of resolving the specific performance problem targeted by each respective chapter.

As a point of clarification, throughout this text reference will be made interchangeably to *supervisory* and *management* practices. Differentiation that is sometimes made between supervision and management will not be made here. Basically, the two terms will both be used to refer to applications within human service settings that are designed to impact staff performance. When considered in this light, the job of a human service manager or supervisor consists of two main functions: (a) to take specific actions to *change* the day-to-day work performance of staff when such performance is problematic or less than optimal; and (b) to take specific actions to *maintain* the routine work activities of staff when their performance is appropriate and acceptable. Hence, a supervisor should be considered a behavior change agent, with staff behavior the first-level focus of the supervisor's behavior change practices, and client welfare the second-level focus. Elaboration on the delineation of a supervisor's job will be provided in subsequent chapters.

REFERENCES

Baer, D.M., Wolf, M.M., & Risley, T.R. (1968). Some current dimensions of applied behavior analysis. *Journal of Applied Behavior Analysis, 1,* 91–97.

Barlow, D.H., & Hersen, M. (1984). *Single case experimental designs: Strategies for studying behavior change.* New York: Pergamon Press.

Blatt, B. (1976). Purgatory. In M. Rosen, G.R. Clark & M.S. Kivitz (Eds.), *The History of Mental Retardation: Collected Papers Vol. 2* (pp. 345–360). Baltimore: University Park Press.

Developmental Dimensions International. (1974). *Interaction management system.* Pittsburgh, PA.

Foxx, R.M., McMorrow, M.J., Bechtel, R., Busch, L., Foxx, C.L., & Bittle, R.G. (1986). The lack of effects of enriched and automated environments on the adaptive and maladaptive behavior of mentally retarded persons. *Behavioral Residential Treatment, 1,* 105–124.

Gardner, J.M. (1973). Training the trainers. A review of research on teaching behavior modification. In R.D. Rubin, J.P. Brady, & J.D. Henderson (Eds.), *Advances in behavior therapy Vol. 4* (pp. 145–158). New York: Academic Press.

Greene, B.F., Willis, B.S., Levy, R., & Bailey, J.S. (1978). Measuring client gains from staff-implemented programs. *Journal of Applied Behavior Analysis, 11,* 395–412.

Gross, A.M., & Ekstrand, M. (1983). Increasing and maintaining rates of teacher praise: A study using public posting and feedback fading. *Behavior Modification, 7,* 126–135.

Iwata, B.A., Bailey, J.S., Brown, K.M., Foshee, T.J., & Alpern, M. (1976). A performance-based lottery to improve residential care and training by institutional staff. *Journal of Applied Behavior Analysis, 9,* 417–431.

Jones, F.H., & Eimers, R.C. (1975). Role playing to train elementary teachers to use a classroom management "skill package." *Journal of Applied Behavior Analysis, 8,* 421–433.

Kast, F.E., & Rosenzweig, J.E. (1974). *Organization and management.* New York: McGraw-Hill.

Kazdin, A.E. (1977). Artifact, bias and complexity of assessment: The ABCs of reliability. *Journal of Applied Behavior Analysis, 10,* 141–150.

Kazdin, A.E. (1980). Acceptability of alternative treatments for deviant child behavior. *Journal of Applied Behavior Analysis, 13,* 259–273.

Kunz, G.G.R., Lutzker, J.R., Cuvo, A.J., Eddleman, J., Lutzker, S.Z., Megson, D., & Gulley, B. (1982). Evaluating strategies to improve careprovider performance on health and developmental tasks in an infant care facility. *Journal of Applied Behavior Analysis, 15,* 521–531.

Lovett, S.B., Bosmajian, C.P., Frederiksen, L.W., & Elder, J.P. (1983). Monitoring professional service delivery: An organizational level intervention. *Behavior Therapy, 14,* 170–177.

Parsons, M.B., Schepis, M.M., Reid, D.H., McCarn, J.E., & Green, C.W. (1987). Expanding the impact of behavioral staff management: A large-scale, long-term application in schools serving severely handicapped students. *Journal of Applied Behavior Analysis, 20,* 139–150.

Prue, D.M., Krapfl, J.E., Noah, J.C., Cannon, S., & Maley, R.F. (1980). Managing the treatment activities of state hospital staff. *Journal of Organizational Behavior Management, 2*(3), 165–181.

Realon, R.E., Wheeler, A.J., Spring, B., & Springer, M. (1986). Evaluating the quality of training delivered by direct care staff in a state mental retardation center. *Behavioral Residential Treatment, 1,* 199–212.

Reid, D.H. (1987). *Developing a research program in human service agencies: A practitioner's guidebook.* Springfield, IL: Charles C Thomas.

Reid, D.H., & Shoemaker, J. (1984). Behavioral supervision: Methods of improving institutional staff performance. In W.P. Christian, G.T. Hannah, & T.J. Glahn (Eds.), *Programming effective human services: Strategies for institutional change and client transition* (pp. 39–61). New York: Plenum Press.

Reid, D.H., & Whitman, T.L. (1983). Behavioral staff management in institutions: A critical review of effectiveness and acceptability. *Analysis and Intervention in Developmental Disabilities, 3,* 131–149.

Repp, A.C., & Deitz, D.E.D. (1979). Improving administrative-related staff behaviors at a state institution. *Mental Retardation, 17,* 185–192.

Shoemaker, J., & Reid, D.H. (1980). Decreasing chronic absenteeism among institutional staff: Effects of a low-cost attendance program. *Journal of Organizational Behavior Management, 2*(4), 317–328.

Skinner, B.F. (1969). *Contingencies of reinforcement: A theoretical analysis.* New York: Appleton-Century-Crofts.

Sperbeck, D.J., & Whitbourne, S.K. (1981). Dependency in the institutional setting: A behavioral training program for geriatric staff. *The Gerontologist, 21,* 268–275.

Stogdill, R.M. (1974). *Handbook of leadership: A survey of theory and research.* New York: The Free Press.

Whitman, T.L., Scibak, J.W., & Reid, D.H. (1983). *Behavior modification with the severely and profoundly retarded: Research and application.* New York: Academic Press.

Willis, J., & Giles, D. (1976). *Great experiments in behavior modification.* Indianapolis: Hackett Publishing Co.

Chapter 2

STRUCTURING AND MONITORING
STAFF PERFORMANCE

A s noted in the preceding chapter, organizational behavior management approaches generally can be categorized into antecedent or consequence procedures. These two general types of management strategies can be combined into a generic model of behavioral supervision that, in essence, can be applied to any given problem with staff performance. A brief summarization of the basic components that comprise the model is presented in Figure 2-1. The rectangular boxes in Figure 2-1 represent the primary action steps involved in behavioral supervision, with the first three boxes (i.e. those at the top of the flowchart) representing antecedent procedures and the bottom two boxes representing consequence components.

Using Figure 2-1 as a guide, the first step in behavioral supervision is to *define* precisely what it is that staff are expected to do. Next, a *monitoring system* should be established in order to provide a supervisor with objective information regarding how well or poorly staff are performing their (previously) defined work responsibilities. If staff are performing adequately, the supervisor should then provide a positive *consequence* for such performance. In contrast, if staff are not performing adequately, a supervisor must first decide if the inadequate performance is due to lack of know-how on the part of staff. If insufficient knowledge regarding how to perform expected job responsibilities is indeed the problem, then a staff *training* component should be implemented to teach staff how to perform the specified work skills. On the other hand, if staff have the skills to complete their assigned duties and work performance is still inadequate, then a negative *consequence* such as corrective feedback should be provided by the supervisor.

The description of the basic components of behavioral supervision as just presented represents a very simplified account of effective management of staff performance. There are numerous considerations that must

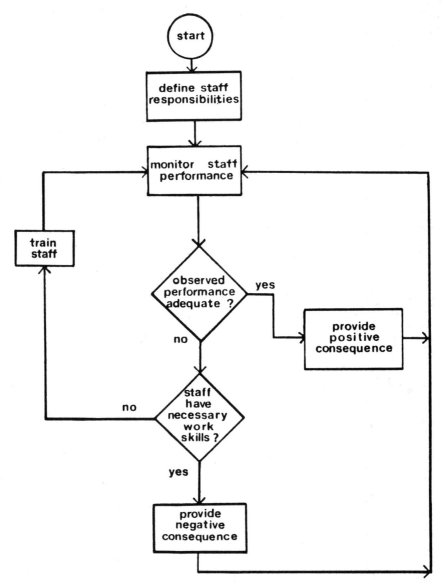

Figure 2-1. Generic model of behavioral supervision processes.

be taken into account in order to effectively implement each of the component steps, and there are numerous ways of implementing each step. Nevertheless, the brief representation of the process as depicted in Figure 2-1 along with the preceding summary can serve as a foundation for developing effective supervisory programs. This chapter and the next two chapters discuss the necessary considerations and variations in implementing each component of the supervisory model, and subsequent chapters describe how the procedures constituting the overall model have been used to improve respective problems with staff performance. The specific focus of this chapter is on the first two steps in the model: defining and monitoring staff performance responsibilities.

Defining Staff Performance Responsibilities

If staff are going to satisfactorily fulfill their work responsibilities, they must of course be cognizant of what those responsibilities involve. Hence, before a supervisor can realistically expect that staff will complete their work tasks appropriately, the supervisor must identify or define those tasks for the staff. In some ways, stressing the need to define work responsibilities in this manner may seem to represent a simple statement of the obvious: people really cannot be expected to do something if they are not aware of what it is that they are supposed to do. However, as this chapter section will indicate, there are several important reasons why it is necessary to assert the need to define work responsibilities. Most importantly in this regard, in many cases supervisors neglect to delineate specific work responsibilities for staff because they (mistakenly) assume that staff already know what their work duties entail.

Another reason it is important to ensure that staff work duties are clearly articulated pertains to the nature of many human service jobs. Jobs in human service settings often involve a wide variety of different responsibilities. Preschool teaching jobs, for example, consist of a diversity of tasks such as meeting the basic care needs of toddlers (toileting, feeding, etc.), teaching appropriate social skills, managing temper tantrums, assisting children in overcoming problems in being away from their parents for the first time, and ensuring the cleanliness and orderliness of the physical environment. Similarly, work duties for nursing home staff include providing certain types of medical care, conducting recreational activities, assisting with basic care needs, interacting with family members of clients, maintaining certain administrative records, etc. When staff are charged with multiple responsibilities as just exemplified, unless a supervisor specifies staff work duties it is not always apparent to staff which tasks are the most important (i.e. the supervisor and staff may place different priorities on different tasks), nor is it apparent which tasks should be fulfilled at certain time periods.

An additional characteristic of a number of human service jobs that heightens the importance of defining performance responsibilities is that staff members often receive job-related directives from several different sources. To illustrate, institutional direct care staff may receive directives regarding what they should do through verbal instructions from their shift supervisor, via an all-staff memorandum from a senior-level administrator, through individual consultation from an agency psychologist, and/or by a phone call from a client's mother. When directives come from several different sources, staff can be faced with confusing and/or conflicting expectations regarding what they should do at any given time unless a responsible supervisor clarifies job expectations.

A final reason for specifying work responsibilities is that such specification can sometimes have the effect of improving what staff are already doing on a routine basis. That is, even when general job expectations are apparent and staff are attempting to fulfill work responsibilities to varying degrees, increasing the specificity of the job assignments can improve the proficiency with which work tasks are completed (Iwata, Bailey, Brown, Foshee, & Alpern, 1976). Because of the performance-improvement effect of certain types of job specification, these particular processes will be discussed more in-depth in Chapter 4 which focuses on management procedures for changing ongoing job performances. A brief exemplification of what is meant by job specification will be provided here, however, to help set the occasion for understanding how the behavioral supervision model (again, see Figure 2-1) can be used effectively.

Clearly defining performance responsibilities involves specifying the exact activities or behaviors in which staff are expected to engage. For many work responsibilities a simple statement from a supervisor will usually suffice for providing staff with the necessary information. Simply telling staff, for example, that they must sign their time cards before the end of the workweek will generally inform staff sufficiently to allow them to complete that particular work task. In contrast, more complex performance responsibilities typically require a more detailed delineation. Essentially, the more activities or behaviors required of staff to perform a respective job task, the more specific the delineation of duties must be in order to ensure that staff are aware of what is expected of them. To illustrate, many staff in institutional settings serving psychiatric or developmentally disabled populations are likely to encounter aggressive attacks on themselves from certain clients. Staff persons need to know how to appropriately respond in such situations in order to prevent harm to themselves, to the aggressive client and/or to other clients—a response process that requires that staff know a number of specific action steps. An example of how the response process can be specifically defined regarding what staff should do when attacked by an aggressive client is presented in Table 2-1.

Table 2-1
COMPONENT STEPS FOR SELF-DEFENSE PROCEDURE

Step Number	Behavioral Definitions
1	Staff member (S) stands within reach of resident (R) within 5s of hit
2	S states R's name and instructs incompatible response within 10s of the hit
3	S physically prompts desired response within 10s of instructions or within 20s of hit
4	S blocks punch with same-side arm, with hand fisted (thumb contacting fingers) and using forearm (between wrist and elbow joint)
5	S blocks kick by raising same-side leg 6 in. with foot partially occluding support leg and torso turning approximately 90° to the side
6	S releases clothing grab by thumb pry within 5s of grab
7	S releases body part grab by thumb or rotating out within 5s of grab
8	S lifts and holds chair between self and R's chair within 5s of attack
9	S states criteria for use of self-defense technique as per policy: to protect people (any) and property

Reprinted with permission from van den Pol, R.A., Reid, D.H., and Fuqua, R.W. (1983): Peer training of safety-related skills to institutional staff: Benefits for trainers and trainees. *Journal of Applied Behavior Analysis, 16,* 139–156.

The process of breaking complex staff performance responsibilities down into a sequence of specific behaviors as exemplified in Table 2-1 involves *task-analyzing* staff job duties. Task analysis has been successfully used to simplify and clearly articulate specific actions required of staff in a wide variety of non-human service work roles ranging from repairing and maintaining jet engines (McCormick & Ilgen, 1980, chap. 4) to janitorial jobs (Cuvo, Leaf, & Borakove, 1978). Task analyses can also be applied to essentially any performance responsibility in human service settings (see Alavosius & Sulzer-Azaroff, 1986; Christian, 1983; van den Pol, Reid, & Fuqua, 1983, for examples and/or discussion of task-analyzing human service jobs).

Although the primary purpose of precisely defining staff work duties is to ensure that staff are aware of what is expected of them, defining job expectations also facilitates other steps in the supervisory model. By delineating staff behaviors that are necessary to fulfill given performance responsibilities, completing the staff *training* component of the behavioral supervision model is enhanced. That is, in those cases where simply making staff aware of their job duties (i.e. defining job roles) is insufficient to ensure adequate staff *know-how* in regard to performing satisfactorily, a formal staff training program is necessary—and such training is facilitated if the job skills that are to be trained have been well specified (see Chapter 3 for a discussion of staff training procedures).

One of the most effective means of defining specific work duties and presenting those duties to staff in a manner that facilitates staff training endeavors is *performance checklists* (Risley & Favell, 1979). Checklists consist of a *concise* written listing of the key behaviors that must occur in order to appropriately complete a job task and, where appropriate, the sequence in which the behaviors should occur. To illustrate, Figure 2-2 presents a checklist that was used to help train direct care staff in an institution how to follow physical therapists' prescriptions for positioning nonambulatory, physically handicapped clients in various therapeutic body positions. As depicted in Figure 2-2, a checklist is essentially a brief written version of a job duty that has been task analyzed.

There are a number of advantages of using performance checklists with staff work responsibilities. First, as alluded to earlier, checklists facilitate staff training endeavors (again, see Chapter 3 for elaboration). Second, relative to lengthier narrative descriptions of job responsibilities that often exist in human service agencies, checklists are easy for staff to read. Relatedly, checklists tend to focus staff attention more to the *specific actions* expected of the staff relative to job descriptions written in text format. Third, checklists can function as a permanent product to periodically remind staff regarding their expected work duties. That is, once staff have participated in a training program utilizing a checklist designed to teach certain skills to staff, the staff can maintain a copy of the checklist and occasionally refer to the copy if they become uncertain regarding how to perform part of their assigned responsibilities.

When considering the process of carefully defining staff job responsibilities, it becomes apparent that this step in the behavioral supervision model can become rather effortful and time-consuming for a supervisor. Because the job of human service staff typically involves a myriad of different tasks as described earlier, concerns arise regarding how practical it is to specify and/or task analyze all aspects of the jobs of all staff in a

POSITIONING

	Client's initials	RL	KW	KJ	DW	DA	GF	RS
II. SIDE LYING (continued)								
3. if possible, the top arm is flexed, brought forward, and supported by a pillow?								
4. the client's bottom leg is straight with knees and toes forward (if possible) and the top leg flexed, brought forward and supported by a pillow?								
B. If client has <u>windblown legs</u>, did caregiver ensure that:				█				█
1. client is placed on side opposite to that on which legs are pulled?				█				█
2. client has a pillow under knees, if necessary, to prevent the pull of gravity from being too strong?				█				█
3. client has a pillow between knees?				█				█
C. If client has <u>scoliosis</u>, did caregiver ensure that: client is placed on the hump side?							█	
D. If client has <u>extension</u>, did caregiver: 1. position with head and shoulders forward?		█		█		█		
2. flex client's legs at hips and knees?		█				█		
III. SITTING Did caregiver ensure that the client: 1. is in his or her own chair?								
2. has hips and knees flexed at right angles?								
3. has lower back against the back of the chair?								
4. has feet flat on foot support?								
5. has seat belt fastened tightly, low across lap?								
6. has all supportive belts fastened?								
	Total rated	/	/	/	/	/	/	/

COMMENTS: _____

Figure 2-2. A checklist used to help train staff to conduct prescribed physical therapy regimes (therapeutic body positioning) with multiply physically handicapped persons. Three body positions (supine, prone, and side) are described in terms of client characteristics and related staff responsibilities. Staff performance relating to each dimension of a client's position is observed and recorded as appropriate (yes "*1*"), inappropriate (no "*'*") or not applicable (NA or a blacked-out scoring segment). Reprinted from Stephens, T.C. & Lattimore, J. (1983). Prescriptive checklist for positioning residential clients. *Physical Therapy, 63,* 1113–1115, with permission from the American Physical Therapy Association.

given human service agency. In essence, it really is not very practical to expect that supervisors can precisely define *all* staff duties. Consequently, two guidelines are offered in regard to which performance responsibilities should be carefully defined (Whitman, Scibak, & Reid, 1983, chap. 11). The first guideline is that *those duties that are most important relative to the overall mission of the human service agency should be precisely articulated.* If, for example, the primary mission of an agency is to educate clients (e.g. a school), then job duties that relate to client teaching endeavors should be clearly defined. If, on the other hand, the primary mission of an agency is to provide certain types of health care (e.g. as in certain living units within nursing homes), then health care routines should be precisely delineated for staff. Ultimately, it is the job of the supervisor in accordance with his/her superiors to determine which staff responsibilities relate most clearly to an agency's primary service mission.

The second guideline pertaining to which job responsibilities should be carefully defined is that *those staff performance areas that at any given time are seriously interfering with the fulfillment of an agency's primary mission should be delineated.* A variety of problems with staff performance can arise that in and of themselves do not relate directly to important agency functions but nevertheless serve to detract from the fulfillment of those functions. For example, staff may be particularly disgruntled about something, which tends to focus staff time and effort on the (perceived) source of disgruntlement in contrast to focusing on the services that staff should be providing. In such cases it is usually worth the supervisor's time to precisely define what staff are actually *doing* (e.g. bickering between colleagues, taking extended breaks to talk about their displeasures) that interferes with the completion of their primary duties. Subsequently, the occasion is then set for the supervisor to take action using a behavioral supervisory strategy to redirect staff behavior to something more appropriate to the goals of the agency.

Monitoring Staff Performance Responsibilities

The second major step in the behavioral supervision model, monitoring, involves the systematic observation of staff performance. The primary purpose of this step is to obtain objective and representative information regarding how well or poorly staff are performing their previously defined job tasks. The data resulting from the monitoring can subsequently be used by a supervisor to make informed decisions concerning whether to take supervisory action to change inadequate staff performance or to take steps to maintain satisfactory job behavior.

The importance of supervisors knowing what their staff are doing is quite well accepted in the management field in general — as well as from a common sense standpoint. However, the manner in which many supervisors in the human services attempt to obtain knowledge about staff performance often leaves much to be desired. Typically, supervisors have no systematic means of observing staff performance. Rather, supervisors observe staff behavior on an infrequent, inconsistent and/or haphazard basis. Such a process can easily result in a nonrepresentative view of staff performance. Further, nonsystematic monitoring of staff performance can result in some staff persons being observed much more frequently than other staff persons. A related problem with unsystematic monitoring processes is that because a supervisor does not have a very substantial data base regarding staff performance (i.e. because the supervisor has not systematically observed staff behavior), the supervisor must rely on the recommendations of other persons in the agency in order to evaluate the performance of a given staff person. Unfortunately, those other persons also usually have not systematically observed staff work activities and, consequently, are not able to provide the supervisor with very representative and/or accurate evaluative information.

Although the primary benefit of systematically monitoring staff performance is to allow a supervisor to make *informed* decisions regarding what, if any, supervisory actions should be taken, there is another beneficial outcome of systematic monitoring. Specifically, the availability of objective and accurate data on staff performance allows a supervisor to evaluate a respective staff member's performance in a manner that is more fair to the staff person relative to evaluations made without such data. If a supervisor can demonstrate to staff members the objective process on which performance evaluations are based (and that the same process is used with all staff persons), then staff are more likely to be responsive to evaluations from a supervisor than if staff know that a supervisor is inconsistent in how he/she evaluates performances of different staff persons. Again, however, most supervisors do not systematically monitor staff work behavior and, consequently, do not have a means of evaluating staff performance that staff perceive as fair. The latter situation is a relatively common source of discontent among staff in human service agencies.

An issue that is frequently expressed in regard to supervisors directly monitoring staff performance is that the monitoring may be *reactive* (Greene, Willis, Levy, & Bailey, 1978; Hay, Nelson, & Hay, 1977; Repp & Deitz, 1979). That is, staff may react to the supervisor's presence when he/she is observing staff by performing differently (i.e. more appropriately) relative to when the supervisor is not conducting observations. Hence, supervisors may obtain an inaccurate account of staff performance that is biased to reflect more appropriate staff work behavior than what routinely occurs. Concern over the potential reactivity of observation processes is indeed a serious issue. Many supervisors have undoubtedly experienced the reactive effect of their presence in terms of entering a staff work area and witnessing the staff immediately change what they are doing (e.g. begin to work more diligently).

Concerns over potential reactivity, although serious, should not discourage the use of systematic monitoring processes with staff performance. Observation systems can be designed relatively easily to prevent or greatly diminish reactive effects on staff performance if several guidelines are followed (see discussion later in this chapter). Actually, where systematic monitoring processes have been formally evaluated in regard to potential reactive effects, research has indicated that such effects may be minimal or nonexistent; staff do not necessarily perform significantly differently when they are being observed versus when they are not being observed (Hagen, Craighead, & Paul, 1975; Ivancic, Reid, Iwata, Faw, & Page, 1981), although there have also been conflicting results in this regard (Hay et al., 1977). Even if monitoring systems are not designed and/or implemented in a manner that prevents staff reactivity though, such systems can still be useful from a performance-improvement standpoint. A supervisor's overt monitoring of staff performance at times may serve to improve staff work behavior in much the same way as supervisor modeling functions (see Chapter 4 for a discussion of the behavior change characteristics of supervisor modeling). However, the primary function of systematically monitoring staff performance is not to change staff work behavior per se, and, as will be discussed later, monitoring systems generally should be designed to prevent reactive effects in order to provide a supervisor with a true picture of routine staff work activity.

Types of Monitoring Systems

Processes for observing staff performance can be categorized into either *formal* or *informal* monitoring systems. Generally, the most objective and representative data base regarding staff work behavior is obtained from the former type of system.

Formal monitoring systems. Formal monitoring systems are characterized by their reliance on *highly systematic* procedures. These systems are based on a well-defined set of staff behaviors that are formally written, and the occurrence or nonoccurrence of those behaviors is observed on an established, regularly occurring time schedule. Additionally, formal observation sheets are prepared to facilitate the monitor's task of observing staff work behavior as well as making frequent and timely records of the observed performance. A variety of formal monitoring processes have been used in organizational behavior management research and application, with the most popular representing *time sampling, duration* and *permanent product* monitoring systems.

Time sampling monitoring systems represent the most frequently used observation procedures with staff performance, at least within the applied behavioral research on staff work behavior. Time sampling involves making brief or momentary observations (and recordings) of what staff are doing at preestablished points in time. This type of observational process is often used to obtain information on the types of work activity staff are engaging in across the entire workday or large portions thereof (Brown, Willis, & Reid, 1981; Burg, Reid, & Lattimore, 1979).

The most significant advantage of a time sampling system is that the process requires a relatively small amount of a supervisor's time to conduct while simultaneously allowing a considerable amount of information to be obtained on staff performance. Time sampling systems can also be implemented in a flexible fashion in regard to when a supervisor conducts the observations, because the entire staff work period does not have to be monitored, only intermittent samples of the period. Additionally, such systems can be used without causing staff to be very uncomfortable, because the staff are not continuously observed for very long (i.e. only a few seconds) during any given observation period (see discussion later in this chapter regarding staff persons' acceptability of supervisory monitoring systems).

A second type of monitoring system, duration monitoring, consists of procedures for observing staff performance throughout the entire time that staff are engaging in a designated work activity. Whereas time sampling procedures just described are used to sample brief occurrences of work activity intermittently at different times during a work period, duration monitoring is applicable when staff are expected to complete a specified, time-limited activity during a part of the overall work routine. For example, Figure 2-3 illustrates an observation form used as part of a duration monitoring system for observing and making records of staff performance during fire drills in a residential setting for mentally retarded persons (van den Pol et al., 1983). On the lefthand side of the observation sheet, the staff behaviors that should occur during a fire drill are listed. Columns for recording the (in)appropriate occurrence of each behavior for each fire drill are presented across the top of the sheet. Using the form displayed in Figure 2-3, a monitor observed an individual staff person's performance throughout a given fire drill and recorded the person's performance on the observation sheet. Similar types of duration monitoring processes have been used to observe staff members' proficiency in conducting skill-acquisition teaching regimes with students (Page, Iwata, & Reid, 1982), lifting and transfer tasks with nonambulatory clients (Alavosius & Sulzer-Azaroff, 1986) and medical care with handicapped persons during seizures (van den Pol et al., 1983).

Duration monitoring systems as just exemplified are most useful for evaluating staff performance when the entire set of work behaviors involved in a performance area must be observed in order to accurately evaluate the performance. Such systems require a supervisor to be present at the exact time that a respective staff person is scheduled to engage in a designated work task and, consequently, cannot be used by a supervisor with as much flexibility as time sampling systems. Duration monitoring can also require a supervisor to continuously observe a staff person's behavior for a long time period during a given monitoring session relative to time sampling systems—a factor that can increase staffs' uncomfortableness with supervisory monitoring.

The third type of formal observation system, permanent product monitoring, is typically the easiest type of performance monitoring to conduct. Permanent product monitoring refers to observing the outcome of a staff member's work that affects a change in the physical work environment in contrast to directly observing a staff person's behavior. A common application of permanent product monitoring is with work tasks that require staff to prepare some type of written document or record (see Chapter 8 for elaboration on documentation responsibilities of staff). In such cases, a supervisor can indirectly monitor staff performance by reviewing the written product to determine if the work was indeed completed, as well as if the work was punctual and of sufficient

Monitoring Form For
Fire Drills

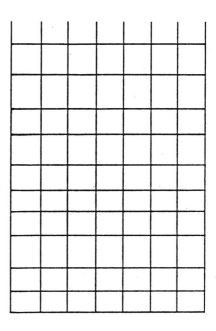

Staff Behaviors	Successive Fire Drills*						
	1st	2nd	3rd	4th	5th	6th	7th
1. Staff (S) removes residents (R) from room; closest first or simultaneously							
2. S IDs nearest fire alarm box, by touching, pointing or verbally							
3. S calls Boiler Room, Maintenance and reports location							
4. S gets nearest fire extinguisher							
5. S IDs use of safety, trigger and sweeping motion via demonstration							
On Appropriate Cue From Drill Instructor:							
6. S closes doors and windows							
7. S unplugs and turns lights off							
8. S waits at exit door until evacuation signal is given							
9. S counts residents							
10. S uses 1st, 2nd or 3rd escape route							

*Score "+" for appropriately completed, "-" for not completed or inappropriately completed, or "NA" for not applicable

Figure 2-3. Example of an observation form used as part of a duration monitoring system — in this case to monitor staff performance during fire drills in an institutional setting for developmentally disabled persons.

quality. Permanent product monitoring processes have been used to evaluate staff's preparation of written training programs for students (Page et al., 1981; Hundert, 1982), written progress notes regarding clients' responsiveness to training endeavors (Repp & Deitz, 1979), staff time and attendance records (Repp & Deitz, 1979), written suggestions from staff to an agency's management (Quilitch, 1978) and completion of civil commitment forms for admitting persons to psychiatric hospitals (Jones, Morris, & Barnard, 1986). Permanent product monitoring can also be easily applied to other types of outcomes of staff performance such as the cleanliness of the physical environment for which staff are responsible (Quilitch, de Longchamps, Warden, & Szczepaniak, 1977) and the availability of prescribed materials for clients to use during leisure time (Risley & Favell, 1979). In some ways, measuring indices of client welfare for which staff are responsible (Chapter 1) can also be considered a type of permanent product monitoring. Monitoring processes for client welfare as a function of staff performance are discussed later in this chapter.

As alluded to previously, the most significant advantage of permanent product monitoring systems is the ease with which these types of systems can be implemented relative to other types of monitoring procedures. Because there is a *permanent* product (or at least an outcome that is stationary for a period of time) that results from staff performance, a supervisor can review the product essentially at his/her convenience. Consequently, the supervisor is not affected by the time and schedule restrictions that characterize duration recording and, to a lesser degree, time sampling. Additionally, less time is often required to monitor the outcome of staff performance than to observe staff work behavior directly. Staff persons also generally seem to be more comfortable with a supervisor monitoring the outcome of their work relative to observing their work behavior directly. However, permanent product monitoring is of course limited to those aspects of staff work responsibilities that result in a change in the physical environment—an outcome that can be relatively infrequent with many human service jobs.

As noted earlier, the most accurate and representative information regarding staff work performance can be obtained through *formal* monitoring systems of the types just exemplified. Unfortunately, though, as with the process of defining staff job duties discussed previously, it is not realistic to expect that a formal monitoring system can be developed, implemented and maintained for *all* aspects of staff work responsibilities. Hence, and again similar to the process of defining job responsibilities, formal monitoring systems should generally be reserved for those staff work duties that are either the most vital to a respective agency's overall mission, or for those work behaviors that are most problematic at any given time. When formal monitoring of certain staff performances is indeed impractical, *informal monitoring* often can still be conducted on a more time-efficient basis to obtain useful information as part of a behavioral supervision program.

Informal Monitoring Systems. Every supervisor essentially engages in informal monitoring to some degree. That is, during the course of the routine workday a supervisor typically comes into contact with staff for whom the supervisor is responsible, providing the supervisor with the opportunity to observe various aspects of the staffs' work behavior. Such informal observations can be quite helpful for obtaining information on how well staff are performing, assuming that there is a degree of systematization added to the observation process, albeit less systematization than what characterizes formal monitoring systems. Systematization is necessary to overcome the inadvertent obtainment of inaccurate and/or nonrepresentative information on staff performance.

Several procedures generally must be incorporated into informal monitoring processes as part of a supervisor's regular work routine if such processes are to result in accurate data collection on staff performance. First, a supervisor must have a very clear definition of what constitutes satisfactory performance whenever he/she happens to observe a staff member's work activity. Many informal monitoring processes involve only a brief observation of staff performance at any given moment, and, without a clear expectation of what staff should be doing, a supervisor will not have sufficient time to thoroughly think about the observed activity to determine if staff are performing acceptably. Second, a supervisor should strive to ensure that his/her observation of staff work performance involves as many of the staff individuals that work for the supervisor as possible and not just a (nonrepresentative) sample of a few staff persons. Probably the best means of accomplishing the latter goal is for a supervisor to incorporate a quick time sampling process within the informal monitoring routine. For example, when a supervisor first enters a respective staff work station for whatever reason, he/she could immediately take a quick look around the work station and make a mental note regarding how many of all the staff who are present are engaging in appropriate work activity and how many are not. By immediately observing the performance of all staff in this manner, an objective idea (albeit based on a small sample of work behavior) can be obtained about how well a work unit of staff is functioning.

The amount of accurate information that a supervisor can obtain on staff performance from informal time sampling systems as just exemplified is usually directly proportional to the frequency with which a supervisor conducts such observations. Hence, a supervisor should strive to make as many observations as possible (or solicit the assistance of reliable others in making observations). Of course, a supervisor must schedule his/her time efficiently to allow opportunities for informal monitoring along with time for fulfillment of other supervisory responsibilities. One advantageous means of conducting frequent observations is for a supervisor to monitor work performance while simultaneously completing other duties. To illustrate, a supervisor can respond to telephone calls from staff members by returning the calls in person in contrast to responding by telephone. By returning a staff member's phone call in person, the supervisor must enter the staff person's work area—which provides the supervisor with an opportunity to conduct a quick time sample observation within the work unit immediately before he/she interacts with the staff member. It is also helpful for a supervisor to limit all meetings or office work to no more than an hour or so in duration whenever possible. By scheduling office time in this manner, a supervisor ensures that he/she can leave a meeting room or office, at least briefly, intermittently throughout the workday, thereby again allowing the opportunity for relatively frequent observations of staff performance. In this respect, it is often advantageous for a supervisor to maintain records (e.g. a weekly tally sheet) regarding how frequently he/she conducts informal observations in various staff work stations—a process that may help a supervisor to maintain an adequate frequency of monitoring staff performance (cf. Burg et al., 1979; Burgio, Whitman, & Reid, 1983).

Even with the types of time-saving procedures as just noted, informally monitoring staff performance can nevertheless require a relatively substantial amount of a supervisor's time. Indeed, a rather common complaint among many supervisors is that they do not have sufficient time to monitor staff performance given numerous other supervisory and administrative responsibilities. However, monitoring staff work activity should not be viewed as a supervisory duty that is secondary in importance to other supervisory tasks (and therefore subject to omission in lieu of completing other duties). It must be remembered that a supervisor's job is to change or maintain staff work behavior, and frequently monitoring staff performance is a necessary step in successfully performing that job on a routine basis. There is also a beneficial side effect of frequent informal monitoring in regard to a supervisor regularly visiting staff work stations: often, staff tend to view such supervisors with more acceptance or respect relative to supervisors who rarely are seen outside of offices or meetings.

Special Concerns with Staff Monitoring Systems

Managing Staff Discomfort. A frequent impediment to supervisors' effective utilization of formal monitoring systems with staff performance is staff dislike of such systems. In short, many staff persons do not like to have their behavior systematically observed by supervisors (or any other persons). Such dislike can be due to a variety of factors, including, for example, staff being self-conscious about their (lack of) certain work skills, staff feeling insulted that their supervisor thinks he/she needs to monitor their performance, and staff thinking that their supervisor does not trust them if he/she has to monitor their behavior. Whatever the cause, supervisors usually need to be prepared to deal with at least some staff discontent when attempting to monitor staff performance on a systematic basis and to take steps to prevent or minimize the potential discontent.

Several guidelines can be useful for reducing staff discomfort with performance monitoring systems. First, it is helpful if supervisors explain openly and honestly what is being observed and why. In most cases, there is no good reason for a supervisor *not* to share the intent of a monitoring system with staff persons. Essentially, staff should know what they are supposed to do (i.e. first step in behavioral supervision) and the focus of the monitoring should likewise be on what staff are supposed to do. Consequently, a supervisor should be able to inform staff rather easily regarding what constitutes the focus of the observations. A supervisor can also openly explain to staff persons that the best way for him/her to know if respective performances are being proficiently completed is to observe staff work activity directly. It can also be helpful to explain that a supervisor is in a much better position to make sound supervisory decisions and to treat staff fairly in regard to work assignments, pay raises, disciplinary actions, etc., if the supervisor has first-hand knowledge regarding staff performance.

A second guideline in regard to reducing staff discomfort with performance monitoring is for a supervisor to conduct observations of work performance without being excessively obtrusive. A supervisor should strive to observe staff behavior in a manner that is least likely to stand out in regard to the normal work environment. For example, a generally undesirable monitoring approach is for a supervisor to overtly stare at a given staff person and/or to closely follow a staff member around while obviously making frequent notations on a clipboard. A more acceptable practice would be for a supervisor to partially join in a work activity or discussion with staff while making quick intermittent observations, and then later briefly record the results of the observations when staff attention is not directly focused on the supervisor. This does not mean that a supervisor should be secretive about observing performance—again, a supervisor should inform staff that he/she will be making observations. Rather, it means that a supervisor should simply try to make observations in a manner that causes the least amount of reaction among staff.

A third guideline is for a supervisor to provide staff with results of the monitoring relatively quickly after the monitoring is completed. If staff persons consistently receive information that results from the monitoring, they generally become more knowledgeable regarding the purpose of the observations. Consequently, whatever inaccurate perceptions staff may have held regarding why a supervisor is monitoring their performance are likely to be diminished (provided that the supervisor has been honest with staff regarding the purpose of the observations).

When attempting to avoid discomfort on the part of staff in regard to performance monitoring systems, supervisors sometimes use *covert* observation procedures. That is, supervisors attempt to observe staff performance secretly without staffs' awareness of the monitoring. Covert systems are also implemented in an attempt to avoid reactivity on the part of staff in terms of staff changing their work behavior when they know that a monitor is present. Rarely, however, do the justifications of a covert observation system outweigh the disadvantages associated with this type of performance monitoring process.

The main problem with covert monitoring systems is the very serious discontent such systems generate among staff. Of course, it is assumed that because the monitoring is conducted covertly, staff will not be aware of the monitoring and consequently will not become discontented. In actuality, though, most formal monitoring systems cannot be implemented in a manner that results in representative and accurate data collection on staff performance without staff becoming at least somewhat aware of the monitoring. When staff do become aware of a supervisor's covert attempts to monitor their performance, staff inevitably view the supervisor in a considerably less than respectful light. Staff often, for example, view such a supervisor as being sneaky or distrustful. When staff have these types of feelings about their supervisor, the supervisor's task of changing and/or maintaining staff work performance is at best difficult and, at worst, essentially impossible.

Because of staff nonacceptance of covert monitoring, this approach to observing staff work performance generally is not recommended for supervisory use. There is one type of situation, however, in which covert monitoring may be necessary. Specifically, if there is relatively good reason for a supervisor to suspect that some kind of very serious inappropriate activity is occurring in a staff work unit—an activity that staff would clearly not engage in if the supervisor was present—then covert monitoring may be necessary in order to essentially catch, and stop, the activity. Such an approach periodically is needed in certain human service agencies in order to stop client exploitation or abuse, theft of agency property, and/or utilization of illegal substances.

Reducing Staff Reactivity to Monitoring Systems. Potential problems with staff reactivity to performance monitoring systems were described earlier. One means of overcoming such problems is for a supervisor to monitor performance by conducting a quick time sample observation of staff performance *immediately* upon entering a staff work station. In this manner, if indeed staff do tend to react to a supervisor's presence by changing their ongoing work behavior, a supervisor can still obtain a brief yet accurate picture of staff performance before staff have time to change their work behavior. In contrast, if a supervisor conducts a time sample observation after he/she has been in the work unit awhile, staff will have had more time to change what they were doing.

Another means of reducing reactivity is for a supervisor to conduct *highly frequent* observations of staff work activity. Typically, any reactivity staff may have to a supervisor's presence is likely to diminish across successive and numerous supervisory observations (cf. Wildman & Erickson, 1977). In addition, a supervisor should not inform staff precisely when he/she will be observing staff work behavior such that staff will not be able to prepare (i.e. change their performance) when they expect a forthcoming observation. A supervisor should inform staff that observations will be forthcoming as discussed earlier but not in terms of the exact time and/or place of the observations. As also mentioned earlier, a supervisor should attempt to conduct observations of staff performance as unobtrusively as possible. Keeping monitoring processes relatively unobtrusive not only reduces staff discomfort with being monitored as noted previously but also helps to reduce staff reactivity to monitoring (Kazdin, 1979; Wildman & Erickson, 1977).

Internal Versus External Monitoring Systems. Internal monitoring systems refer to observation procedures that are conducted by someone who is an integral part of a given staff work unit or conducted by someone who has direct supervisory authority over the work unit. For example, in an institutional living unit, an internal monitor may be a living unit supervisor, the supervisor's secretary, or the team psychologist for the living unit (provided that the latter two persons work exclusively, or at least predominantly, in the living unit). In contrast, *external* monitoring systems are conducted by personnel who are not integrally involved with, or directly responsible for, a respective staff work unit. Using the example of an institutional living unit, an external monitor would be a representative from another institutional living unit or from a department that is in a separate part of the institution's organizational structure (e.g. staff development or quality-assurance department).

There are a number of advantages to internal monitoring systems relative to external approaches. First, because an internal monitor is a person whom staff are accustomed to seeing in the staff work area, the monitor's presence is not an unusual event for staff relative to the presence of an external monitor. It is therefore usually easier for an internal monitor to conduct observations of staff performance unobtrusively and, consequently, with less of a reactive and discomforting effect on staff members. Second, the work activities involved in monitoring staff performance can be considered an integral component (i.e. part of the supervisory process) of the internal monitor's overall job responsibilities, particularly if the monitor is a supervisor of the staff. In contrast, external monitoring usually represents a separate job in and of itself for an agency representative, which requires part or all of an agency staff position exclusively for monitoring. External monitors also are not in a role that allows them to directly respond to information stemming from the monitoring but only to summarize the information to present (second-hand) to a supervisor.

In contrast to the advantages of internal monitoring, a disadvantage that is often cited is that internal monitors are likely to distort the information they obtain in a positively biased fashion (Favell, Favell, Riddle, & Risley, 1984; Risley & Favell, 1979). That is, because internal monitors are evaluating staff performance that they are at least partially responsible for, such monitors may tend to view the performance as being more desirable than would an external monitor who has less investment in how well staff are performing. Whether or not this type of biasing process occurs has not been formally evaluated in staff management, at least to our knowledge. Based on our experience, biased data presentation on the part of internal monitors does not appear to be a consistent problem. Actually, a number of supervisors tend to be particularly critical of staff performance areas for which they are responsible and, subsequently, present data on staff work behavior in an overly negative light. Regardless, safeguards against potentially inaccurate data presentation can be built into internal monitoring systems by intermittently conducting a small number of external observations in addition to the internal checks. Comparisons can then be made between the outcomes of the internal and external monitoring procedures to detect potential differences, and subsequently make whatever changes may be needed in the monitoring processes.

In regard to the advantages of *external* monitoring systems, there are two generally recognized benefits. The first is that these approaches to observing staff performance are not assumed to run the risk of resulting in inaccurate data presentation as are internal systems. Again, though, our experience suggests that internal monitoring systems typically are not seriously characterized by such problems. The second advantage of external systems is that an external monitor, by the nature of his/her designated job responsibilities, usually has more time for conducting systematic observations of staff performance than does an internal monitor. Nevertheless, essentially all of the advantages just noted with internal monitoring systems do not exist with external systems. Also, we have found that agency staff persons who have a full-time responsibility of (externally) monitoring staff work behavior on a formal basis generally do not enjoy that type of job for very long, resulting in a subsequent turnover problem among persons employed to be external monitors.

Monitoring Staff Performance Through Indices of Client Welfare. A method of monitoring staff performance that has been noted only briefly up to this point involves observing indices of client welfare to reflect the adequacy with which staff perform their work. Indeed, because the main mission of any given human service agency is to improve client welfare, it is only logical that the (non)proficiency with which agency staff fulfill that mission be directly monitored (see Chapter 1 for elaboration). We have not focused on monitoring systems for client welfare in this chapter, however, for several reasons. In particular, numerous descriptions are available regarding monitoring systems for client welfare for many kinds of human service settings, including, for example, schools (Parsons, Schepis, Reid, McCarn, & Green, 1987), institutions for the developmentally disabled (Greene et al., 1978) and mentally ill (Pomerleau, Bobrove, & Smith, 1973), nursing homes (Burgio, Burgio, Engel, & Tice, 1986), and preschools (Kunz et al., 1982). To repeat such descriptions here would be needlessly redundant. Also, there is a variety of staff performance responsibilities that, when fulfilled, do not necessarily result in direct and/or readily apparent changes in client behavior (e.g. housekeeping responsibilities, certain recordkeeping duties—see Chapter 8 for elaboration). Monitoring indices of client welfare for those types of staff responsibilities would not be very informative for supervisors in regard to knowing how well staff are performing.

Another reason for not emphasizing monitoring systems for client welfare in this chapter is that there are some areas of client welfare that, although they may be directly affected by staff performance, are affected very slowly over a long period of time. To illustrate, some profoundly handicapped young children are medically at risk due to extremely low body weight and are heavily dependent on the proficiency with which caregiving staff conduct feeding regimes to obtain and/or maintain a healthy body weight (Korabek, Reid, & Ivancic, 1981). The weight of such children often changes very slowly—too slowly to allow day-by-day judgments as to the adequacy with which staff feed respective meals (i.e. daily weight gain would not be expected). In such cases, a more immediately informative means of monitoring staff feeding performance than observing daily weight increments of the children would be to observe, for example, the amount of prescribed food intake that staff successfully feed to a given child per meal such as the percent of food consumed or number of bites of food consumed (Korabek et al., 1981). Such monitoring could be supplemented with less frequent monitoring (e.g. weekly or monthly) of client weight gain or loss.

Although monitoring of staff performance via changes in client welfare is not emphasized in this chapter for the reasons just noted, the importance of observing client behavior as part of the overall management of a human service agency should not be underestimated (see Chapter 1). Throughout the second section of this text numerous examples of monitoring systems for client welfare as a function of training and managing staff performance will be presented. Suffice it to say at this point that, wherever possible, *both* client behavior and staff behavior should be systematically monitored by human service managers. However, in situations such as those just exemplified in which client welfare is not really expected to change as a direct result of changes in staff performance, staff work behavior warrants monitoring in and of itself for the reasons noted throughout this chapter, as well as for those reasons that will be noted periodically throughout the remainder of this text.

Staff Self-Monitoring. A final consideration regarding performance monitoring systems that warrants mentioning is staff *self-monitoring*. Self-monitoring or self-recording involves staff maintaining records on their own work behavior. This type of observation process has been used in a variety of work situations including, for example, direct care staff maintaining records of how often they conduct therapeutic interactions with institutionalized clients (Burgio et al., 1983) and middle-management supervisors recording how often they provide performance feedback to their staff (Reid et al., 1985). However, because self-monitoring often affects the behavior of the staff who are recording their own performance, this procedure is really considered more of a *management* or *consequence process* in behavioral supervision than a performance monitoring approach per se. Consequently, a more detailed discussion of staff self-monitoring is provided in Chapter 4.

REFERENCES

Alavosius, M.P., & Sulzer-Azaroff, B. (1986). The effects of performance feedback on the safety of client lifting and transfer. *Journal of Applied Behavior Analysis, 19,* 261–267.

Brown, K.M., Willis, B.S., & Reid, D.H. (1981). Differential effects of supervisor verbal feedback and feedback plus approval on institutional staff performance. *Journal of Organizational Behavior Management, 3*(1), 57–68.

Burg, M.M., Reid, D.H., & Lattimore, J. (1979). Use of a self-recording and supervision program to change institutional staff behavior. *Journal of Applied Behavior Analysis, 12,* 363–375.

Burgio, L.D., Burgio, K.L., Engel, B.T., & Tice, L.M. (1986). Increasing distance and independence of ambulation in elderly nursing home residents. *Journal of Applied Behavior Analysis, 19,* 357–366.

Burgio, L.D., Whitman, T.L., & Reid, D.H. (1983). A participative management approach for improving direct-care staff performance in an institutional setting. *Journal of Applied Behavior Analysis, 16,* 37–53.

Christian, W.P. (1983). A case study in the programming and maintenance of institutional change. *Journal of Organizational Behavior Management, 5*(3/4), 99–153.

Cuvo, A.J., Leaf, R.B., & Borakove, L.S. (1978). Teaching janitorial skills to the mentally retarded: Acquisition, generalization, and maintenance. *Journal of Applied Behavior Analysis, 11,* 345–355.

Favell, J.E., Favell, J.E., Riddle, J.I., & Risley, T.R. (1984). Promoting change in mental retardation facilities: Getting services from the paper to the people. In W.P. Christian, G.T. Hannah, & T.J. Glahn (Eds.), *Programming effective human services: Strategies for institutional change and client transition* (pp. 15–37). New York: Plenum.

Greene, B.F., Willis, B.S., Levy, R., & Bailey, J.S. (1978). Measuring client gains from staff-implemented programs. *Journal of Applied Behavior Analysis, 11,* 395–412.

Hagen, R.L., Craighead, W.E., & Paul, G.L. (1975). Staff reactivity to evaluative behavioral observations. *Behavior Therapy, 6,* 201–205.

Hay, L.R., Nelson, R.O., & Hay, W.M. (1977). The use of teachers as behavioral observers. *Journal of Applied Behavior Analysis, 10,* 345–348.

Hundert, J. (1982). Training teachers in generalized writing of behavior modification programs for multihandicapped deaf children. *Journal of Applied Behavior Analysis, 15,* 111–122.

Ivancic, M.T., Reid, D.H., Iwata, B.A., Faw, G.D., & Page, T.J. (1981). Evaluating a supervision program for developing and maintaining therapeutic staff-resident interactions during institutional care routines. *Journal of Applied Behavior Analysis, 14,* 95–107.

Iwata, B.A., Bailey, J.S., Brown, K.M., Foshee, T.J., & Alpern, M. (1986). A performance-based lottery to improve residential care and training by institutional staff. *Journal of Applied Behavior Analysis, 9,* 417–431.

Jones, H.H., Morris, E.K., & Barnard, J.D. (1986). Increasing staff completion of civil commitment forms through instructions and graphed group performance feedback. *Journal of Organizational Behavior Management, 7*(3/4), 29–43.

Kazdin, A.E. (1979). Unobtrusive measures in behavioral assessment. *Journal of Applied Behavior Analysis, 12,* 713–724.

Korabek, C.A., Reid, D.H., & Ivancic, M.T. (1981). Improving needed food intake of profoundly handicapped children through effective supervision of institutional staff performance. *Applied Research in Mental Retardation, 2,* 69–88.

Kunz, G.G.R., Lutzker, J.R., Cuvo, A.J., Eddleman, J., Lutzker, S.Z., Megson, D., & Gulley, B. (1982). Evaluating strategies to improve careprovider performance on health and developmental tasks in an infant care facility. *Journal of Applied Behavior Analysis, 15,* 521–531.

McCormick, E.J., & Ilgen, D.R. (1980). *Industrial psychology, second edition.* Englewood Cliffs, NJ: Prentice-Hall.

Page, T.J., Christian, J.G., Iwata, B.A., Reid, D.H., Crow, R.E., & Dorsey, M.F. (1981). Evaluating and training interdisciplinary teams in writing IPP goals and objectives. *Mental Retardation, 19,* 25–27.

Page, T.J., Iwata, B.A., & Reid, D.H. (1982). Pyramidal training: A large-scale application with institutional staff. *Journal of Applied Behavior Analysis, 15,* 335–351.

Parsons, M.B., Schepis, M.M., Reid, D.H., McCarn, J.E., & Green, C.W. (1987). Expanding the impact of behavioral staff management: A large-scale, long-term application in schools serving severely handicapped students. *Journal of Applied Behavior Analysis, 20,* 139–150.

Pomerleau, O.F., Bobrove, P.H., & Smith, R.H. (1973). Rewarding psychiatric aides for the behavioral improvement of assigned patients. *Journal of Applied Behavior Analysis, 6,* 383–390.

Quilitch, H.R. (1978). Using a simple feedback procedure to reinforce the submission of written suggestions by mental health employees. *Journal of Organizational Behavior Management, 1*(2), 155–163.

Quilitch, H.R., de Longchamps, G.D., Warden, R.A., & Szczepaniak, C.J. (1977).

The effects of announced health inspections upon employee cleaning performance. *Journal of Organizational Behavior Management, 1*(1), 79–88.

Reid, D.H., Parsons, M.B., McCarn, J.E., Green, C.W., Phillips, J.F., & Schepis, M.M. (1985). Providing a more appropriate education for severely handicapped persons: Increasing and validating functional classroom tasks. *Journal of Applied Behavior Analysis, 18,* 289–301.

Repp, A.C., & Deitz, D.E.D. (1979). Improving administrative-related staff behaviors at a state institution. *Mental Retardation, 17,* 185–192.

Risley, T.R., & Favell, J. (1979). Constructing a living environment in an institution. In L.A. Hamerlynck (Ed.), *Behavioral systems for the developmentally disabled: II. Institutional, clinic, and community environments* (pp. 3–24). New York: Brunner/ Mazel.

van den Pol, R.A., Reid, D.H., & Fuqua, R.W. (1983). Peer training of safety-related skills to institutional staff: Benefits for trainers and trainees. *Journal of Applied Behavior Analysis, 16,* 139–156.

Whitman, T.L., Scibak, J.W., & Reid, D.H. (1983). *Behavior modification with the severely and profoundly retarded: Research and application.* New York: Academic Press.

Wildman, B.G. & Erickson, M.T. (1977). Methodological problems in behavioral observation. In J.D. Cone & R.P. Hawkins (Eds.), *Behavioral assessment: New directions in clinical psychology* (pp. 255–273). New York: Brunner/Mazel.

Chapter 3

STAFF TRAINING

A critical determinant of the proficiency with which human service staff fulfill their job roles is the amount and quality of the work skills that staff possess. In short, staff must *know how* to competently perform the varied tasks that constitute their assigned responsibilities. Even though the ability of staff to proficiently perform their duties does not guarantee that staff will consistently complete those duties on a day-to-day basis (Reid & Whitman, 1983), if staff *do not* have the necessary work skills, then there is no possibility of the duties being completed satisfactorily. In order to ensure that staff do indeed have the skills to perform their work tasks, staff *training* programs are often necessary in human service organizations.

The importance of staff training is particularly apparent in regard to the performance of paraprofessional staff (Bensberg & Barnett, 1966; Miller & Lewin, 1980). Paraprofessional staff typically are hired into human service jobs such as teacher aides, institutional direct care attendants, group home personnel, etc., without any formal education or training to specifically prepare them for their work responsibilities (Burch, Reiss, & Bailey, 1987). It is subsequently incumbent upon managers in respective human service agencies to ensure that these staff persons receive adequate training in order to be able to perform their job duties adequately.

Staff training programs are also frequently needed for professional staff in human service settings. Although professionals receive formal educational preparation for working in a human service field prior to assuming employment, and therefore do not require as much initial training within an agency as paraprofessional staff, professionals nevertheless often require training for other reasons. For example, many human service agencies require skills of professional personnel that are idiosyncratic to a given agency—special skills that could not be expected to be acquired prior to working in a respective agency (e.g. Fitzgerald et al., 1984; van den Pol, Reid, & Fuqua, 1983). There are also frequent

45

developments in applied research that can affect current service provision, and professionals must receive periodic training in such developments in order to maintain state-of-the-art skills in their particular professions.

Because of the well-recognized need for staff training, a very considerable amount of applied behavioral research has been reported on methods of teaching job skills to human service staff. It is the purpose of this chapter to describe the staff training procedures that have been addressed in the research, along with the relative advantages and disadvantages of each procedure. Before providing such a description, however, a fundamental characteristic of staff training endeavors warrants mention in regard to the behavioral supervision model discussed in Chapter 2. Specifically, staff training should be viewed as a step in the model that is *often necessary* for improving routine staff performance *but rarely sufficient* in this regard. This feature of staff training has been demonstrated in numerous investigations in human service settings (Adams, Tallon & Rimell, 1980; Edwards & Bergman, 1982; Gardner, 1972; McKeown, Adams & Forehand, 1975). Unfortunately, though, staff training programs have not always been viewed in this light. Rather, in many ways staff training programs have been considered as a kind of cure-all for staff performance problems in human service provision. The latter view has resulted in a considerable amount of wasted time on the part of human service managers and staff in regard to resolving problematic staff performance. Again, although staff training is frequently very important, it nevertheless represents only one of the necessary steps in effective supervision.

Focus and Format of Chapter

In accordance with the orientation of the entire text, this chapter addresses staff training research and application that is behavioral in nature. More specifically, the focus is on investigations and program applications in which there was a reliance on *behavioral procedures* as the mechanism to teach new skills to staff. In addition, investigations will be included in which *applied behavior analysis research* designs were used to evaluate the staff training procedures, even though the training procedures themselves may not represent typical behavioral approaches.

The format of the chapter consists of three main sections. First, a review of behavioral staff training procedures will be provided. Second, the staff work skills that have been targeted in the behavioral staff training literature will be discussed. Finally, an evaluative summary of effective staff training procedures will be presented based on the research to date, along with a discussion of issues yet to be resolved with this component of staff supervision.

Behavioral Training Strategies
Used to Teach New Work Skills to Staff

The most prevalent behavioral approach to training new work skills to staff consists of *multifaceted programs* (Whitman, Scibak, & Reid, 1983, chap. 11). Multifaceted approaches involve the use of a large number of behavior change procedures that are combined into one training program. However, there is also a basic set of procedures that represents the core of the multifaceted programs. The latter procedures include verbal instruction, written instruction, performance modeling, performance practice, and feedback. This chapter section describes each of these core procedures.

Verbal Instruction

One of the most common procedures used in staff training programs is verbal instruction. Verbal instruction involves a vocal presentation to staff of the rationale for certain job skills along with related background information and/or a description of the actual job skills per se. Verbal instruction as part of staff training programs has been provided by specialty (expert) personnel who are external to a given human service organization such as university consultants (Katz & Lutzker, 1980; Langone, Koorland, & Oseroff, 1987) as well as by individuals who work within the organization on a routine basis (Fabry & Reid, 1978; Page, Iwata, & Reid, 1982). Verbal instruction has been provided in both a group format with staff (Fitzgerald et al., 1984; Ivancic, Reid, Iwata, Faw, & Page, 1981) and a one-trainer-to-one-staff-person situation (Kissel, Whitman, & Reid, 1983; Stoddard, McIlvane, McDonagh, & Kledaras, 1986). Most frequently, verbal instruction has been presented through direct person(s)-to-person(s) contact in the form of an interaction between a supervisor or designated trainer and a staff member (e.g. Page et al., 1982). In a relatively small number of cases, audiovisual formats such as computer-assisted programs (Singer, Sowers, & Irvin, 1986) and slide-tape presentations (Edwards & Bergman, 1982) have also been employed that do not rely on an interpersonal interaction between a trainer and trainee.

Verbal instruction as a means of teaching work skills to staff can be advantageous in several ways. In particular, verbal instruction often sets the occasion for two-way communication between the trainer and trainee regarding the subject matter being trained. Such communication allows for an ongoing question-and-answer process which enhances the individualization of the training based on specific staff needs. Verbal instruction is also a rather traditionally accepted means of training, in that it probably is the most frequently used staff training approach. In contrast to these advantages, however, there are also several notable disadvantages to verbal instruction. Most importantly, verbal instruction when used as the sole means of training staff often does not result in satisfactory levels of skill acquisition on the part of staff trainees (Gardner, 1972). The ineffectiveness may be due to a variety of factors, including the inability of the presenter to communicate effectively and/or inattentiveness of the (trainee) audience.

All things considered, and based on a rather substantial amount of staff training research (see Gardner, 1972; Whitman et al., 1983, chap. 11, for reviews), verbal instruction generally is best suited for teaching *verbal* skills to staff (i.e. the ability to discuss the subject matter) in contrast to teaching *performance* skills (how to actually do a job). Job-related verbal skills can be important for staff, in that being able to articulate the requirements of a job task can enhance the staffs' understanding of what it is they are supposed to do. However, being able to discuss and/or understand the requirements of a job does not ensure that staff will be able to perform the job. From a service provision standpoint, the latter skills are the more important.

Written Instruction

Another popular staff training procedure is written instruction. As with instructions presented vocally, written instruction can be presented in a variety of formats including self-instructional manuals that are prepared by an agency specifically for training one type of job skill to staff (Fitzgerald et al., 1984; Ford, 1983; Hundert, 1982) and commercially available, published papers or books for training a variety of more general work skills (McKeown et al., 1975; Stumphauzer & Davis, 1983a). Performance checklists as described in Chapter 2 can also be used to instruct staff in how to perform a particular skill (Inge & Snell, 1985) as can pictorial presentation of work duties (Fitzgerald et al., 1984; Stoddard et al., 1986).

A primary advantage of written instruction is that it reduces or eliminates the need for an on-site trainer. That is, staff can receive the instruction without constant trainer supervision. To illustrate, written information in the form of a Personalized System of Instruction (Ford, 1983) was used to train institutional staff by providing them with successive units of written material that they could study at their own pace. Another advantage of written instruction is that, frequently, written material is more likely to ensure a complete description of specific job tasks relative to verbal instruction. Written instruction can also provide a permanent referent for staff, in that they can review the information on an as-needed basis (see similar discussion in Chapter 2 regarding performance checklists).

In contrast to the advantages of written instruction as just noted, a disadvantage of this approach to staff training is that staff must be able to read and understand what is written, and not all human service staff are sufficiently skillful in this area. Insufficient staff reading ability can be particularly problematic for some paraprofessional staff who lack a high school education. An additional disadvantage of written instruction is that if published papers or commercially available materials are used, the content of the written information is sometimes too general to be of value to staff for application in their particular work setting. Finally, if used as the sole training mechanism, written instruction provides limited or no opportunity for clarification and/or discussion between a staff trainer and trainee.

Performance Modeling

The two training procedures just described, verbal and written instruction, are in essence based on *verbal* skills of the staff trainer and trainee. Such procedures center on individuals' ability to speak clearly, listen carefully, and/or read and write proficiently. In contrast, performance modeling as a staff training procedure centers more on *performance* skills: a trainer's ability to proficiently demonstrate or perform the task being trained and a trainee's ability to observe the performance. Using performance modeling or demonstration, the task(s) to be taught can be physically demonstrated via live (Fitzgerald et al., 1984; Mansdorf & Burstein, 1986) or filmed (Ascione & Borg, 1983; Kissel et al., 1983) models.

A necessary component in the effective use of modeling as a means of training staff is the availability of a trainer (model) who has performance expertise in a given skill area. Generally, investigations on modeling have relied on certain personnel indigenous to a respective human service agency to function as models for training other staff in the agency. For example, occupational therapists have functioned as staff trainers to model certain motor development procedures for caregiving staff to conduct with physically handicapped clients (Inge & Snell, 1985). Programmatically skilled supervisors of direct care staff and psychologists have also functioned as trainers to model specific client-related behavior management skills (Mansdorf & Burstein, 1986; Page et al., 1982). Experienced peers have likewise served as models for less experienced colleagues as a means of teaching institutional caregiving routines (van den Pol et al., 1983) as well as teaching appropriate interaction styles in group home settings (Maloney, Phillips, Fixsen, & Wolf, 1975).

Frequently, when modeling is used to train staff, the modeling is conducted in a simulated work situation. Such situations often involve trainers and/or trainees role-playing client behavior (Jones & Eimers, 1975) according to a planned script in order to ensure that each skill targeted to be taught to staff is demonstrated. However, modeling can also be conducted in a less structured manner by a trainer in the trainees' actual work site involving the clients for whom the trainees are responsible (Templeman, Fredericks, Bunse, & Moses, 1983).

A major advantage of performance modeling is that it is often easier for staff to comprehend what a work skill entails if they view firsthand the procedure relative to if they listen to, or read, a description of the task. If the procedures that are demonstrated have to be altered during training due to an unanticipated environmental event, then staff can also see how the trainer adjusts the procedures to accommodate various changes in the work setting. An additional advantage of modeling is that staff do not have to have the degree of academic skills (i.e. reading and writing) to benefit from modeling approaches to training relative to written instruction.

Although performance modeling, whether live or filmed, can be a relatively effective means of teaching new skills to staff, there are also some disadvantages. One disadvantage is that, as just noted, an experienced practitioner must be available to perform the task proficiently in the modeling situation, and such personnel may not always be available in certain settings. Further, some practitioners who are proficient in conducting a particular work task feel uncomfortable performing the task in front of their peers and, consequently, are not very willing to engage in this type of staff training process. In regard to the use of video or filmed demonstrations in lieu of a live model, the necessary equipment may not be readily accessible for training staff and/or the equipment may require an unrealistic financial outlay for a given human service agency.

Performance Practice

Like modeling, performance practice involves more of a reliance on performance or motor skills than verbal skills. However, whereas modeling primarily entails proficient motor skills on the part of a staff trainer, performance practice centers on the motor skills of the staff trainee. That is, performance practice involves a trainee rehearsing the targeted skill that is being trained by the staff trainer. Performance practice typically follows verbal instruction, written instruction, and/or performance modeling as part of a staff training program. The former training procedures are initially used by a trainer to introduce and describe the work behavior(s) expected of staff, followed in turn by the trainees practicing the work skill. Trainees may practice the targeted work activities in the environment in which they routinely work (Stoddard et al., 1986) and/or in simulated work situations (Delamater, Connors, & Wells, 1984; Mansdorf & Burstein, 1986; Watson & Uzzell, 1980; Zlomke & Benjamin, 1983).

One rather unusual type of performance practice that has been used at times in staff training programs is verbal and/or written practice or recall. In this type of performance practice, staff essentially describe to a trainer what the work skill entails after the trainer has instructed the staff (Filler, Hecimovic, & Blue, 1978). Verbal or written recall is used primarily to help verify that the trainee has gained some (verbal) understanding of the job task being trained.

From a trainer's perspective, performance practice is most advantageous, in that it provides the trainer with clear information as to whether the staff trainee has indeed acquired the skill being trained. Actually, the only way a trainer should ever be convinced that his/her staff training program has been effective is to *see* the staff person competently perform the targeted work skill. Performance practice frequently has the additional advantage of assisting a staff member to gain confidence in his/her ability to implement the particular procedure being trained. However, performance practice can also be rather disadvantageous, in that only a few staff can be trained at any one time (i.e. only as many staff can be trained whose performance can be observed by the staff trainer). In addition, certain staff may feel uncomfortable performing the skill being trained in front of the trainer, especially if the staff question their level of proficiency in performing the task.

Performance Feedback

The final procedure that is usually incorporated within multifaceted approaches to staff training is performance feedback. When used as part of a staff training program, feedback refers to information provided to a staff trainee regarding the (non)proficiency with which the trainee has performed the skill being trained. Feedback is usually provided by a staff trainer immediately after a trainee has practiced the skill being trained in order to inform the trainee whether he/she has mastered the skill or if the trainee needs to change certain aspects of his/her performance.

There is a wide variety of methods of presenting feedback to staff persons as part of training endeavors, ranging from rather formal computer-generated information on performance (Singer et al., 1986) to informal comments from a supervisor (Page et al., 1982). Although there are relative advantages and disadvantages to each of the various methods of presenting feedback, essentially every procedure can be effective to some degree (see Reid & Green, in press, for a review on the use of feedback in organizational behavior management research on staff training). Actually, feedback is one of the most effective means of improving staff performance. The significance of feedback in this regard has been most apparent in management research and application that focus on changing routine staff performance in the daily work setting (i.e. improving staffs' implementation of work skills that they know *how* to perform but nevertheless are not performing) rather than on staff training per se (i.e. teaching new work skills to staff). For this reason, a detailed discussion of performance feedback procedures will be provided in Chapter 4 which specifically addresses changing staffs' day-to-day application of their work skills. Suffice it to say at this point that performance feedback is usually an integral component of effective multifaceted approaches to staff training.

Types of Skills Targeted in Behavioral Research on Staff Training

Due in essence to the multitude of different types of job responsibilities within and across human service agencies, organizational behavior management research in staff training has focused on a wide variety of job skills. Such skills range from staffs' ability to apply treatment proce-

dures for improving client functioning to staffs' completion of environmental maintenance routines and administrative duties. This chapter
section discusses the major types of skills that have been addressed in the
staff training research.

Training Staff to Use Multi-Varied
Behavioral Treatment Strategies With Clients

A widely accepted treatment model for teaching adaptive skills to
clients as well as remediating client behavior problems in human service
organizations is behavior modification (see *Journal of Applied Behavior
Analysis,* Volumes 1–20). A necessary component in the effective use of
behavior modification procedures for meeting client habilitative needs
is that staff who are responsible for implementing the procedures must
be skilled in such applications; the staff must be adequately *trained* to
carry out the treatment strategies. Consequently, a number of staff training programs have been developed for training human service staff in
the general use of a multi-varied set of behavior modification principles
and procedures. In particular, paraprofessional staff in institutional and
community settings serving mentally retarded persons have participated
in numerous training programs focusing on a general knowledge of the
basic principles and practices of behavior modification (Ford, 1983;
Gage, Fredericks, Johnson-Dorn, & Lindley-Southard, 1982; Gardner,
1972; Rosen, Yerushalmi & Walker, 1986; Schinke & Wong, 1978; Zlomke
& Benjamin, 1983). Using multifaceted programs involving essentially
all of the staff training procedures discussed in the preceding section,
these programs have taught staff a wide variety of behavior modification
skills such as appropriate terminology, data collection procedures, client
assessment strategies, and a variety of skills that are necessary for developing and writing individualized client treatment programs.

Professional staff have also participated in a large number of training
programs focusing on multi-varied behavior modification treatment
approaches with clients in such settings as schools (Anderson, Kratochwill,
& Bergan, 1986) and community mental health centers (Stumphauzer &
Davis, 1983a; 1983b). Koegel, Russo, and Rincover (1977), for example,
trained teachers of autistic children to competently apply a comprehensive,
prototypical set of behavior modification procedures for use with their
students. The Koegel et al. program focused on training teachers how to
prompt students to help them engage in appropriate activities, to shape
and refine student skills, and to deliver consequences to maintain stu-

dent skills. Similar types of behavior modification procedures have also been targeted in a number of other teacher training programs (e.g. Hundert, 1982; Langone et al., 1987; McKeown et al., 1975; Templeman et al., 1983). As with the training procedures used with paraprofessional staff, the staff training programs with professional teachers involved primarily multifaceted training approaches using most if not all of the procedures described in the preceding section.

Training Staff to Use Singular Habilitative Strategies With Clients

Each of the organizational behavior management studies just noted represents a rather comprehensive approach to staff training. The comprehensiveness is reflected in the use of a number of different procedures (e.g. verbal and written instructions, performance modeling and practice, feedback) *to train* the staff as well as a number of different skills *to be trained to* the staff as exemplified in the Koegel et al. (1977) study. Generally, however, most staff training programs that have focused on teaching staff how to implement behavior modification strategies with clients have been much less comprehensive. Most studies have focused on training staff to proficiently implement only one or a few specific types of behavior modification procedures, and have used only a subset of the training procedures described in the preceding section to conduct the staff training activities.

A number of studies have focused on training staff, both paraprofessionals and professionals, how to *reinforce* appropriate client behavior (Adams et al., 1980; Gross & Ekstrand, 1983; Hall, Panyan, Rabon, & Broden, 1968; Neef, Shafer, Egel, Cataldo, & Parrish, 1983; Panyan & Patterson, 1974; Speidel & Tharp, 1978; Van Houton & Sullivan, 1975). Several staff training programs have also taught staff to *punish* aberrant client behavior (Katz & Lutzker, 1980; Mansdorf & Burstein, 1986). A number of investigations have likewise examined methods of training staff to use behavioral treatment procedures specifically designed to *teach self-help skills* to mentally retarded persons (Kissel et al., 1983; Watson & Uzzell, 1980). Similarly, conducting specific *self-care routines* with dependent clients has been targeted in the behavioral research on staff training, including appropriate feeding techniques with physically and mentally handicapped persons (Edwards & Bergman, 1982), safely lifting clients in and out of wheelchairs (Stoddard et al., 1986), properly positioning nonambulatory clients (Inge & Snell, 1985), and responding to client seizures (van den Pol et al., 1983). Other staff training programs have focused on *teaching manual signing* skills to institutional staff in order to enhance staff communication with nonverbal clients during routine daily activities (Fitzgerald et al., 1984) and on teaching institutional direct care staff and teachers to *conduct purposeful learning activities* with severely and profoundly handicapped persons (Burch et al., 1987; Green, Canipe, Way, & Reid, 1986; Reid et al., 1985).

Training Administrative and Supervisory Skills to Staff

The focus of the staff training programs in the preceding section involved staff skills that directly impact client welfare such as teaching clients new skills, providing personal care to dependent clients, etc. Although improving client welfare is the primary mission of human service agencies (and, therefore, staff skills that directly affect that welfare are of utmost importance), there are numerous other staff activities that must occur in human service settings in order to allow staff to have the opportunity to provide direct services to clients. Staff must also be trained in how to conduct these types of (nonclient) duties. One such set of duties is administrative responsibilities. Administrative duties generally refer to those work tasks that are not performed directly with clients but impact on the ultimate ability of an agency to provide appropriate services to clients (see Chapter 8 for a more detailed discussion of administrative responsibilities).

Several studies in the organizational behavior management area have identified administrative-related skills as training needs of staff. Due to the necessity of qualitative program planning now mandated by many regulatory bodies (e.g. Intermediate Care Facility Standards governing treatment provision in residential facilities for the mentally retarded, Public Law 94-142 governing school programs for children with special needs), researchers have focused on how to teach staff to develop client treatment goals and objectives in accordance with regulatory guidelines (Page et al., 1981). Training staff (e.g. teachers) how to write treatment programs to meet identified client goals has also been the focus of staff training research (Hundert, 1982). Relatedly, training staff to evaluate treatment goals and corresponding implementation strategies has been targeted by staff training researchers (Maher, 1981).

Another type of nonclient-oriented responsibility targeted in the staff training research is supervisory skills (i.e. how to change and maintain staff work behavior). To date, researchers have evaluated methods of teaching supervisors to give feedback to staff in institutional (Page et al. 1982) and group home settings (Davis, McEachern, Christensen, & Vant Voort, 1987), as well as improving supervisors' general interpersonal skills (Clark et al., 1985). In essence, these studies have attempted to demonstrate how to teach supervisors subsets of the types of procedures that have been discussed in this and preceding chapters, as well as procedures that will be described in subsequent chapters.

Evaluative Summary of Behavioral Research and Application in Staff Training

As indicated in the two preceding sections, there has been a very considerable amount of organizational behavior management research on methods of training job skills to human service staff. Such research has resulted in the development of a variety of training programs that can be used to teach numerous types of work skills. Based on the training research that has been conducted, a number of data-based conclusions can be made regarding effective versus non-effective approaches for training human service staff. However, the technology of staff training is by no means complete. This chapter section summarizes the primary conclusions that can be drawn from the staff training research, as well as the gaps that exist in our current knowledge base.

Overall Role of Staff Training as Part of Behavioral Supervision

The role of staff training within an organizational behavior management approach to supervision was noted earlier. To reiterate, staff training should be viewed as a component of behavioral supervision that is *often necessary* for improving staff performance *but rarely sufficient* in this regard. This feature of staff training is repeated here because it represents probably the most important conclusion that can be made from the staff training research. In short, staff training in and of itself should not be relied on to resolve very many staff performance problems—staff training should be used to *help* solve problems with staff work behavior in conjunction with the other components of the behavioral supervision model (Chapter 2).

Essentially, there are three reasons why staff training endeavors are often not sufficient for improving day-to-day staff performance. First, staff training programs do not always sufficiently teach staff how to perform the skills that are addressed in the training programs. The ineffectiveness of training attempts in this respect is most notable in regard to those training procedures that rely primarily on *verbal* teaching strategies (e.g. verbal instruction in the form of classroom lectures, discussion groups, instructional films). As noted earlier, verbal teaching strategies are often ineffective for teaching how to *perform* a work task. When considering the wealth of reports of staff training programs that *are* effective, however (and particularly the multifaceted programs described previously), there really seems to be no acceptable reason for conducting training programs that do not effectively teach staff how to perform a particular work skill. Numerous means of effectively training staff are described in the reports referenced throughout this chapter and the interested reader is referred to those reports for procedural elaboration (see also summary section at the end of this chapter).

The second reason why staff training programs are rarely sufficient for improving staff job performance is that even when the programs effectively teach staff to perform a skill, staff trainees frequently do not maintain the newly acquired skill for very long (van den Pol et al., 1983). Part of the problem in this regard is that many of the early behavioral investigations on staff training procedures did not examine the durability of trainee skills that were initially acquired through staff training programs. Although more recent investigations have focused on skill maintenance, this feature continues to be omitted in much of the staff training research. To illustrate, of the 40-plus staff training studies referenced in this chapter, essentially half did not report data on the long-term maintenance of initial behavior changes among staff trainees.

Because the difficulty in maintaining skills taught to staff is due to a number of factors, an in-depth discussion of methods of overcoming problems with skill durability is beyond the scope of this chapter. However, a relevant discussion is provided in Chapter 4 regarding antecedent versus consequence supervisory procedures (see also Whitman et al., 1983, chap. 3, for discussion on this topic). At this point, suffice it to say that in order to maintain staff skills that are taught via a staff training program, supervisors must be prepared to conduct follow-up supervisory procedures to assist staffs' skill maintenance as part of the day-to-day work routine (see Chapter 4).

A third reason for the somewhat qualified impact of staff training on routine staff performance relates to *insufficient skill generalization.* Frequently, staff may be able to perform a work skill within the training situation but cannot, or do not, perform the skill during the regular job situation (i.e.

the skill does not generalize across situations). The primary problem underlying difficulties in skill generalization is that the conditions in which staff perform a skill during staff training are often quite different than the routine work conditions in which staff are ultimately expected to apply the skill. The differences may be due, for example, to different physical environments (e.g. a staff training classroom versus a staff work site in a nursing home, school, mental health center, etc.), different work materials used in staff training programs relative to the materials available in the daily work setting (e.g. simulated equipment versus actual job tools), and fewer distractions in staff training routines relative to the actual job site (e.g. the latter situation typically involves more staff peers and other personnel, more clients, more supervisory demands on staff, etc.). One major means of overcoming the problems with lack of skill generalization is to conduct staff training through an *on-the-job* format (Horton, 1975). As discussed in the next section though, some controversy currently exists over the relative merits of on-the-job approaches to staff training.

Classroom-Based Training Versus On-The-Job Training

Traditionally, staff training programs in human service settings have been characterized by a reliance on verbally oriented training procedures conducted in classroom-type settings separate from staff work areas (e.g. Frazier, 1972). One of the major impacts of organizational behavior management research on staff training has been the development and application of more performance-oriented training procedures implemented in the routine work environment of staff. Generally, these two rather divergent approaches to staff training represent two ends of a continuum of training procedures. Specifically, on the one end, staff training can be conducted entirely in a classroom with primarily verbal training procedures (Edwards & Bergman, 1982). On the other end of the continuum, training can be conducted entirely within the natural job site with performance training strategies (Ringer, 1973), although almost all of the latter procedures still entail at least some verbal formats (e.g. instructional comments from a trainer). Various training approaches also fall within the two ends of the continuum such as those programs that involve implementation of both verbal and performance procedures in a classroom, and implementation of some of both types of procedures in the routine work site (e.g. Faw, Reid, Schepis, Fitzgerald, & Welty, 1981). The relative merits of the performance-oriented procedures have been noted earlier, as has the advantage of on-the-job training in terms of reducing problems with skill generalization. However, to date the research does not provide sufficient data to conclude the degree to which *both* approaches to training should be incorporated into multifaceted staff training programs (i.e. at what point on the continuum the most effective approaches exist).

All things considered, there are advantages and disadvantages to both of the approaches to staff training just noted. Table 3-1 summarizes the most apparent characteristics that usually exist in this regard with the different training formats. At this point, a reasonable conclusion based on the available research data, albeit a conservative conclusion, is that those training programs designed to improve some aspect of day-to-day staff performance *should include at least some performance training strategies conducted at least in part within the trainees' routine work site*. Before an objective delineation of the relative amounts of the different types of *verbal, classroom-based* procedures that should be incorporated into staff training programs can be made, additional research is needed.

Table 3-1
GENERAL ADVANTAGES AND DISADVANTAGES OF CLASSROOM-BASED VS. ON-THE-JOB TRAINING

Training Format	*Advantages*	*Disadvantages*
Classroom-Based	Efficient use of trainer time	Difficult for supervisors to arrange while ensuring fulfillment of staff work duties.
	Facilitates staff acquisition of verbal knowledge of job duties	
	Easy for staff trainer to schedule	Difficult to ensure consistent staff attentiveness to training
	Minimizes distractions for staff during training	Difficult to determine and/or ensure that staff can actually perform the skills discussed in the classroom
	Traditionally accepted approach to training	
On-The-Job	Minimizes problems with skill generalization	Usually requires (time-consuming) 1:1 trainer-to-trainee working arrangement
	Enhances determination of trainee proficiency of skills being trained	Frequent distractions during training
	Facilitates application of trained skills within routine work site	Can interfere with ongoing work in the job site
		Difficult for trainer to schedule

Methodological (In)Adequacies of Behavioral Staff Training Research

As would generally be expected with any area of research, the methodological sophistication of investigations on staff training procedures has generally improved from the earlier investigations to the more recent studies. Nevertheless, continued improvement in the research methodology is needed in order to resolve existing problems with staff training procedures as noted periodically in this chapter. In particular, as alluded to in the preceding section, additional research is needed to more thoroughly compare various approaches to staff training. Such comparison research is needed to evaluate not only the relative *effectiveness* of different training procedures but also the *efficiency* in regard to the amount of skill acquisition of trainees relative to trainer time and expense investment in the respective training programs (cf. Ford, 1983).

Another major area in need of research is the *acceptability* (Chapter 1) of different training approaches. Specifically, the degree to which staff trainers and trainees enjoy, or are accepting of, various training formats warrants investigation. Procedural acceptability can be a significant variable that affects the ultimate utility of a staff training program in a human service agency (see Reid & Green, in press, for discussion). To date, less than one-fourth of the investigations on staff training procedures have evaluated trainer or trainee acceptance of the training programs (see Fitzgerald et al., 1984; Maher, 1981; van den Pol et al., 1983, for representative examples of acceptability measures in staff training research).

An additional area in need of research attention pertains to those staff training programs that are designed to teach staff certain skills to directly impact client welfare (e.g. how to conduct therapy or personal care regimens with clients). Essentially, if these programs are to be considered truly effective, then it must be demonstrated that staff acquired the targeted skills *and* that the staff could indeed apply the skills with their clients (Chapter 1). The latter demonstration requires an apparent improvement in client welfare as a function of the staffs' acquisition (and application) of the designated skills (Greene, Willis, Levy, & Bailey, 1978). Although several investigations have demonstrated that client welfare can be enhanced by training certain skills to staff (e.g., Fabry & Reid, 1978; Faw et al., 1981; Keogel et al., 1977), the majority of studies have not evaluated whether staff participation in a training program targeting client-treatment or caregiving skills results in any improvement in client welfare.

Summary: A Prototypical Approach to Staff Training

Throughout this chapter the relative advantages and disadvantages of various staff training procedures have been noted, as well as some general suggestions regarding the circumstances most appropriate for implementing respective procedures. This chapter section summarizes the previously presented information into a prototypical approach to staff training. Of course, given the multiplicity of job responsibilities in human service agencies, we do not suggest that our recommended training strategy would be appropriate in every situation. Respective training formats ultimately need to be based on the specific circumstances in which staff training is needed. The educational background of trainees, for example, can affect the amount and type of training that is likely to be effective (Page et al., 1981). The amount of time that is expected to be encompassed in training can likewise impact how, and/or by whom, training should be conducted (van den Pol et al., 1983) as can the verbal versus performance nature of the skills to be taught to trainees (Gardner, 1972). Nevertheless, our review of the staff training research, as well as our own experience, suggests that there is a prototypical staff training approach that can be effectively applied to meet many staff training needs.

The basic components of a prototypical staff training program are presented in Table 3-2 (cf. Reid, Parsons, & Schepis, in press). The first two steps represented in Table 3-2 are essentially the first two steps of the generic behavioral supervision model (Chapter 2). The remaining steps reflect training procedures discussed in this chapter, each of which can usually be implemented in a variety of formats (as also discussed in this chapter).

An important ingredient in the success of the training approach summarized in Table 3-2 is the involvement of the supervisor of the staff trainees. Whenever possible, the person responsible for training staff should be the day-to-day supervisor of the staff. The advantages of staff supervisors functioning in a staff training capacity have been discussed elsewhere (Parsons et al., 1987; Reid et al., in press) and will be only briefly summarized here. The first advantage is that by requiring a supervisor to train important skills to staff, the probability that the

Table 3-2

COMPONENT STEPS OF A PROTOTYPICAL STAFF TRAINING PROGRAM

Step	*Procedural Summary*
1	Specify work behaviors to be taught to staff.
2	Provide staff with checklist description of the work behaviors specified in Step 1.
3	Verbally describe the work behaviors on the checklist to staff, along with the rationale for the importance of the skills.
4	Physically demonstrate the target behaviors for staff.
5	Observe staff practice the target behaviors.
6	Provide corrective and/or approving feedback to staff based on their demonstration of the target behaviors.
7	Continue Steps 4, 5 and 6 until staff are observed to perform the target behaviors adequately.

supervisor him/herself is competent in the targeted work skills is enhanced relative to a supervisor not being involved in training, and such competency facilitates the supervisor's task of effectively managing staff performance. Second, once a supervisor trains staff in respective work skills, he/she is in an advantageous position to carry out necessary procedures to help staff apply and maintain their newly acquired work skills (see Chapter 4 for elaboration). Finally, the involvement of the supervisor in staff training programs often helps to impress upon staff the importance of the skills being trained and, relatedly, that the supervisor values the participation of staff in the training programs.

Recommending that supervisors be responsible for staff training endeavors does not imply that there is no need for agency personnel to be employed solely for staff training purposes (e.g. staff development departments). Rather, it means that, frequently, the target audience for staff training personnel should be primarily supervisors and, secondarily, staff members under the supervisors' domain of responsibility. Most desirably, staff training personnel should work in close conjunction with supervisory persons in order to train agency staff. In some cases, such as those training needs that continuously occur (e.g. orienting new staff), supervisors may initially conduct training endeavors in order to ensure the supervisors' competence in the skill area being addressed, and staff training personnel may conduct subsequent training programs with the supervisors' awareness of the occurrence and outcome of the training.

Staff training personnel and supervisors may also divide among themselves certain components of training programs in order to minimize the work load involved in training staff. Regardless of which particular strategy is used, however, it is again stressed that an important component in the overall success of the training endeavor is usually at least some significant involvement on the part of the supervisor. The following chapter discusses more specifically what such involvement should entail.

REFERENCES

Adams, G.L., Tallon, R.J., & Rimell, P. (1980). A comparison of lecture versus role-playing in the training of the use of positive reinforcement. *Journal of Organizational Behavior Management, 2*(3), 205–212.

Anderson, T.K., Kratochwill, T.R., & Bergan, J.R. (1986). Training teachers in behavioral consultation and training: An analysis of verbal behaviors. *Journal of School Psychology, 24*, 229–241.

Ascione, F.R., & Borg, W.R. (1983). A teacher-training program to enhance mainstreamed, handicapped pupils' self-concepts. *Journal of School Psychology, 21*, 297–309.

Bensberg, G.J., & Barnett, C.D. (1966). *Attendant training in southern residential facilities for the mentally retarded.* Atlanta: Southern Regional Education Board.

Burch, M.R., Reiss, M.L., & Bailey, J.S. (1987). A competency-based "hands-on" training package for direct care staff. *Journal of the Association for Persons with Severe Handicaps, 12*, 67–71.

Clark, H.B., Wood, R., Kuehnel, T., Flanagan, S., Mosk, M., & Northrup, J.T. (1985). Preliminary validation and training of supervisory interactional skills. *Journal of Organizational Behavior Management, 7*(1/2), 95–115.

Davis, J.R., McEachern, M.A., Christensen, J., & Vant Voort, C. (1987). Behavioral skills workshop for staff and supervisor in a community residence for developmentally handicapped adults. *Behavioral Residential Treatment, 2*(1), 25–36.

Delamater, A.M., Connors, C.K., & Wells, K.C. (1984). A comparison of staff training procedures: Behavioral applications in the child psychiatric inpatient setting. *Behavior Modification, 8*, 39–58.

Edwards, G., & Bergman, J.S. (1982). Evaluation of a feeding training program for caregivers of individuals who are severely physically handicapped. *Journal of the Association for the Severely Handicapped, 7*, 93–101.

Fabry, P.L., & Reid, D.H. (1978). Teaching foster grandparents to train severely handicapped persons. *Journal of Applied Behavior Analysis, 11*, 111–123.

Faw, G.D., Reid, D.H., Schepis, M.M., Fitzgerald, J.R., & Welty, P.A. (1981). Involving institutional staff in the development and maintenance of sign language skills with profoundly retarded persons. *Journal of Applied Behavior Analysis, 14*, 411–423.

Filler, J., Hecimovic, A., & Blue, S. (1978). An analysis of the effectiveness of a preservice workshop for educators of severely handicapped young students. *AAESPH Review, 3,* 174–177.

Fitzgerald, J.R., Reid, D.H., Schepis, M.M., Faw, G.D., Welty, P.A., & Pyfer, L.M. (1984). A rapid training procedure for teaching manual sign language skills to multidisciplinary institutional staff. *Applied Research in Mental Retardation, 5,* 451–469.

Ford, J.E. (1983). Application of a personalized system of instruction to a large, personnel training program. *Journal of Organizational Behavior Management, 5*(3/4), 57–65.

Frazier, T.W. (1972). Training institutional staff in behavior modification principles and techniques. In R.D. Ruben, H. Fensterheim, J.D. Henderson & L.P. Ullmann (Eds.), *Advances in Behavior Therapy: Proceedings of the Fourth Conference of the Association for Advancement of Behavior Therapy* (pp. 171–178). New York: Academic Press.

Gage, M.A., Fredericks, H.D.B., Johnson-Dorn, N., & Lindley-Southard, B. (1982). Inservice training for staffs of group homes and work activity centers serving developmentally disabled adults. *The Journal of the Association for Persons with Severe Handicaps, 7,* 60–70.

Gardner, J.M. (1972). Teaching behavior modification to nonprofessionals. *Journal of Applied Behavior Analysis, 5,* 517–521.

Green, C.W., Canipe, V.S., Way, P.J., & Reid, D.H. (1986). Improving the functional utility and effectiveness of classroom services for students with profound multiple handicaps. *The Journal of the Association for Persons with Severe Handicaps, 11*(3), 162–170.

Greene, B.F., Willis, B.S., Levy, R., & Bailey, J.S. (1978). Measuring client gains from staff-implemented programs. *Journal of Applied Behavior Analysis, 11,* 395–412.

Gross, A.M., & Ekstrand, M. (1983). Increasing and maintaining rates of teacher praise: A study using public posting and feedback fading. *Behavior Modification, 7,* 126–135.

Hall, R.V., Panyan, M., Rabon, D., & Broden, M. (1968). Instructing beginning teachers in reinforcement procedures which improve classroom control. *Journal of Applied Behavior Analysis, 1,* 315–322.

Horton, G.O. (1975). Generalization of teacher behavior as a function of subject matter specific discrimination training. *Journal of Applied Behavior Analysis, 8,* 311–319.

Hundert, J. (1982). Training teachers in generalized writing of behavior modification programs for multihandicapped deaf children. *Journal of Applied Behavior Analysis, 15,* 111–122.

Inge, K.J., & Snell, M.E. (1985). Teaching positioning and handling techniques to public school personnel through inservice training. *The Journal of the Association for Persons With Severe Handicaps, 10,* 105–110.

Ivancic, M.T., Reid, D.H., Iwata, B.A., Faw, G.D., & Page, T.J. (1981). Evaluating a supervision program for developing and maintaining therapeutic staff-resident interactions during institutional care routines. *Journal of Applied Behavior Analysis, 14,* 95–107.

Jones, F.H., & Eimers, R.C. (1975). Role playing to train elementary teachers to use a classroom management "skill package." *Journal of Applied Behavior Analysis, 8,* 421–433.

Katz, R.C., & Lutzker, J.R. (1980). A comparison of three methods for training timeout. *Behavior Research of Severe Developmental Disabilities, 1,* 123–130.

Kissel, R.C., Whitman, T.L., & Reid, D.H. (1983). An institutional staff training and self-management program for developing multiple self-care skills in severely/ profoundly retarded individuals. *Journal of Applied Behavior Analysis, 16,* 395–415.

Koegel, R.L., Russo, D.C., & Rincover, A. (1977). Assessing and training teachers in the generalized use of behavior modification with autistic children. *Journal of Applied Behavior Analysis, 10,* 197–205.

Langone, J., Koorland, M., & Oseroff, A. (1987). Producing changes in the instructional behavior of teachers of the mentally handicapped through inservice education. *Education and Treatment of Children, 10,* 146–164.

McKeown, Jr., D., Adams, H.E., & Forehand, R. (1975). Generalization to the classroom of principles of behavior modification taught to teachers. *Behavior Research and Therapy, 13,* 85–92.

Maher, C. A. (1981). Training of managers in program planning and evaluation: Comparison of two approaches. *Journal of Organizational Behavior Management, 3*(1), 45–56.

Maloney, D.M., Phillips, E.L., Fixsen, D.L., & Wolf, M.M. (1975). Training techniques for staff in group homes for juvenile defenders: An analysis. *Criminal Justice and Behavior, 2,* 195–215.

Mansdorf, I.J., & Burstein, Y. (1986). Case manager: A clinical tool for training residential treatment staff. *Behavioral Residential Treatment, 1,* 155–167.

Miller, R., & Lewin, L.M. (1980). Training and management of the psychiatric aide: A critical review. *Journal of Organizational Behavior Management, 2*(4), 295–315.

Neef, N.A., Shafer, M.S., Egel, A.L., Cataldo, M.F., & Parrish, J.M. (1983). The class specific effects of compliance training with "do" and "don't" requests: Analogue analysis and classroom application. *Journal of Applied Behavior Analysis, 16,* 81–99.

Page, T.J., Christian, J.G., Iwata, B.A., Reid, D.H., Crow, R.E., & Dorsey, M.F. (1981). Evaluating and training interdisciplinary teams in writing IPP goals and objectives. *Mental Retardation, 19,* 25–27.

Page, T.J., Iwata, B.A., & Reid, D.H. (1982). Pyramidal training: A large-scale application with institutional staff. *Journal of Applied Behavior Analysis, 15,* 335–351.

Panyan, M.C., & Patterson, E.T. (1974). Teaching attendants the applied aspects of behavior modification. *Mental Retardation, 12,* 30–32.

Parsons, M.B., Schepis, M.M., Reid, D.H., McCarn, J.E., & Green, C.W. (1987). Expanding the impact of behavioral staff management: A large-scale, long-term application in schools serving severely handicapped students. *Journal of Applied Behavior Analysis, 20,* 139–150.

Reid, D.H., & Green, C.W. (in press). Staff training. In J.L. Matson (Ed.), *Handbook of behavior modification for persons with mental retardation* (2nd Edition). New York: Plenum Press.

Reid, D.H., Parsons, M.B., McCarn, J.E., Green, C.W., Phillips, J.F., & Schepis, M.M. (1985). Providing a more appropriate education for severely handicapped persons: Increasing and validating functional classroom tasks. *Journal of Applied Behavior Analysis, 18,* 289–301.

Reid, D.H., Parsons, M.B., & Schepis, M.M. (in press). Management practices that affect the relative utility of aversive and nonaversive procedures. In S.L. Harris & J.S. Handleman (Eds.), *Life threatening behavior: Aversive and nonaversive interventions.* Newark, NJ: Rutgers University Press.

Reid, D.H., & Whitman, T.L. (1983). Behavioral staff management in institutions: A critical review of effectiveness and acceptability. *Analysis and Intervention in Developmental Disabilities, 3,* 131–149.

Ringer, V.M.J. (1973). The use of a "token helper" in the management of classroom behavior problems and in teacher training. *Journal of Applied Behavior Analysis, 6,* 671–677.

Rosen, H.S., Yerushalmi, C.J., & Walker, J.C. (1986). Training community residential staff: Evaluation and follow-up. *Behavioral Residential Treatment, 1,* 15–38.

Schinke, S.P. & Wong, S.E. (1978). Teaching child care workers: A behavioral approach. *Child Care Quarterly, 7*(1), 45–61.

Singer, G., Sowers, J., & Irvin, K. (1986). Computer-assisted video instruction for training paraprofessionals in rural special education. *Journal of Special Education Technology, 8,* 27–34.

Speidel, G.E., & Tharp, R.G. (1978). Teacher training workshop strategy: Instructions, discrimination training, modeling, guided practice, and video feedback. *Behavior Therapy, 9,* 735–739.

Stoddard, L.T., McIlvane, W.J., McDonagh, E.C., & Kledaras, J.B. (1986). The use of picture programs in teaching direct care staff. *Applied Research in Mental Retardation, 7,* 349–358.

Stumphauzer, J.S., & Davis, L.C. (1983a). Training Mexican American mental health personnel in behavior therapy. *Journal of Behavior Therapy and Experimental Psychiatry, 14,* 215–217.

Stumphauzer, J.S., & Davis, L.C. (1983b). Training Asian American mental health personnel in behavior modification. *Journal of Community Psychology, 11,* 43–47.

Templeman, T.P., Fredericks, H.D.B., Bunse, C., & Moses, C. (1983). Teaching research in-service training model. *Education and Training of the Mentally Retarded, 18,* 245–252.

van den Pol, R.A., Reid, D.H., & Fuqua, R.W. (1983). Peer training of safety-related skills to institutional staff: Benefits for trainers and trainees. *Journal of Applied Behavior Analysis, 16,* 139–156.

Van Houton, R., & Sullivan, K. (1975). Effects of an audio-cueing system on the rate of teacher praise. *Journal of Applied Behavior Analysis, 8,* 197–201.

Watson, L.S., Jr., & Uzzell, R. (1980). A program for teaching behavior modification skills to institutional staff. *Applied Research in Mental Retardation, 1,* 41–53.

Whitman, T.L., Scibak, J.W., & Reid, D.H. (1983). *Behavior modification with the severely and profoundly retarded: Research and application.* New York: Academic Press.

Zlomke, L.C., & Benjamin, V.A., Jr. (1983). Staff in-service: Measuring effectiveness through client behavior change. *Education and Training of the Mentally Retarded, 18,* 125–130.

Chapter 4

PROCEDURES FOR CHANGING
ONGOING WORK PERFORMANCE

I n essence, the primary function of the management procedures discussed
to this point is to set the occasion for the implementation of supervisory strategies that affect significant changes in ongoing staff performance.
Once important areas of staff work behavior that warrant changing have
been clearly delineated along with the implementation of a corresponding
monitoring system (Chapter 2), and necessary staff training has been
conducted (Chapter 3), then a supervisor can effectively go about improving the day-to-day work performance of his/her staff. This chapter describes
management practices that can be used to change such performance.

The procedures to be discussed in this chapter represent the real
essence of organizational behavior management and effective supervision.
In this regard, earlier it was noted that it is not really feasible to precisely
delineate and systematically monitor a large number of different areas of
staff performance simultaneously. Consequently, as also noted, those
particular supervisory steps should be reserved for very important and/or
problematic staff performance areas. In contrast, the types of strategies
discussed in this chapter should not be reserved for certain situations—
they should be a major component of a supervisor's daily work routine.
The management procedures to be described represent the most critical
actions that enable a supervisor to proficiently fulfill his/her role of
changing and maintaining staff work performance.

A rather varied and large number of performance change strategies
have been developed through applied research in organizational behavior management. Many of these staff management procedures involve
several procedural components that are very similar to staff training
approaches (Chapter 3). However, there has been somewhat more research
on the efficacy of the individual procedural components involved in
managing staff performance relative to the research on staff training. As
with the behavioral supervisory procedures discussed in preceding

69

chapters, the staff management approaches for directly changing ongoing work performance are generally grouped into either *antecedent* or *consequence* strategies (Whitman, Scibak, & Reid, 1983, chap. 11). A small but important number of approaches also focus on *self-management* procedures (Burgio, Whitman, & Reid, 1983). Additionally, several behavioral supervisory approaches combine a large number of antecedent, consequence and/or self-management strategies into *multifaceted* management programs (Reid & Shoemaker, 1984). We will describe the basic organizational behavior management procedures according to these general groupings. Within the chapter sections discussing these four groups, a description of the different types of respective procedures will be presented along with a summary of some of their more common advantages and disadvantages.

Antecedent Supervisory Procedures

Antecedent supervisory procedures, like antecedent behavioral approaches in general (Chapter 1), are strategies that are conducted *before* staff are expected to perform a certain work duty, with the intent that the strategies will increase the likelihood that staff will indeed complete the targeted work assignment as part of the daily job routine, and do so proficiently. In this regard, the staff training strategies discussed in the preceding chapter represent a subgroup of antecedent procedures. However, antecedent procedures used within staff *training* programs for teaching new work skills typically are conducted before antecedent strategies designed for *managing* ongoing staff performance as part of organizational behavior management applications. Antecedent procedures help to ensure that staff know and/or remember what they are expected to do as well as assist staff in essentially getting started to perform a given work responsibility. Generally, antecedent procedures involve instructional strategies, increasing job structure, performance modeling, and differentiated prompting.

Instructional Strategies

Instructional strategies refer to staff management processes in which a supervisor attempts to impact staff performance by informing staff in writing and/or verbally (vocally) regarding what staff are expected to do (Whitman et al., 1983, chap. 11). These types of management procedures are very similar to the instructional strategies discussed previously under staff training (Chapter 3) and are based on the existing delineation of staff performance responsibilities (Chapter 2). However, when used as (part of) an ongoing staff management program—that is, to change staff's performance of something they already know how to do in contrast to identifying or training a *new* performance skill—instructional strategies provide less information about a job responsibility than instructional procedures used in staff training programs or in initial performance delineation processes. To illustrate, instructions as part of a job specification step may, for example, inform recreation staff *what* type of activities to conduct with nursing home residents during evening hours, and instructions within a training endeavor may show staff *how* to conduct the activities. In contrast, instructions as part of an on-the-job staff management program may simply *direct and/or remind* which individual staff are to conduct those types of activities with respective groups of residents on certain evenings.

Attempting to change various staff performances through instructions represents the most frequently utilized staff management procedure in typical human service settings. Instructions from supervisors via a staff memorandum, a phone call or a brief meeting are all very commonplace, usually occurring repeatedly during the workday on the part of most supervisors. The popularity of instructional strategies probably exists because these procedures represent rather natural means of attempting to change another person's behavior. The first thing (and often the only thing) most of us do when we want people to do something is to ask or tell the individuals what we want them to do. Instructional strategies also have the advantage of generally being easy for a supervisor to do and requiring minimal planning or preparation on the part of a supervisor.

Despite the ease and naturalness with which instructional strategies can be applied by most supervisors, these types of approaches to managing staff performance, like their instructional counterparts in staff training, in and of themselves, are not consistently effective (Reitz & Hawkins, 1982). Because of the inconsistent efficacy, instructional strategies generally have not been used in isolation by applied behavioral researchers when attempting to demonstrate a method of improving staff work performance; instructional strategies are usually combined with other staff management procedures (e.g. Greene, Willis, Levy & Bailey, 1978; Ivancic, Reid, Iwata, Faw, & Page, 1981). However, under certain conditions, instructional approaches to staff management can be effective. The basic condition that usually must exist in order for instructions to function effectively is that the change in staff performance that is instructed by a supervisor must not represent a major and/or permanent alteration in staffs' routine work activities. To illustrate, asking a staff member to attend a brief meeting is often effective in achieving the staff member's attendance at the meeting; such an action does not require a major and/or lasting change in regard to the staff person's usual work routine. In contrast, asking a staff member to discontinue talking to emotionally disturbed clients working in a sheltered workshop in a child-like manner and to engage in age-appropriate, adult-like interactions with the clients is not likely to bring about significant changes in how the staff member interacts with clients. To comply with the latter supervisory request, the staff member would have to change an interpersonal interaction style that he/she has probably been used to engaging in for a long period of time and, consequently, it is not easy for the staff person to change. Furthermore, compliance with the supervisory directive would require the staff member to remember to act differently in the future every time he/she talks to a client during the work day, week, month, etc. — which also represents a difficult task for the staff person.

Increasing Job Structure

An antecedent management procedure that is quite similar to instructions is increasing job structure. Increasing the structure of a staff person's job refers to a very precise elaboration regarding *what* a staff person is expected to do (i.e. performance specification noted previously in this chapter and discussed in-depth in Chapter 2) as well as *when* and *how often* it should be done, *where* the job duty should occur and *with whom* (e.g. which clients), and/or with which work *materials* it should involve (Reid & Whitman, 1983; Sneed & Bible, 1979). In essence, the difference between instructions and increasing job structure is the amount of direction given to a staff member, with the latter procedure providing considerably more information. Whereas instructions represent a frequently occurring approach to staff management, increasing job structure occurs relatively infrequently. The relative infrequency of use of the latter procedure is due most likely to the increased work effort required of a supervisor to precisely describe all the important procedural parameters of the various duties expected of staff. To thoroughly describe all aspects of staff job duties also requires a supervisor to clearly break down those duties into discrete work behaviors required of staff (Chapter 2).

Increasing job structure is usually more effective than its simpler counterpart, instructions, in that precisely presenting all the important job parameters to a staff person can bring about more consistent and/or comprehensive changes in staff performance. For example, specification and presentation of the exact types of personal care that institutional direct care staff should provide to profoundly handicapped clients, as well as when the care should occur and which staff were responsible for taking care of each client, resulted in improvement in the personal care provided to clients in a state institution (Iwata, Bailey, Brown, Foshee, & Alpern, 1976). In addition to being somewhat more effective than instructions, increasing the structure of staff performance responsibilities can be beneficial in other ways for supervisors who oversee a number of staff persons, who in turn have shared responsibility over groups of clients. In these situations, unless there is sufficient job structure, the responsibilities of individual staff persons with given clients are not always very evident such that it is difficult to hold each staff member accountable for the care provided to a particular client.

A disadvantage of increasing job structure is that, similar to essentially all antecedent interventions, this approach to managing staff performance is not consistently successful in changing work behavior and/or does not bring about very large or durable changes in staff performance (Seys & Duker, 1978). In addition, increasing job structure does not seem to be consistently well received among staff members. Some staff persons (and particularly professionally trained staff) prefer to have more flexibility in performing their responsibilities than what is allowed when a supervisor delineates a large amount of job structure. Professional staff often prefer to have only the goals of their work efforts identified and then use their own means of achieving those goals. In this regard, it is the supervisor's responsibility to determine—using an acute observational awareness of staff responsiveness to supervisory actions—which staff persons perform best with and without a large degree of job structure. For staff persons who do not like a lot of structure to their jobs, a supervisor may use this strategy as a consequence (see "Consequence Procedures" later in this chapter). That is, staff may be allowed to perform without very much job structure provided their performance is satisfactory. If their performance becomes less than satisfactory, then a supervisor may impose increased job structure until an appropriate level of performance is observed.

Performance Modeling

A somewhat less common antecedent procedure than instructions and increasing job structure, and somewhat more effective, is performance modeling. Modeling refers to a supervisor or his/her designee physically demonstrating for staff the work activities that the supervisor wants the staff to perform. When used in this regard as a staff management procedure, modeling is different than when used in a staff training endeavor. In staff training, modeling is used to (help) teach staff how to perform a work activity that staff do not know how to perform, whereas in staff management, modeling is used to prompt staff to perform an activity that they know how to perform but are not actually doing. Modeling has been successfully used to improve several different types of performance areas such as increasing staff's implementation of designated self-help training procedures with mentally retarded students (Gladstone & Spencer, 1977) and increasing staff's implementation of recreational activities with institutionalized psychiatric patients (Wallace, Davis, Liberman, & Baker, 1973).

As just implied, modeling is relatively advantageous, in that there is somewhat more documentation regarding its effectiveness than other antecedent management procedures. Supervisory modeling also has the advantage of often being very well received by staff persons (Whitman et al., 1983, chap. 11). Many staff like to see supervisors present in the staffs' actual work site helping staff to perform their job (which is an outcome of modeling if it is conducted within the routine work setting). Supervisory modeling essentially has the effect of showing staff that the supervisor is well aware of the work that is required of staff and that the supervisor cares about what the staff are doing. By participating in staff work activities through performance modeling, a supervisor can also gain some rather insightful awareness of some of the subtle characteristics of a staff member's job—an awareness that can be useful in designing means of assisting staff to improve their performance. Of course, to successfully model desired staff performances in the routine work site, a supervisor must be *able* to proficiently engage in the targeted performance area, which is not always feasible for some supervisors (Reid & Green, in press). Additionally, modeling can require a considerable amount of time and effort on the part of a supervisor relative to other types of antecedent management procedures.

Differentiated Prompting

The final antecedent procedure to be discussed, differentiated prompting, is a relatively little used variation of instructional approaches to staff management. Differentiated prompting refers in essence to a signal given to a staff member that does not provide any specific procedural information about a staff member's job per se but nevertheless serves to remind the staff person to do something. For example, differentiated prompts in the form of auditory signals over an intercom system have been used to increase teachers' rates of praising certain student behaviors in classrooms (Van Houten & Sullivan, 1975). In this case, the auditory signals did not specifically *instruct* the teachers to do something but, rather, served in essence to *remind* them to do something they had previously been instructed to do. Hence, the prompting is differential, in that even though the signal does not provide descriptive or procedural information specific to a given job duty, it is differentially directed to a certain work activity based on previous instructions to perform a job. In the Van Houten and Sullivan study just noted, for example, the auditory signals normally would have had no meaning for the teachers, except that the teachers had been previously instructed to engage in a certain work responsibility (i.e. reinforcing specified student behaviors) when they heard the intercom signal.

Although differentiated prompting procedures such as auditory signaling can impact staff performance, such procedures can be perceived by staff as being somewhat strange and/or artificial (e.g. hearing "beeps" over an intercom every few minutes). In this regard, staff may view supervisors in a less than respectable light when staff perceive supervisory actions to be rather bizarre. However, there are certain differentiated prompting procedures that can be incorporated within typical work environments relatively easily without appearing awkward or strange. In particular, a supervisor's mere *presence* in the staff work site can serve as a differentiated prompt if the supervisor has recently instructed staff regarding a desired work activity and the supervisor has informed staff that he/she will be coming around to see how staff are performing the designated task (Parsons, Schepis, Reid, McCarn, & Green, 1987). Staff may respond to the supervisor in this respect, because the supervisor's presence serves to remind the staff to do the specific task that the supervisor recently requested them to do. In other cases, staff may change their

performance when they see the supervisor, because the staff are appre-
hensive about what the supervisor might do if he/she observes staff not
engaging in the appropriate work activity. Alternatively, and more desirably from the point of view of this text, staff may change their performance when they see the supervisor because they *want* the supervisor to
see them engaging in appropriate work and they *look forward* to the
supervisor's subsequent positive reaction (see "Consequence" section
later in this chapter).

In addition to simply being present in the staff work environment as a
means of informal differentiated prompting, a supervisor can use casual
conversation to encourage staff to perform certain activities. For example,
in a staff management program designed to evoke teachers' use of certain
types of newly developed classroom curricular activities, the school
principal visited the teachers' classrooms on an impromptu basis and
casually asked them questions regarding the new activities in order to
prompt the teachers' attention to the new responsibility (Reid et al., 1985).
This type of casual interaction within the staffs' routine work setting has
an advantage similar to that with performance modeling noted earlier, in
that staff can be quite appreciative of the supervisor taking the time to
interact with them in such a manner. Of course, for a supervisor to
effectively prompt and essentially interact with staff in this way, the
supervisor must be at least somewhat skilled interpersonally—a skill
that not all human service supervisors possess (Reid & Green, in press).

Consequence Staff Management Procedures

Of all the procedures for changing and/or maintaining staff performance, from both a staff *training* and staff *management* perspective,
the most effective are the consequence procedures. The most valuable
contribution of organizational behavior management in regard to supervising human service provision has been the demonstration of the systematic use of performance consequences to make significant improvements
in day-to-day staff performance. The purpose of this section is to describe
the varied types of consequence procedures that can be, and have been,
used to manage staff performance along with the relative advantages and
disadvantages of the different procedures. For organizational purposes,
consequence procedures are categorized into two general groups. The
first group (and by far the larger) involves the explicit application of
performance feedback. The second group includes those strategies that

involve the application of consequences other than performance feedback, including the use of special privileges, tangible items and monetary bonuses.

Performance Feedback Procedures

As with performance feedback procedures used in staff training (Chapter 3), feedback strategies used to manage ongoing work behavior entail the presentation of information regarding some aspect of staff members' proficiency in conducting their work (Ford, 1980). In its purest form, feedback entails no explicit approving or disapproving components, only a description of the work that occurred. However, in organizational behavior management applications, feedback is usually accompanied by some explicit value judgments such as supervisor praise (e.g. Montegar, Reid, Madsen, & Ewell, 1977) or at least implicit value components such as comparing staff performance to some preestablished work goal (e.g. Burg, Reid, & Lattimore, 1979). The inclusion of information regarding the judged adequacy of work performance along with purely descriptive feedback is due primarily to the increased efficacy of feedback procedures when the former components are included (Realon, Lewallen, & Wheeler, 1983). For example, feedback provided by a supervisor to institutional direct care staff regarding their work performance effectively decreased the amount of time staff spent in non-work-related activities but did not result in increases in work performance deemed as most desirable by their supervisor — in this case, therapeutic interactions with profoundly handicapped persons (Brown, Willis, & Reid, 1981). It was only when the supervisor specifically praised the latter type of performance along with the feedback presentation that interactions increased. Because of data such as that provided by Brown et al., as well as our own experience, we recommend that some explicit approving and/or disapproving components always be provided with feedback procedures. Actually, it has become somewhat commonplace to refer to approving and/or disapproving information provided with nonjudgmental descriptive information under the general label of feedback. Our use of the term feedback throughout the remainder of this text will refer to the format which includes specific approving and/or disapproving components.

In many ways, descriptive information about performance (i.e. feedback) is at least implicitly involved in any consequence application. Some aspect of performance is usually described or referred to, for example, when staff receive positive consequences (e.g. praise) or negative consequences (e.g. a verbal reprimand) from a supervisor. Nevertheless, the use of performance feedback is much more explicit and/or pervasive in some consequence applications than in others. This section describes the former types of procedures, which include a variety of formats for presenting feedback. Each format has its own advantages and disadvantages, some of which are the same as the relative attributes of feedback procedures discussed previously with staff training. However, there are also advantages and disadvantages of the various procedures that are more idiosyncratic to staff management applications.

Verbal feedback. Verbal feedback is probably the most frequently used type of performance feedback. Verbal feedback from a supervisor has been used singularly as a consequence procedure to manage day-to-day staff performance (e.g. Brown et al., 1981; Montegar et al., 1977) as well as in conjunction with a number of other staff management procedures (e.g. Parsons et al., 1987; Ivancic et al., 1981). Verbal feedback can be provided to staff members individually (Montegar et al., 1977) and/or in a group context (Faw, Reid, Schepis, Fitzgerald, & Welty, 1981).

Perhaps the most important advantage of verbal feedback—in addition to its efficacy—is that it can be provided very readily with minimal or no preparation on the part of a supervisor. That is, although verbal feedback can be provided on a scheduled, structured basis in conjunction with a systematic monitoring program (e.g. once per week at a routinely scheduled staff meeting), it can also be provided on an impromptu basis by a supervisor whenever he/she observes commendable staff performance during the ongoing work routine (e.g. when a supervisor happens to be walking through a given staff work area). In addition, verbal feedback facilitates a two-way interaction between a supervisor and a staff member, in that the two persons must meet on a face-to-face basis. Such an interaction, albeit usually brief, allows a supervisor the opportunity to learn more about his/her staff persons based on how they respond to the feedback and whatever work-related information that they might add to the interaction in an incidental manner. Knowledge about staff persons in regard to their likes and dislikes concerning the work situation can of course be valuable in assisting a supervisor to determine the most effective (and acceptable) means to manage staff performance. The act of a supervisor initiating interactions (i.e. in order to provide verbal feedback) with staff also represents a management strategy that is usually well accepted by staff (Korabek, Reid, & Ivancic, 1981).

If verbal feedback is to be used effectively to change and/or maintain some aspect of staff performance during the routine course of the workday (and is to be well received as just noted), a crucial guideline must be followed: the feedback must be *sincere*. If a supervisor attempts to verbally praise staff performance, for example, when the supervisor really does not care about that particular performance area and/or is not really pleased with it, the resulting outcome is not likely to be very beneficial. Staff members, like any adults, can usually detect insincere or superficial attempts by a supervisor to be nice about something. In such cases, the supervisory praise is not likely to function as a reinforcer for staff performance and, consequently, there will be no improvement in staff behavior.

The importance of sincerity in regard to the provision of feedback is not restricted to verbal feedback. All formats for providing feedback that will be discussed in subsequent sections require sincerity on the part of the supervisor. Actually, discussing the importance of sincerity when considering praising other persons' actions perhaps is simply stating the obvious. However, we highlight the importance of sincerity here because supervisors can inadvertently find themselves in the situation of providing insincere feedback relatively easily. The latter situation occurs, for example, when a supervisor has been providing feedback to the same staff persons regarding the same specific performance area for an extended time period. The feedback may have been sincere when initially provided, but over time, the supervisor's concern for the designated performance area waned (e.g. because the performance area no longer represented a management crisis with staff behavior); yet, the supervisor continues to give feedback because he/she thinks feedback must be provided as part of the supervisory role. Again, feedback provided without a true concern for the targeted performance area is not likely to be well received by staff. If a supervisor cannot be sincere for whatever reason in providing feedback to staff, then the supervisor should find some other means of managing staff performance.

Similar to the criterion of sincerity when providing feedback is the issue of a supervisor *appearing sincere*. That is, a supervisor must first be sincere and then be able to *express* his/her sincerity to staff. Without the latter feature, even if a supervisor is seriously concerned about a staff performance area, such concern will not be evident to staff. Relatedly, to maximize the effectiveness of feedback, a supervisor needs to be able to comment on staffs' performance in an interpersonally *pleasant* manner.

These characteristics of the effective use of verbal feedback (i.e. *how* feedback is presented during an interaction with a staff member) represent the most serious disadvantage of this method of providing feedback: some supervisors simply do not have the interpersonal skills to verbally provide feedback in a style that appears sincere and is well received by staff. Some supervisors also do not feel comfortable praising staff regarding their behavior, and the uncomfortableness has a detrimental effect on the style with which the feedback is presented. Hence, verbal feedback should not be the sole or dominant management strategy for every supervisor.

Written Feedback. The most readily available alternative to verbal feedback is written feedback. Written feedback has been used in two general ways in organizational behavior management research in human service settings. One way has involved privately written information (e.g. Shoemaker & Reid, 1980) that provides feedback on performance to an individual employee, usually through a memorandum from a supervisor (Repp & Deitz, 1979). Privately written feedback is advantageous in one sense, in that it can provide a permanent record of information for a staff member. Consequently, the record (e.g. a memorandum) can serve to prompt the staff person to continue the performance that was initially written about—provided that the staff member periodically looks at the written record. More importantly, however, written feedback does not require the interpersonal skills on the part of a supervisor for face-to-face interactions with staff persons as does verbal feedback, only a modest degree of writing skills. Some supervisors also do not feel as uncomfortable writing about a staff person's performance relative to talking to the staff person (i.e. verbal feedback). Another advantage of privately written feedback is that it is often easier for a supervisor to schedule time to prepare written feedback relative to verbal feedback. Whereas the provision of verbal feedback requires a supervisor to coordinate his/her schedule with the availability of a given staff person, privately written feedback can be prepared by a supervisor at his/her convenience and subsequently sent to the staff member.

An example of a rather formal type of privately written feedback is provided in Figure 4-1. Figure 4-1 presents a *Green Stamp Award* used at Western Carolina Center, a state residential facility serving developmentally disabled persons in North Carolina. The Green Stamp is professionally printed with the agency's letterhead and state seal, along with the statement, "I like your work at Western Carolina Center because. . . . " A supervisor can complete the statement by positively commenting on some aspect of a staff person's behavior. To increase the impact of the feedback, the Green Stamp also indicates that a copy via a perforated section of the stamp will be sent to the staff personnel office. Such a copy allows a permanent record of the feedback (and the staff member's commendable performance) to be maintained.

A somewhat subtle advantage of formal, written feedback mechanisms such as the Green Stamp Award is that the availability of the feedback form or award can serve to facilitate the supervisor's task of providing feedback as well as to prompt him/her to give feedback. Because the feedback is partially prepared in regard to the information permanently printed on the stamp, the supervisor's task is made easier relative to having to prepare all aspects of the feedback. Relatedly, simply having a blank feedback form available (e.g. maintaining a small pile of forms on a supervisor's desk) can function to remind a supervisor to give positive feedback in a manner as just described. In this regard, those feedback procedures (as well as any organizational behavior management procedures) that are relatively easy and time efficient to implement by a supervisor are most desirable. A supervisor in a human service setting typically has many responsibilities, and those supervisory strategies that require a lot of work and/or time on the part of a supervisor are not likely to be used very often (i.e. the procedures generally are not very acceptable to supervisors).

In contrast to the advantages of privately written feedback as just noted, there are some notable disadvantages of this management strategy. Unlike verbal feedback, privately written feedback does not involve face-to-face interactions between a supervisor and a staff member. Consequently, all the advantages of such interpersonal interactions discussed previously do not exist with written feedback. Further, there is some cost involved with written feedback, such as professionally preparing a feedback form like a Green Stamp Award. If privately written feedback is provided in typed format to possibly enhance its professionalism or formal nature, the availability of a secretary is often required as well as a given amount (albeit usually minimal) of the latter's time. Also, whereas some supervisors do not feel comfortable giving verbal feedback to staff, other supervisors are uncomfortable *writing* to staff about the latter's performance.

The second general means of providing written feedback is through public presentation of the information, typically referred to as *public*

WESTERN CAROLINA CENTER

Green Stamp Award

Presented to:

Jim Mentor

I really like your work at Western Carolina Center because:

of the extra hours worked voluntarily during the recent snow emergency.

Awarded by: *Lance Best*

Date: *11/4/87*

This award will be considered in promotions, increment, and job opportunities.

Figure 4-1. Example of a type of privately written feedback. The Green Stamp Award, developed at Western Carolina Center, is used by supervisors to write commendations to staff persons concerning their work performance.

posting. Public posting involves presenting information (i.e. feedback) on staff performance on display for all staff persons to view in a given work place. A variety of formats for publicly displaying feedback have been used effectively in human service agencies (Greene et al., 1978; Hutchison, Jarman, & Bailey, 1980; Panyan, Boozer, & Morris, 1970; Quilitch, 1975; Welsch, Ludwig, Radiker, & Krapfl, 1973). To illustrate, Figure 4-2 presents an example of a "Pats-On-The-Back" system used by a school principal to publicly praise commendable staff performance as one consequence component of a comprehensive management program used to improve the classroom performance of educators (Parsons et al., 1987). The feedback form as exemplified in Figure 4-2 was displayed in the school corridor and could be viewed by all staff in the school.

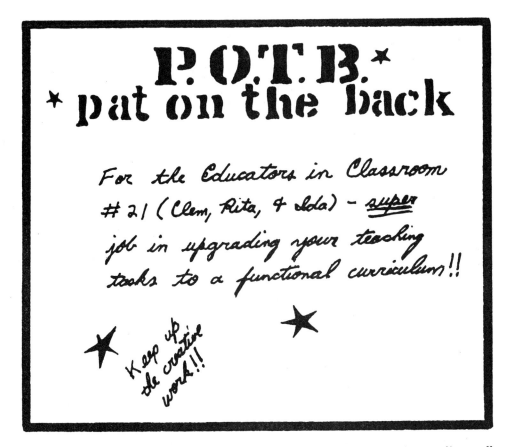

Figure 4-2. Example of an *informal* means of publicly posting feedback regarding staff performance. The Pats-On-The-Back format was drawn from Parsons et al. (1987).

Another format for publicly posting feedback involves displaying graphs that numerically quantify specific performances. For example, bar graphs that quantified staff absentee records were a key part of a management program used to reduce staff absenteeism in a state mental retardation facility (Reid, Schuh-Wear, & Brannon, 1978). A more formal format for publicly posting feedback is presented in Figure 4-3. Figure 4-3 represents an illustration of an official agency award used to publicly praise commendable work performance (in this case, effective application of treatment programs by institutional staff) that is framed and permanently displayed in a work unit.

Publicly posted feedback in its various formats as just exemplified has basically the same advantages as privately written feedback in terms of a behavior change procedure. For example, like privately written feedback, publicly posted feedback does not require the degree of interpersonal interaction skills that verbal feedback requires. Also, publicly posted feedback provides a permanent record of the feedback. However, there is also a major advantage of publicly posted feedback that privately written feedback does not share. Because posted feedback presents information on a given staff person's performance for other agency staff to view, publicly posted feedback sets the occasion for a number of consequences to be provided to the individual staff person. Due to the multiple consequences associated with publicly posted feedback, this strategy can be a more powerful behavior change procedure than privately written feedback. To illustrate, the Pats-On-The-Back feedback form noted earlier provides positive feedback to a staff person directly from a supervisor *and* sets the occasion for other staff members to review the information that is publicly displayed and then for those staff members to comment favorably to the staff person identified on the form. Hence, the latter staff member receives feedback from several different sources (i.e. the supervisor who wrote the information and the staff peers who commented on the information once they read it).

Unfortunately, the same feature of publicly posted feedback that can make this form of feedback quite powerful (its *public* nature) also represents the most serious disadvantage of this management strategy. The process of staff members viewing information about another staff person's performance at times can have an unexpected *negative* impact on the latter's work activity. Other staff members may, for example, be jealous of the staff member whose performance is publicly lauded by a supervisor and consequently chide or otherwise chastise the staff person. Such

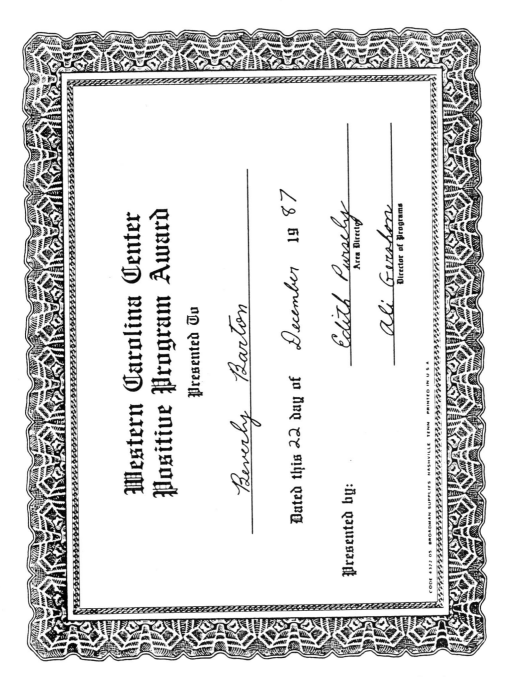

Figure 4-3. Example of a *formal* means of publicly posting feedback regarding staff performance —in this case referring to performance involving client training programs. The Positive Program Award can be framed and posted permanently on a work unit wall.

staff activities can have the effect of punishing the staff person's perform-ance that is publicly praised by the supervisor. In addition, some staff persons simply do not like to be the center of attention among their work peers, and being the recipient of publicly posted feedback can have the effect of essentially putting a staff person in such a situation.

The potentially negative features of publicly posted feedback as just noted have been discussed in regard to publicly posting *positive* information about staff performance such as the Pats-On-The-Back format. If *negative* information concerning staff work activities is presented publicly such as a posted reprimand, there can be even more serious disadvantages with public posting. Publicly posting negative feedback is frequently viewed as a rather insensitive or even cruel means of supervising and generally is received quite unfavorably by the staff person whose performance is targeted as well as by his/her staff colleagues. Due to this feature of publicly posting negative feedback, as well as the problems associated with any supervisory procedure that lacks acceptability among staff (Chapter 1), we do not recommend this form of feedback delivery for use by supervisors.

One method of public posting that decreases the likelihood of some of the problems that can occur with this type of feedback procedure is to publicly display information on client welfare for which staff are respon-sible in contrast to displaying information about staff performance per se. Such a process has been used in a variety of work situations (e.g. Greene et al., 1978; Ivancic et al., 1981; Reitz & Hawkins, 1982). For example, in a comprehensive program to increase the proficiency with which direct care staff fed profoundly handicapped children who were medically at risk due to pediatric eating impairments, Korabek et al. (1981) publicly posted the amount of food intake of each child per meal as well as the monthly weights of each child.

The advantages of posting client information in lieu of information on staff performance are severalfold. First, such a process removes staff some-what from the center of attention. Again, some staff persons do not like to be in such a situation. Second, the process focuses attention on the most important variable within human service agencies: client welfare. By viewing publicly displayed information on client variables, supervisors and staff may be more likely to think about their performance in light of how it impacts the identified areas of client welfare. Of course, the confi-dentiality of clients must be taken into consideration in regard to how and where (as well as *if*) information on client welfare is to be displayed.

Nonfeedback Consequences

The consequence procedures discussed to this point involve the explicit presentation of feedback to staff regarding their performance. In discussing the variety of formats for presenting feedback it was noted that, in essence, all consequence procedures involve performance feedback to some degree. However, it was also noted that there are certain types of consequences that, when presented, are not designed to provide detailed, descriptive information on job behavior per se. The latter procedures are intended instead to present in a more general fashion something that staff presumably like in order to reinforce staff performance. Such consequence processes may involve giving staff desired items or special work privileges, allowing staff to participate in enjoyable events, or officially commending various performances through special-recognition ceremonies.

Generally, the most common nonfeedback consequence *item* used in staff management has been money (Katz, Johnson, & Gelfand, 1972; Pomerleau, Bobrove, & Smith, 1973; Pommer & Streedbeck, 1974; Realon, Wheeler, Spring, & Springer, 1986). Many human service systems provide some kind of merit system in which pay increases are provided to staff for exhibiting performance that is considered to be more than satisfactory. Other items that have been used in staff management include free meals (Shoemaker & Reid, 1980), commercial trading stamps (Bricker, Morgan, & Grabowski, 1972; Hollander & Plutchik, 1972; Hollander, Plutchik, & Horner, 1973), and discount coupons for purchasing store items at reduced cost (Fox, Hopkins, & Anger, 1987). Several types of special *privileges* and/or *events* have also been used as consequences in applied research in human service agencies such as the opportunity to arrange desired work schedules involving preferred days off (Iwata et al., 1976; Reid et al., 1978), to be relieved of undesired work duties (Shoemaker & Reid, 1980), to have a free lunch with a supervisor (Shoemaker & Reid, 1980), and to take trips off the work site area (Seys & Duker, 1978). Finally, *special-recognition ceremonies* have included such activities as being recognized publicly within an agency as staff person of the week (Pomerleau et al., 1973) or recognized via special comments in an agency newsletter (Patterson, Cooke, & Liberman, 1972).

The examples just provided reflect the types of consequences that have been used in organizational behavior management research in human service agencies. The variety of these types of consequences that are potentially available to human service managers is essentially endless, depending on the creativity of respective managers. From a more applied, nonresearch perspective, Appendix A describes the variety of consequences that managers in state mental retardation institutions located throughout the United States report that they use with their staff members. As indicated in the consequences presented in Appendix A, which range from providing free child care to increasing staff input into managerial decisions, managers can indeed be quite creative in providing positive outcomes for staff work performance.

When considering the relative advantages and disadvantages of non-feedback consequences, special concern must be directed to the specific type of consequence that is used, in that each type has its own idiosyncratic attributes. For example, some items may be desirable to staff persons but are too difficult for a supervisor to obtain on a routine basis (e.g. commercial trading stamps). Other items such as monetary bonuses based on exemplary work may be disallowed by union contracts. Further, the *purpose* of each consequence program must be considered. In this regard, the primary goal of consequence systems in organizational behavior management research has been to *reinforce* desired staff performances in order to increase the frequency of those work behaviors. As alluded to in Chapter 1, if consequence programs are to have reinforcing effects on targeted work behaviors of staff, then the programs must be administered in accordance with certain principles of behavior change (cf. Miller, 1978). For instance, the consequences generally must be provided contingently and consistently following *only* those specific work behaviors that are targeted for change and the consequences typically must be provided frequently. Many of the types of consequences discussed in this section, along with those exemplified in Appendix A, were not provided to staff in such a manner. Some of the special-recognition consequences, for example, only involved a general description of the (commendable) performance of staff persons and were provided very infrequently, such as only once per year.

Because many nonfeedback consequence programs are not administered in accordance with established principles of behavior change, such programs should not be assumed to effect major and/or long-lasting changes in staff work performance during the daily work routine. However, the purpose of these types of systems is not always to directly change daily work performance per se. Rather, such programs are sometimes used to express special appreciation (albeit on an infrequent basis) in an effort to simply do something nice for a staff person who has done a good job.

Using (nonfeedback) consequences in this manner may have no other effect than helping a staff person feel good about his/her work situation. Although such an effect may not be immediately reflected in improved job performance, such an outcome can be advantageous in terms of overcoming problems with poor morale among staff persons. Elaboration on how behavioral staff management procedures can be used to remedy problems with staff morale is provided in Chapter 10.

Although many applications of nonfeedback consequences in human service agencies are not likely to significantly affect routine work performances of staff as just noted, they can be effective if used in a more behavioral manner. If target behaviors of staff are identified and the consequences are frequently provided based on the specific occurrence of those behaviors, then staff performance is likely to be altered (see Reid & Whitman, 1983, for a review of effective consequence applications). One of the reasons that such approaches can be effective (and a major advantage of nonfeedback consequence programs) is that many of the specific consequences are often highly desirable among staff and staff will work (more and/or better) to earn the consequences. The *novelty* of the special items or events relative to the routine work situation can also enhance the value of the consequences, at least for a while. However, the novelty aspect also relates to a major disadvantage of nonfeedback consequences. Specifically, because many of the approaches involve resources and/or routines that are not typically available to a supervisor, the systems are financially costly to implement (e.g. paying for food to provide free meals to staff) and/or are effortful for a supervisor to develop and maintain (e.g. continuously rearranging staff work schedules to allow desired days off). Elaboration on the problems with financing and implementing these types of systems is provided elsewhere (Reid, Parsons, & Schepis, in press). Overall, it is relatively common to see nonfeedback systems initially attempted by a supervisor and then soon abandoned because the systems are too expensive or burdensome for the supervisor to continue to use.

Self-Management Procedures

The third type of staff management procedure to be discussed, *self-management* strategies, involves many of the antecedent and consequence procedures described previously in this chapter. However, whereas the management approaches discussed earlier are dependent upon supervisors for implementation, the self-management strategies are primarily dependent upon the staff members themselves for implementation. In this regard it may seem somewhat contradictory to talk about *staff-* or *self*-management strategies as a means of supervision. A basic premise of this text is that a supervisor must assume responsibility, and be held accountable, for the performance of his/her staff supervisees. Hence, it is the supervisor's *responsibility* to manage staff performance. Nevertheless, one means for a supervisor to manage the performance of his/her staff is to systematically involve the staff in managing their own performance, within guidelines established by the supervisor.

In essence, the locus of control in regard to managing staff performance in human service settings can be considered to fall along a continuum (Kissel, Whitman, & Reid, 1983). On one end of the continuum, staff performance is under the total control of the supervisor, whereas on the other end, the staff are in total control of their work performance. Although these two ends of the continuum are somewhat hypothetical in that neither the supervisor nor the staff are probably ever in total control of the work situation, the continuum between the two ends is a realistic representation of how control of staff performance can vary within an organization. The types of procedures discussed so far in this chapter fall toward the supervisor-controlled end of the continuum, whereas the self-management procedures fall toward the staff-controlled end. With the self-management procedures staff are more responsible for managing their work performance and the supervisor is less responsible, although the latter's responsibility is never completely relinquished.

Basically, there are three types of self-management procedures that have been investigated in organizational behavior management research in human service settings. The first type of procedure is *self-recording* through which staff maintain records of their performance. Recording information on one's own behavior seems to have the effect of increasing an individual's awareness of what he/she should be doing (Jones, Nelson, & Kazdin, 1977) and consequently can serve to change the frequency with which an individual engages in the behavior that is being recorded. For example, institutional direct care staff increased their frequency of therapeutic interactions with severely and profoundly mentally retarded persons when the staff self-recorded their frequency of such interactions (Burg et al., 1979).

Self-recording as a means of managing staff performance (under the direction of the supervisor) can be relatively advantageous, in that it reduces the amount of time and effort on the part of a supervisor to manage staff work activities because staff are performing part of the supervisory functions. Also, self-recording can be helpful, because the process results in a permanent product of staff performance (i.e. the self-recorded information). Assuming that the self-recorded information is accurate—which is usually the case if intermittent supervisory checks on staff performance are conducted along with the staff self-recording— the information can be used to document that certain job duties have been completed. However, to date self-recording as a staff management procedure has been investigated too infrequently to determine its true efficacy. Also, all things considered, self-recording really is a specific performance action required of staff, and certain staff may be reluctant, forget, or even refuse to maintain records of their work behavior. In such cases, if more external (i.e. supervisory) management procedures are required to evoke staffs' self-recording (which in turn is intended to improve work behavior), the utility of self-recording procedures would have to be questioned (Burg et al., 1979).

A second type of self-management procedure is *goal-setting* in which staff participate with their supervisor in establishing goals or standards for their work performance. For example, preschool staff may be asked by a supervisor to determine the number of new types of learning activities that they should implement each month with their children (i.e. in contrast to the preschool director mandating that there be a certain number of new activities). Similarly, clinicians in a mental health clinic may be asked to set a goal for reducing the interval between the time they terminate a client's case and when they complete the corre- sponding termination report.

To date, the research on staff goal-setting has not systematically investi- gated the effects of this procedure per se but, rather, has included goal-setting as one part of a comprehensive staff management program (e.g. Burgio et al., 1983). Future research is warranted on this self- management procedure because there can be a certain intuitive appeal to involving staff in the determination of what is expected of them; people would seem to work harder to achieve a goal they agree with, and helping to establish a performance goal should increase the likelihood that staff would agree with the goal. Additionally, goal-setting is gener- ally a less time-consuming self-management procedure for staff than self-recording.

The third type of self-management procedure, *self-reinforcement,* refers to staff explicitly providing themselves with a positive consequence following a pre-specified work performance. To illustrate, in an attempt to increase therapeutic staff interactions with institutionalized clients, staff were asked to praise themselves for increasing such interactions (Burgio et al., 1983). This particular self-management strategy has been applied very infrequently in organizational behavior management research in human service settings. The relative lack of research in this regard may be because self-reinforcement seems to have more disadvantages on a practical level than other self-management procedures. Instructing staff to praise themselves, for example, for their performance can appear to many staff to represent a rather strange request from a supervisor and the staff may feel uncomfortable engaging in the process. Similarly, many supervisors may have reluctance in requesting their staff to engage in self-reinforcement because it is clearly not a typical supervisory activity. Nevertheless, self-reinforcement has been used effectively by adults to change their behavior in a variety of nonwork situations (see Jones et al., 1977, for an overview). Also, staff can be involved in self-reinforcement on a more normal basis by simply having input into what the consequences will be that the supervisor provides to the staff contingent on the latter's performance (Seys & Duker, 1978; Spreat et al., 1985). Continued research on this potential management strategy is needed to more clearly determine its (non)utility.

In many ways, the rather novel self-management procedures as just described are similar to a more traditional managerial strategy, *participative management* (see Ivancic et al., 1981, for a summary of the similarities and differences between self-management and participative management). The basic ideas underlying behavioral self-management and more traditional participative management approaches can be viewed similarly, in that attempts are made to improve work performance by involving staff in the management of their work situation. However, there are also some serious differences in the two managerial approaches. In particular, the self-management processes discussed here refer to clearly delineated, specific actions for supervisors and staff to engage in, whereas procedures that constitute more traditional participative management approaches are not as well articulated in terms of exactly what supervisors and supervisees should do. Hence, the applicability of the self-management approaches is facilitated relative to the traditional participative management approaches. Relatedly, it is much more straightforward to evaluate the (non)effectiveness of specific self-management strategies than of participative management approaches, because with the latter, it is not entirely clear which activities on the part of supervisors and staff actually constitute the management approach.

Multifaceted Supervisory Procedures

The final major group of behavioral supervisory procedures is *multifaceted* interventions. As with multifaceted staff training programs, multifaceted management approaches are characterized by the incorporation of a large number of antecedent, consequence and/or self-management components into one supervisory intervention (Whitman et al., 1983, chap. 11). For example, a multifaceted management procedure used to increase the proficiency with which institutional direct care staff provided personal care for profoundly handicapped clients included verbal and written instructions, supervisory modeling, verbal feedback, privately written and publicly posted feedback, and staff self-recording (Korabek et al., 1981). Similarly, a multifaceted management intervention used to improve the functional utility of classroom teaching tasks provided by teachers for severely handicapped students included verbal and written instructions, differentiated prompting, verbal feedback, privately written and publicly posted feedback, and staff goal setting (Parsons et al., 1987).

The rationale behind the use of multifaceted management programs is basically an attempt to maximize the probability of resolving a given problem with staff performance (Ivancic et al., 1981). By combining a number of procedural components—each of which at times can singularly bring about behavior change—into one management intervention, the probability of resolving the performance problem of concern is enhanced relative to relying on only one component procedure. That is, if only one procedure (e.g. modeling) is used and that procedure is not effective, then the performance problem will not be resolved. In contrast, if the (modeling) procedure is used in conjunction with other procedures (e.g. verbal feedback, publicly posted feedback, self-recording), then one or more of the latter procedures may result in improved performance even if the former component is ineffective.

The apparent advantage of multifaceted interventions is that, because of the inclusion of a number of behavioral management components, this type of supervisory approach is generally very effective. Multifaceted interventions have resulted in large improvements in staff performance in a number of investigations in human service settings involving both professional (Parsons et al., 1987; Reid et al., 1985) and paraprofessional staff (Ivancic et al., 1981; Korabek et al., 1981; Shoemaker & Reid, 1980). Indeed, as will be discussed in subsequent chapters, multifaceted interventions often represent the management strategy of choice for resolving specific performance problems of staff because of their consistent effectiveness.

Although the simultaneous use of a number of managerial components enhances the effectiveness of multifaceted interventions relative to other supervisory strategies, this feature also represents the major disadvantage of multifaceted programs: they require a considerable amount of a supervisor's time for successful implementation. Because of the time requirement, it is quite unrealistic to attempt to use multifaceted approaches with very many performance areas of staff at any given point in time. In this regard, a general guideline that can be helpful for determining when to use this type of supervisory approach is similar to that noted in Chapter 2 for delineating and monitoring staff performance: multifaceted programs should be reserved for those staff performance areas that either relate to the most important aspect of an agency's functioning, or to an aspect that is causing the most problems for an agency at a particular time period (Reid & Shoemaker, 1984).

REFERENCES

Bricker, W.A., Morgan, D.G., & Grabowski, J.G. (1972). Development and maintenance of a behavior modification repertoire of cottage attendants through TV feedback. *American Journal of Mental Deficiency, 77,* 128–136.

Brown, K.M., Willis, B.S., & Reid, D.H. (1981). Differential effects of supervisor verbal feedback and feedback plus approval on institutional staff performance. *Journal of Organizational Behavior Management, 3*(1), 57–68.

Burg, M.M., Reid, D.H., & Lattimore, J. (1979). Use of a self-recording and supervision program to change institutional staff behavior. *Journal of Applied Behavior Analysis, 12,* 363–375.

Burgio, L.D., Whitman, T.L., & Reid, D.H. (1983). A participative management approach for improving direct-care staff performance in an institutional setting. *Journal of Applied Behavior Analysis, 16,* 37–53.

Faw, G.D., Reid, D.H., Schepis, M.M., Fitzgerald, J.R., & Welty, P.A. (1981). Involving institutional staff in the development and maintenance of sign language skills with profoundly retarded persons. *Journal of Applied Behavior Analysis, 14,* 411–423.

Ford, J.E. (1980). A classification system for feedback procedures. *Journal of Organizational Behavior Management, 2*(3), 183–191.

Fox, D.K., Hopkins, B.L., & Anger, W.K. (1987). The long-term effects of a token economy on safety performance in open-pit mining. *Journal of Applied Behavior Analysis, 20,* 215–224.

Gladstone, B.W., & Spencer, C.J. (1977). The effects of modelling on the contingent praise of mental retardation counsellors. *Journal of Applied Behavior Analysis, 10,* 75–84.

Greene, B.F., Willis, B.S., Levy, R., & Bailey, J.S. (1978). Measuring client gains from staff-implemented programs. *Journal of Applied Behavior Analysis, 11,* 395–412.

Hollander, M.A., & Plutchik, R. (1972). A reinforcement program for psychiatric attendants. *Journal of Behavior Therapy and Experimental Psychiatry, 3,* 297–300.

Hollander, M., Plutchik, R., & Horner, V. (1973). Interaction of patient and attendant reinforcement programs: The "piggyback" effect. *Journal of Consulting and Clinical Psychology, 41,* 43–47.

Hutchison, J.M., Jarman, P.H., & Bailey, J.S. (1980). Public posting with a habilitation team: Effects on attendance and performance. *Behavior Modification, 4,* 57–70.

Ivancic, M.T., Reid, D.H., Iwata, B.A., Faw, G.D., & Page, T.J. (1981). Evaluating a supervision program for developing and maintaining therapeutic staff-resident interactions during institutional care routines. *Journal of Applied Behavior Analysis, 14,* 95–107.

Iwata, B.A., Bailey, J.S., Brown, K.M., Foshee, T.J., & Alpern, M. (1976). A performance-based lottery to improve residential care and training by institutional staff. *Journal of Applied Behavior Analysis, 9,* 417–431.

Jones, R.T., Nelson, R.E., & Kazdin, A.E. (1977). The role of external variables in self-reinforcement: A review. *Behavior Modification, 1,* 147–178.

Katz, R.C., Johnson, C.A., & Gelfand, S. (1972). Modifying the dispensing of reinforcers: Some implications for behavior modification with hospitalized patients. *Behavior Therapy, 3,* 579–588.

Kissel, R.C., Whitman, T.L., & Reid, D.H. (1983). An institutional staff training and self-management program for developing multiple self-care skills in severely/ profoundly retarded individuals. *Journal of Applied Behavior Analysis, 16,* 395–415.

Korabek, C.A., Reid, D.H., & Ivancic, M.T. (1981). Improving needed food intake of profoundly handicapped children through effective supervision of institutional staff performance. *Applied Research in Mental Retardation, 2,* 69–88.

Miller, L.M. (1978). *Behavior management: The new science of managing people at work.* New York: John Wiley & Sons.

Montegar, C.A., Reid, D.H., Madsen, C.H., & Ewell, M.D. (1977). Increasing institutional staff to resident interactions through in-service training and supervisor approval. *Behavior Therapy, 8,* 533–540.

Panyan, M., Boozer, H., & Morris, N. (1970). Feedback to attendants as a reinforcer for applying operant techniques. *Journal of Applied Behavior Analysis, 3,* 1–4.

Parsons, M.B., Schepis, M.M., Reid, D.H., McCarn, J.E., & Green, C.W. (1987). Expanding the impact of behavioral staff management: A large-scale, long-term application in schools serving severely handicapped students. *Journal of Applied Behavior Analysis, 20,* 139–150.

Patterson, R., Cooke, C., & Liberman, R.P. (1972). Reinforcing the reinforcers:

A method of supplying feedback to nursing personnel. *Behavior Therapy, 3,* 444–446.

Pomerleau, O.F., Bobrove, P.H., & Smith, R.H. (1973). Rewarding psychiatric aides for the behavioral improvement of assigned patients. *Journal of Applied Behavior Analysis, 6,* 383–390.

Pommer, D.A., & Streedbeck, D. (1974). Motivating staff performance in an operant learning program for children. *Journal of Applied Behavior Analysis, 7,* 217–221.

Quilitch, H.R. (1975). A comparison of three staff-management procedures. *Journal of Applied Behavior Analysis, 8,* 59–66.

Realon, R.E., Lewallen, J.D., & Wheeler, A.J. (1983). Verbal feedback vs. verbal feedback plus praise: The effects on direct care staff's training behaviors. *Mental Retardation, 21,* 209–212.

Realon, R.E., Wheeler, A.J., Spring, B., & Springer, M. (1986). Evaluating the quality of training delivered by direct care staff in a state mental retardation center. *Behavioral Residential Treatment, 3,* 199–212.

Reid, D.H., & Green, C.W. (in press). Staff training. In J.L. Matson (Ed.), *Handbook of behavior modification for persons with mental retardation* (2nd Edition). New York: Plenum Press.

Reid, D.H., Parsons, M.B., McCarn, J.E., Green, C.W., Phillips, J.F., & Schepis, M.M. (1985). Providing a more appropriate education for severely handicapped persons: Increasing and validating functional classroom tasks. *Journal of Applied Behavior Analysis, 18,* 289–301.

Reid, D.H., Parsons, M.B., & Schepis, M.M. (in press). Management practices that affect the relative utility of aversive and nonaversive procedures. In S.L. Harris & J.S. Handleman (Eds.), *Life threatening behavior: Aversive and nonaversive interventions.* Newark, NJ: Rutgers University Press.

Reid, D.H., Schuh-Wear, C.L., & Brannon, M.E. (1978). Use of a group contingency to decrease staff absenteeism in a state institution. *Behavior Modification, 2,* 251–266.

Reid, D.H., & Shoemaker, J. (1984). Behavioral supervision: Methods of improving institutional staff performance. In W.P. Christian, G.T. Hannah, & T.J. Glahn (Eds.), *Programming effective human services: Strategies for institutional change and client transition* (pp. 39–61). New York: Plenum Press.

Reid, D.H., & Whitman, T.L. (1983). Behavioral staff management in institutions: A critical review of effectiveness and acceptability. *Analysis and Intervention in Developmental Disabilities, 3,* 131–149.

Reitz, A.L., & Hawkins, R.P. (1982). Increasing the attendance of nursing home residents at group recreation activities. *Behavior Therapy, 13,* 283–290.

Repp, A.C., & Deitz, D.E.D. (1979). Improving administrative-related staff behaviors at a state institution. *Mental Retardation, 17,* 185–192.

Seys, D.M., & Duker, P.C. (1978). Improving residential care for the retarded by differential reinforcement of high rates of ward-staff behaviour. *Behavioural Analysis and Modification, 2,* 203–210.

Shoemaker, J., & Reid, D.H. (1980). Decreasing chronic absenteeism among institutional staff: Effects of a low-cost attendance program. *Journal of Organizational Behavior Management, 2*(4), 317–328.

Sneed, T.J., & Bible, G.H. (1979). An administrative procedure for improving staff performance in an institutional setting for retarded persons. *Mental Retardation, 17,* 92–94.

Spreat, S., Piper, T., Deaton, S., Savoy-Paff, D., Brantner, J., Lipinski, D., Dorsey, M., & Baker-Potts, J.C. (1985). The impact of supervisory feedback on staff and client behavior. *Education and Training of the Mentally Retarded, 20,* 196–203.

Van Houten, R., & Sullivan, K. (1975). Effects of an audio-cueing system on the rate of teacher praise. *Journal of Applied Behavior Analysis, 8,* 197–201.

Wallace, C.J., Davis, J.R., Liberman, R.P., & Baker, V. (1973). Modeling and staff behavior. *Journal of Consulting and Clinical Psychology, 41,* 422–425.

Welsch, W.V., Ludwig, C., Radiker, J.E., & Krapfl, J.E. (1973). Effects of feedback on daily completion of behavior modification projects. *Mental Retardation, 11,* 24–26.

Whitman, T.L., Scibak, J.W., & Reid, D.H. (1983). *Behavior modification with the severely and profoundly retarded: Research and application.* New York: Academic Press.

Chapter 5

INCREASING THERAPEUTIC ACTIVITIES IN CONGREGATE LIVING ENVIRONMENTS SERVING DEPENDENT CLIENTS

A common model of service provision within the human services is residential, congregate care. This type of service delivery is characterized most typically by the provision of treatment services to *groups* of clients in residential *living* environments. Generally, clients served within a congregate care setting share a number of common characteristics in order that they might benefit from similar types of residential treatment services. Such services are usually designed for *dependent* clients such as persons who are very young, very elderly or seriously mentally handicapped. Because these types of client populations are so often dependent on caregivers for the fulfillment of many if not most of their wants and needs, congregate care services typically involve training, assisting, and supervising residential clients in essentially all aspects of daily living.

Due to the dependency of clients in congregate care environments on staff as just noted, staff performance is a particularly important issue in this type of human service provision. To illustrate, even the most basic *safety* of residential clients is usually a direct function of how well staff perform their caregiving work tasks (Favell, Favell, Riddle & Risley, 1984). Similarly, from a therapeutic standpoint, the provision of stimulating activities and social interactions which foster client learning and habilitation typically occurs only if staff perform in a competent, and often effortful, manner (Parsons, Cash, & Reid, in press).

The importance of therapeutic activities provided by staff in congregate care settings has probably been most frequently recognized in regard to services for institutionalized, mentally retarded persons (e.g. Christian, Hannah, & Glahn, 1984). Such recognition has been especially widespread since the early 1970s when federal legislation and litigation established the legal right of all mentally retarded people to an appropriate education or habilitation (see Martin, 1984, for a summary). Due

99

primarily to legal requirements, public residential programs that provide congregate care for the mentally retarded have been heavily scrutinized by governmental regulatory agencies in an effort to ensure the provision of therapeutic services to clients. A focus of the regulatory agencies, in addition to health and safety issues, has been the requirement that each client receive training based on individually planned treatment goals, and that such training extend throughout the day as well as in all environments within the residential facility—including congregate living units (Smith, 1983).

The fulfillment of regulatory criteria for residential care and training is relatively straightforward during times of the day when professional staff are available to provide a variety of specialty clinical services (e.g. educational programs in schools, vocational training, speech therapy, occupational therapy) to individual and/or small groups of clients. However, professional clinical services often are brief and occur only intermittently during a client's day. Much of the typical day for an institutionalized client is usually spent in the living area such as a ward or cottage where paraprofessional direct care staff are primarily (or exclusively) responsible for the client's treatment provision. In order to comply with regulatory standards during these latter times, direct care staff are required to provide clients with opportunities to practice and generalize skills that have been learned during more formally structured training sessions provided by professional clinicians. The provision of such opportunities requires that staff interact with clients and engage clients in constructive activities on a rather frequent basis.

Actually, living environments for residential populations such as the elderly and the mentally handicapped present many potential opportunities for clients to learn and/or practice important skills. Similarly, although representing only a partial living environment in that clients do not actually live in the setting, day-care centers in which many young children spend the majority of their waking hours provide numerous learning opportunities within a congregate care situation. Within these kinds of environments, language and communication skills, for example, can be taught incidentally when a client has a need that he/she is attempting to fulfill (Schepis et al., 1982). To illustrate, the name of a leisure material or food item can be advantageously taught (or its application practiced) at the exact moment when the client wants to enjoy the leisure material or eat the food. How to wash one's hands can be similarly taught when a client's hands are clearly dirty or just before or after a meal during the routine course of the day in a living environment. In essence, the range of incidental teaching opportunities that occur within residential, congregate care settings is endless (see Hart & Risley, 1982, for elaboration on incidental teaching).

Although living environments can potentially provide a variety of informal teaching opportunities for residential clients as just exemplified, in actuality such settings rarely are characterized by the frequent provision of teaching activities (Burg, Reid, & Lattimore, 1979; Warren & Mondy, 1971). Rather, in typical congregate living environments for dependent persons, clients are often alone in their beds for long periods of time or are crowded into central dayrooms with no apparent purposeful activity. Such situations are especially problematic for seriously dependent populations, because frequently these individuals do not possess the skills to independently engage in constructive leisure pursuits during unstructured times of the day. Hence, when no specific activity is scheduled to occur within a living environment (e.g. eating, dressing or grooming) and clients are left by staff to be on their own, clients have nothing to do for extended periods of time. An illustration of typical client inactivity in this regard is reflected in Figure 5-1. Figure 5-1 summarizes results of systematic observations of client behavior conducted in 22 living areas of public residential facilities for the mentally retarded during times when clients were not in formal school or vocational programs such as the late afternoon and early evening (Parsons et al., in press). As indicated in Figure 5-1, clients spent essentially two-thirds of their time without engaging in any constructive or purposeful activity (i.e. off-task in Figure 5-1) in contrast to participating in appropriate leisure or learning activities (active treatment). Such conditions not only represent situations in which potential learning opportunities for clients are not taken advantage of but also stand in clear contrast to the legal mandate noted previously regarding active treatment within residential services for the mentally retarded.

In attempting to translate the need for therapeutic activities into services that can actually be provided by direct care staff in congregate care situations, client treatment is perhaps most appropriately viewed in a rather basic form as described by Repp and Barton (1980). Using Repp and Barton's conceptualization, appropriate treatment provision is reflected by clients being active, staff being active, and clients and staff interacting to the habilitative benefit of the client. When treatment provision to dependent clients is considered in these terms, the role of client care

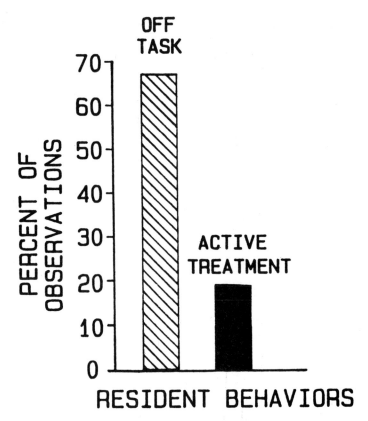

Figure 5-1. Average percentage of observations that involved off-task and active treatment activity among clients in 22 residential units for severely and profoundly mentally retarded persons during nonschool and nonwork periods of the day and evening (i.e. typically nonstructured leisure times). Based on Parsons, M.B., Cash, V.B., & Reid, D.H. (in press). Improving residential treatment services: Implementation and norm-referenced evaluation of a comprehensive management system. *Journal of Applied Behavior Analysis.*

workers clearly appears to be the most salient factor affecting the level of therapeutic activity provided in congregate care environments.

Problems that Mitigate Against Staff Provision of Therapeutic Activities and Interactions With Residential Clients

A number of reasons exist regarding why direct care staff in congregate care environments typically do not interact with clients and/or provide constructive activities at therapeutically sufficient levels. Some reasons relate to the skill levels of the clients. Infants, for example, simply do not have the ability to engage in a wide variety of activities that staff might readily participate in and find enjoyable. Similarly, mentally retarded clients may not possess the social or communication skills to attract, and/or respond to, staff attention in a positive way. In addition, some mentally retarded clients may be physically unattractive or exhibit maladaptive behaviors such as aggression or self-injury to the degree that they repel staff or attract only negative staff attention. In the same vein, involving elderly clients in activities often requires a high degree of physical effort by staff members. In the latter case, the benefit of providing activities to dependent clients may not appear to staff to be worth the effort.

Other factors that are considered to mitigate against frequent and/or positive staff interactions and activities with residential clients involve characteristics of the staff who are typically employed in direct care positions within human service agencies. In particular, few client care workers have any training or formal job preparation prior to employment as a direct care staff member (Zlomke & Benjamin, 1983). Having had no background regarding the characteristics of the clients with whom they will be working, many staff persons are totally unaware of how to work most effectively with clients—and particularly when activities must be provided to *groups* of clients. Successfully interacting with, and providing constructive activities to, groups of clients requires a set of skills considerably different and more complex than those needed to work with individual clients (Reid & Favell, 1984). Hence, staff frequently need to be taught how to provide training and/or therapeutic activities to groups of clients. Unfortunately, the effectiveness of typical in-service training programs that are presented in an attempt to provide the necessary training in this regard is often diminished by the frequently high turnover rate of employees in direct care positions (Zaharia & Baumeister, 1978), such that new staff who are not yet trained usually represent a substantial portion of a given agency's staff population.

Another factor that impedes proficient staff performance is that, due in part to limited educational backgrounds, client care staff frequently perceive their job as only to provide basic care (e.g. bathing, feeding clients) or related housekeeping and paperwork chores in contrast to client habilitation activities. The former duties are somewhat discrete and the benefits or outcomes of staff efforts are more readily apparent than the (longer term) benefits of engaging clients in various therapeutic activities. A somewhat related factor is that new staff members who may be motivated to interact with clients when they begin their employment are often influenced into performing at a less-than-optimal level by modeling the performance of more experienced but less motivated staff (Reid & Whitman, 1983). Similarly, peer pressure applied by experienced staff can influence new staff to perform less diligently (Reid & Whitman, 1983).

Understanding the causes for problematic performances of direct care staff with residential clients can be important for effectively designing management interventions to resolve the problems. However, an over-emphasis on the potential causes needs to be avoided. As discussed in the introductory comments to this text, the focus of effective staff management should not be on conceptualizing the potential reasons for inadequate staff performance but, rather, on workable methods of improving such performance. In this regard, because of the long-standing concern over problems with direct care staffs' treatment provision in congregate care settings, there has been a relatively considerable amount of behavioral research on methods of improving this area of staff performance. In light of such research, the purpose of this chapter is to: (a) summarize and critique the investigations that have been conducted, and (b) synthesize from the investigations the management strategy of choice for increasing direct care staffs' therapeutic interactions with clients in congregate living environments.

Summary of the Research

This section describes the behavioral research that relates directly to increasing staff-client interactions and staff provision of therapeutic activities in congregate care settings. Following a brief discussion of the general characteristics of the studies conducted in this area of staff performance, the more unique aspects of the investigations will be discussed in regard to specific behavior change procedures used with staff performance.

General Procedural Characteristics

The vast majority of the behavioral studies that have focused on improving staff performance in congregate living units have used a combination of antecedent and consequence procedures in a multifaceted approach (Chapter 4). However, most of the multifaceted management interventions generally have included many of the same basic antecedent and consequence components. For example, almost all of the interventions have included some form of staff instructions or training. Instructions to staff regarding how to interact with clients in living units have usually been provided verbally through an in-service meeting (Burg et al., 1979; Montegar, Reid, Madsen & Ewell, 1977; Seys & Duker, 1978), although a few studies have used written directions (Dyer, Schwartz & Luce, 1984; Kunz et al., 1982). Modeling of desired interaction styles for staff has also been used to train staff through demonstration in the living area (Coles & Blunden, 1981; Montegar et al., 1977) and through videotaped examples of appropriate staff interactions with clients (Burch, Reiss & Bailey, 1987).

In addition to the relatively common in-service and modeling approaches, additional antecedent procedures have often been used to further set the occasion for increased staff interactions with clients. In particular, increased structure has been added to the staff work routine by assigning highly specific staff responsibilities regarding interactions with clients (Coles & Blunden, 1981; Parsons et al., in press; Spangler & Marshall, 1983) and/or by scheduling specific time periods for staff to conduct activities with clients (Coles & Blunden, 1981; Parsons et al., in press; Seys & Duker, 1978, 1986; Spangler & Marshall, 1983). The setting of specific expectations or criteria levels for staff interactions has also been used to increase the likelihood that staff will interact frequently with clients (Burg et al., 1979; Seys & Duker, 1986).

With few exceptions (e.g. Burch et al., 1987; Quilitch & Gray, 1974), some form of consequence procedure has been used in all the studies in this area of staff performance. The most frequently used consequence procedure has been supervisory feedback. Common forms of feedback that have been employed include verbal feedback from supervisors (Brown, Willis & Reid, 1981; Coles & Blunden, 1981; Seys & Duker, 1986), publicly posted feedback (Coles & Blunden, 1981; Kunz et al., 1982), and, to a lesser degree, privately written feedback (Parsons et al., in press). Staff have also been trained to provide feedback to themselves regarding their interactions with clients as a form of self-feedback (Burg et al., 1979; Burgio, Whitman & Reid, 1983). A reinforcing consequence that has been used other than feedback was the opportunity to engage in preferred activities with clients (Seys & Duker, 1978). Examples of how the various types of procedures as just noted have been combined into respective multifaceted management programs across investigations is provided in Table 5-1.

Table 5-1

PROCEDURAL COMPONENTS OF MULTIFACETED MANAGEMENT INTERVENTIONS

Reference	Antecedent Procedures			Consequence Procedures		
	Instructions	Job Delineation	Goal Setting	Feedback	Approval	Self Management
Quilitch & Gray (1974)	vocal					
Montegar, Reid, Madsen, & Ewell (1977)	vocal				vocal	
Burg, Reid, & Lattimore (1979)	vocal		supervisor determined			self recording
Coles & Blunden (1981)	vocal & modeling	schedules & roles		vocal, written & publicly posted		
Kunz, Lutzker, Cuvo, Eddleman, Lutzker, Megson & Gulley Exp. 2 (1982)	vocal & written	activity cards		publicly posted		self recording
Burgio, Whitman & Reid (1983)	vocal		participatory			self recording, self feedback & self praise
Spangler & Marshall (1983)		schedules & roles				
Dyer, Schwartz, & Luce (1984)	vocal & written			written & publicly posted	written	
Burch, Reiss, & Bailey (1987)	vocal, written & modeling					

Unique Procedural Characteristics

A number of studies have used a self-control component (Chapter 4) along with various external supervisory procedures to improve staff interactions with groups of clients in living units. However, to date, only one investigation has attempted to evaluate the efficacy of a staff management program that involved staff essentially self-managing their work performance in this area without explicit assistance from managerial personnel (Burgio et al., 1983). In the Burgio et al. investigation, client care workers set their own daily goals of specific numbers of interactions to conduct with clients. Additionally, using a portable recording apparatus, staff recorded the frequency of their interactions and then graphed their rate of interacting as a form of self-feedback. Staff also were instructed to praise themselves for meeting or exceeding the daily goal. These self-control, or behavioral participative management, procedures were effective in significantly increasing staff interactions with clients and, subsequently, the amount of time clients spent in constructive activities (e.g. interacting with staff, manipulating leisure materials). Acceptability data indicated that staff approved of the participative management system relative to other types of management approaches with which the staff were familiar.

Another rather specialized type of management program that has been used to increase institutionalized, mentally retarded persons' engagement with leisure materials involved scheduling a specific period to conduct activities with clients and assigning certain staff the exclusive role of prompting and reinforcing clients to use the materials (Coles & Blunden, 1981; Parsons et al., in press; Spangler & Marshall, 1983). Such a "play manager" or "room manager" role concept is based on the work of LeLaurin and Risley (1972) who introduced the idea of a "zone" arrangement for staff working in day-care centers for infants and toddlers. In a zone concept, staff are responsible for different activities or areas in a room and for working with *all* clients who enter into the assigned area. Such an approach is in contrast to the more common strategy of staff being responsible for only *one* group of clients as they move through different activities and areas throughout the day (see Mansell, Felce, de Kock, & Jenkins, 1982, for elaboration). The zone approach has been successfully used to increase therapeutic staff interactions with institutionalized, mentally retarded clients (e.g. Spangler & Marshall, 1983). However, Coles and Blunden (1981) also reported that high levels of staff interactions with clients (and consequently high levels of appropriate client activity) could not be *maintained* solely by scheduling the activity period and assigning staff the role of play or room manager. In the latter case, a system of staff monitoring and supervisory feedback was necessary to maintain high levels of staff-supported client activity. Similarly, Seys and Duker (1986) found that scheduling staff to conduct training activities did not in and of itself result in more activities being conducted with clients until the additional components of staff self-recording, supervisory prompting and supervisory feedback were employed.

A somewhat more novel approach to improving habilitative activities in living units (at least in terms of the focus of the management intervention) was described by Dyer et al. (1984). The purpose of the Dyer et al. investigation was to increase specially delineated, *purposeful and age-appropriate* activities provided to autistic youth within a residential living environment. That is, rather than only increasing the general *quantity* of staff-client interactions as targeted in most investigations, Dyer et al. focused on improving the *quality* of the activities in an attempt to ensure that staff were interacting with clients in a manner that would maximally assist the clients to function as independently and normally as possible. The management intervention consisted of inservicing supervisors using written instructions regarding what constituted purposeful activities with clients and then posting the instructions in the living areas. Staff were subsequently monitored and provided with written feedback regarding the degree to which the activity that they were conducting met the criteria for an age-appropriate and purposeful activity. Such procedures appeared quite effective for improving the therapeutic quality of client activities provided by the direct care personnel.

The only investigation that pertained to increasing therapeutic client activities in congregate care settings (as congregate care is defined in this chapter) by improving staff behavior that was not conducted in a residential facility serving the developmentally disabled was reported by Kunz et al. (1982) in an infant care facility. In the Kunz et al. study, supervisors instructed individual staff to conduct specified activities with each child and to record the completion of the play activities. Supervisors then totaled the number of play sessions conducted with all children and publicly posted the information for both staff and parents of the young children to review. The percentage of time that children spent engaged in play interactions (with the staff) was substantially increased as a result of the management intervention. Kunz et al. also included acceptability data which indicated that both staff and parents responded relatively favorably to the self-recording and public posting management approach.

As indicated earlier, a number of management programs designed to improve direct care staffs' provision of therapeutic interactions in congregate care situations have used many of the same types of procedures combined into a multifaceted system. In contrast, investigations that evaluated a management procedure singularly at any given time have been relatively rare in this area of staff performance research. Where such research has occurred, some idiosyncratic effects of individual management procedures have been found. Brown et al. (1981), for example, reported that supervisor feedback alone (i.e. only descriptive information of performance without any approving or disapproving comments — see Chapter 4 for elaboration) suppressed the frequency of staff nonwork behavior but did not increase specific client-directed interactions that were of concern to the staff supervisors. The latter staff performance area did not improve until supervisors provided explicit verbal praise along -with the feedback contingent on staff interacting with clients. Seys and Duker (1978) also evaluated several procedures and found that inservicing staff and scheduling of recreational activities (a routine practice in many facilities) was insufficient in regard to improving the amount of time staff spent engaging in such activities with clients. Improvements occurred only when staff helped to set a criterion for an average percent of time to engage in the activities and when consequences (special activities chosen by the staff) were delivered based on staff performing at or above the established criterion level.

Results of the Brown et al. (1981) and Seys and Duker (1978) investigations, albeit based on a relatively small amount of research to date, suggest that all of the various component procedures that have been used in the different multifaceted management programs may not have been necessary for the overall success of the respective programs. As discussed elsewhere in regard to the behavioral staff management research in general (Whitman, Scibak, & Reid, 1983, chap. 11), more investigations involving congregate care that evaluate the relative (non)effects of different components of multifaceted management programs are warranted.

Critique of the Research

The purpose of this section is to critically review the staff management research summarized in the preceding section in order to objectively judge the degree of definitiveness with which conclusions can be made about the utility of respective management procedures. For the sake of efficiency, an in-depth critique of each individual study will not be presented; rather, the focus will be on the general *body* of staff management research that addresses the problem of increasing therapeutic activities provided by staff in congregate living areas serving dependent clients. Special attention will be given to the degree of social significance of the target staff behaviors addressed in the investigations as well as to the validity of the experimental designs employed, the effectiveness of the interventions and the acceptability of the staff management procedures.

Social Significance of the Target Behaviors

The focus of the interventions discussed in this chapter basically has been to evaluate methods of changing staff behavior in order to increase staff interactions with clients through the conducting of various leisure or training activities with clients and/or by prompting clients to appropriately use leisure materials. Because the *ultimate* goal in this regard has been to increase the amount of time clients spend involved in constructive activities, the social significance of the staff behaviors targeted for change through management interventions should really be determined by the benefits *clients* derived from the change in staff performance (Chapter 1). Hence, indices of client activity level as a function of changes in staff behavior must be evaluated. Approximately half of the studies that were reviewed included a measure of client behavior in this regard (e.g. Burg et al., 1979; Burgio et al., 1983; Coles & Blunden, 1981; Dyer et al., 1984; Parsons et al., in press; Quilitch & Gray, 1974; Spangler & Marshall, 1983), each of which reported beneficial changes in client activity that coincided with the implementation of a respective staff management program. These rather consistent outcomes (at least among the investigations that monitored client behavior) suggest that the targeted staff performance areas were indeed important. However, upon closer scrutiny, the nature of the client behaviors that were addressed warrants consideration. Specifically, this area of research as a whole has not attended very carefully to the *quality* of the activities that staff provide to clients.

The research involving severely and profoundly mentally retarded clients, which represents the vast majority of congregate care populations studied, particularly needs increased emphasis on activities that would be more likely to lead to enhanced independent or adaptive functioning of the clients. The majority of the studies reviewed provided very little information about the therapeutic quality of the activities that staff conducted in terms of how those activities related to identified treatment goals for individual clients. Basically, the intent to this point in the research has been to increase *any* type of nonpunitive, staff-evoked activity among groups of clients that is not maladaptive in nature (e.g. aggression, stereotopy). Although such a purpose seems understandable given the historic lack of any useful client activity in most congregate care settings during times when formal treatment programs are not available, a more desirable goal would be to not only increase staff-supported client activity but to ensure that such activity is truly therapeutic. Although elaboration on what constitutes therapeutic or purposeful activity among dependent clients during typical leisure-related times is beyond the scope of this text, numerous descriptions are available elsewhere that would be of benefit to researchers and managers concerned with this area of service provision (Bates, Renzaglia, & Wehman, 1981; Dyer et al., 1984; Parsons et al., in press; Reid, Green, McCarn, Parsons, & Schepis, 1986).

Validity of the Experimental Designs

Generally, the investigations reviewed used adequate experimental designs to sufficiently demonstrate that the various combinations of management procedures described in respective studies were responsible for the reported improvements in staff performance (i.e. adequate internal validity). Only two of the studies appeared somewhat questionable in this respect. In the Spreat et al. (1985) investigation, functional control of the dependent variable (staff behavior) was not apparent, in that a reversal experimental design was used to evaluate effects of supervisory feedback and staff performance did not change when feedback was discontinued (see Baer, Wolf & Risley, 1968, for discussion of necessary behavior changes that allow for valid conclusions when employing reversal designs). Also, in one of the experiments of the Coles and Blunden (1981) study that assessed effects of different variations of a staff monitoring and feedback system, no real control of each procedural variation on staff behavior was apparent. Hence, conclusions regarding effects of the separate interventions are prohibited.

Whereas internal validity was, for the most part, adequate, the external validity of given interventions represents a pervasive weakness in the current research on improving therapeutic activities in congregate living areas. With few exceptions (e.g. Burgio et al., 1983; Dyer et al., 1984;

Parsons et al., in press), research has been limited to demonstration projects involving only one living unit of a state institution. The research has only begun to attempt to demonstrate the efficacy of *wide-scale* applications of behavioral staff management procedures for increasing therapeutic activities in congregate settings. That is, studies demonstrating improvements *throughout* a given agency's staff and client population have been infrequent. Additionally, all but one of the studies reviewed (Kunz et al., 1982) were conducted in residential environments for the mentally retarded or autistic. There is a serious paucity of research on behavioral staff management systems in other congregate care settings including day-care programs for infants, nursing homes for the elderly, psychiatric facilities for the mentally ill and community group homes for the mentally retarded. Although a plausible case can be made to some degree for the application of the staff management procedures with demonstrated effectiveness in institutions for the mentally retarded to other congregate care settings, systematic research is nevertheless needed in settings serving other types of clients in order to empirically demonstrate the generality of the management procedures.

Effectiveness of Management Interventions

As discussed previously, almost all of the studies assessing the impact of staff management procedures on the level of therapeutic activities in congregate living units used multifaceted interventions. Essentially all of the intervention packages resulted in changes in staff performance, providing rather strong support for the efficacy of behavioral management procedures in this area of staff performance. However, relatively little information is available regarding the strength of any one component of the management packages relative to the success of the overall interventions. Among the few component analyses that have been conducted in this area, it appears that antecedent procedures such as staff inservices and staff scheduling alone appear relatively unlikely to significantly change staff behavior, particularly over long periods of time. More research is needed to analyze other individual components to determine specific strategies that are necessary and/or sufficient for changing staff behavior and, ultimately, changing the behavior of dependent clients. In this regard, streamlining management programs by eliminating unnecessary procedures is important if such procedures are to be used frequently in applied settings; human service managers have a number of different job responsibilities to fulfill and essentially do not have time to spend with supervisory strategies that do not effect improvements in staff performance.

In addition to the unclear effectiveness of individual components of multifaceted interventions, a weakness of the behavioral management research in this area relates to the lack of demonstrations of the effectiveness of the management procedures for substantial time periods. With few exceptions (e.g. Dyer et al., 1984; Parsons et al., in press; Seys & Duker, 1978, 1986), studies in the congregate care area have included experimental sessions of less than four hours duration. Approximately half of the studies involved experimental sessions of less than two hours. In residential settings, managers and staff typically are charged with the responsibility of providing treatment services for much longer periods of time. Questions remain as to whether procedures that are effective in improving staff behavior for a two-hour experimental session, for example, can be equally effective when staff are responsible for providing activities throughout the majority of the routine workday. Similarly, the research has not consistently demonstrated which procedures effectively *maintain* staff performance (and client performance) across extended time periods involving work days, weeks, months, etc. Relatively few studies (e.g. Coles & Blunden, 1981; Parsons et al., in press) included follow-up periods greater than six months, although the results of these particular investigations were generally supportive in regard to showing the durability of the initial changes in staff performance that accompanied the supervisory interventions. Which management procedures effectively maintain staff provision of therapeutic activities is a crucial issue when considering the effort that managers must take to ensure quality service provision by direct care staff. Considerable time and energy is often needed to affect initial change with staff, and managers may not be able to exert such effort on a continuous basis month after month in order to maintain initially improved staff performance. Hence, management procedures are needed that, once instituted, require reduced attention from managers to continue to operate. In some respects, maintaining desirable staff behavior may be more difficult than initially evoking such behavior in light of common variables that affect staff performance over the long run in congregate care settings such as program reorganization, hiring of new staff and exposure of staff to the same performance contingencies over a long time period.

Staff Acceptability

A key variable affecting the durability of the effects of staff management procedures relates to the acceptability of the procedures to both client care staff and supervisors. In short, if personnel do not find various procedures very acceptable, the procedures are not likely to be adopted into routine management practices (Chapter 1). Of the studies reviewed, only three included formal measures of staff acceptability (Burgio et al., 1983; Kunz et al., 1982; Spreat et al., 1985), and none of the studies evaluated the acceptability of the procedures among supervisors. Each investigation that evaluated procedural acceptability used a questionnaire format whereby direct care staff answered questions concerning how they felt about the management procedures employed. Although questionnaire responses can be helpful (and the obtained responses were generally positive toward the respective behavioral management procedures), a stronger indication of acceptability is whether or not management procedures continue to be used with staff after a given study is formally finished (cf. van den Pol, Reid, & Fuqua, 1983). Coles and Blunden (1981) provided some encouraging data in this regard by reporting that their activity zone and room manager procedures were used 339 days out of a possible 365 days following the initial experimental intervention. As a whole, however, the research provides little information as to whether staff are likely to view the management procedures positively, or whether supervisors are likely to view the improved staff performance that results from the management interventions as sufficiently reinforcing to maintain the supervisory efforts that are needed to continue the improvements.

Procedures Most Likely to Increase Therapeutic Activities in Congregate Care Environments for Dependent Clients

Although the existing research on staff performance problems discussed in this chapter clearly is not complete as noted in the previous section, the research nevertheless has successfully demonstrated some management interventions that should be helpful to supervisors. Actually, a number of procedures seem likely to improve the level of therapeutic activities provided to groups of dependent clients relative to what typically exists in congregate care settings. The purpose of this section is to describe what appears to be the *most* effective of all the procedures evaluated to date (cf. Parsons et al., in press).

In attempting to improve therapeutic activities provided by direct care personnel in congregate care situations, the first managerial steps are to define and monitor the behaviors of the *clients* that would indicate that the clients are indeed participating in therapeutic activities. As noted earlier, careful attention should be paid to both the quantity and the therapeutic quality of the activities. The primary point here is that a necessary, although not always sufficient, indicator of whether staff are performing satisfactorily in regard to their task of providing therapeutic services to clients in congregate situations is what the clients are actually *doing* during leisure-related periods in living units.

After defining and monitoring the client activities that are desired to occur, the second managerial step is to clearly determine the parameters of what staff should be doing in order to positively effect the designated client activity. Specific client activity periods should be delineated and clear definitions of staff job duties during those periods should be specified. In particular, periods during the day or evening when other more routinely occurring events such as mealtimes are not already scheduled should be identified. These typically nonstructured time periods, which often are two to three hours in duration, should be broken down into small time blocks of 30 to 45 minutes. Longer time periods generally require too much effort on the part of staff to consistently provide one type of therapeutic client activity throughout the period. In essence, client and staff activities should be sufficiently detailed such that staff know what they are to do, when they are to do it, where they are to do it and with whom they should do it—in contrast to staff performance expectations being only generally identified. To illustrate, a rather common type of staff work schedule prepared by supervisors in residential facilities for the mentally retarded is provided in the upper panel of Figure 5-2. In contrast to this type of *general* staff schedule, a *detailed* schedule that is much more likely to set the occasion for appropriate staff performance (and client activity) is exemplified in the bottom panel of the figure.

To further structure activity time periods, staff should be provided with very specific roles or sets of duties, particularly when staff are attempting to engage *groups* of clients in activities. For instance, one staff member could be assigned to care for the basic needs of the clients such as toileting incontinent individuals. This staff member also could have

SAMPLE SCHEDULE 1

STAFF	3:00 - 5:00
Meg	Group 1 - leisure time
Claire	Group 2 - leisure time
Don	Group 2 - leisure time

SAMPLE SCHEDULE 2

3:00-3:30	3:30-4:15	4:15-5:00
Snack	Exercise	Table Games
In diningroom	at gym	In cottage dayroom
Materials: N A	Materials: balls, mini-trampoline, hand weights, exercise bike	Materials: magazines, video game, games in Drawer 1
Staff Roles activity _Meg_ resident care _Claire_	Staff Roles activity _Don_ resident care _Meg_	Staff Roles activity _Claire_ resident care _Don_
trainer _Don_ (work on John's drinking program)	trainer _Claire_ (focus on residents correctly using exercise bike)	trainer _Meg_ (teach Amy & Tom video game usage)

Figure 5-2. Examples of a typical, general staff schedule for conducting group activities with dependent clients in a congregate care situation (top panel) and a more specific, behavioral schedule (bottom panel). Whereas the general schedule indicates only the global nature of what should occur, the specific schedule provides more detailed information such as, for example, delineation of what staff should do (e.g. activity role, trainer role), the designated time periods, the location, and the required materials.

the assigned responsibility of handling any duties that might require that a staff member leave the group in order to, for example, answer a telephone, manage disruptive behavior, or escort a client to the bathroom. A second staff member could be charged with constantly moving about the room in order to briefly interact with clients for 30 to 60 seconds by providing or exchanging leisure materials (Parsons et al., in press), to engage in brief incidental teaching interactions with clients (Schepis et al., 1982) and/or to reinforce clients who are constructively active (Burgio et al., 1983). If additional staff members are available, their role could be to spend longer time periods (e.g. three to five minutes) with individual clients attempting to more formally teach functional skills (Parsons et al., in press). Elaboration on these types of staff roles is provided in Table 5-2. When using this type of role-assignment process, it is helpful if staff alternate roles at least hourly, because some of the job duties are more physically taxing than others and the role rotation will reduce the likelihood of decreases in staff performance due to staff becoming tired.

Table 5-2
EXAMPLES OF ROLE SPECIFICATION FOR DIRECT CARE STAFF DURING GROUP ACTIVITY TIMES IN CONGREGATE CARE SETTINGS

Role	*Duties*
Client Care Coordinator	• assist clients with basic care needs (e.g. toileting)
	• manage client disruptive behavior
	• ensure clients remain in activity area
	• assume activity role when client care is not needed
Client Activity Coordinator	• provide choice of materials for all clients
	• prompt clients in appropriate use of materials
	• reinforce clients for using materials appropriately
	• move from client to client at least every 60 seconds
	• do not leave activity area
Client Trainer	• conduct assigned training programs that require step sequence, multiple trials or that must occur in location away from activity room
	• assume client care or activity role in the absence of either

The process of assigning staff to perform a set of duties for all clients within a given group as exemplified in Table 5-2 and the preceding paragraph is quite different from the frequently used model of assigning one staff person to be responsible for just one subgroup of clients. The former model, which requires that there be at least two staff members assigned to a group of clients in order to fulfill separate roles, has the advantage of ensuring that no client will be left unattended for a long period of time, that basic care needs will be met and that all clients will receive brief teaching-type interactions from staff on a frequent basis. In short, the role assignment model allows for the provision of the maximum amount of active treatment possible given the number of direct care staff on duty (cf. Repp & Barton, 1980). Further, when more than two staff are assigned to a group of clients, the additional staff can fulfill the trainers' role (Table 5-2) in order to increase the amount of systematic, formal training provided to individual clients within the group. Organizing staff duties according to the same set of clearly articulated job roles across all living units also provides sufficient structure such that when staff are required to substitute in other living units that are periodically short-staffed, the staff are more knowledgeable about what they are expected to do relative to having to determine for themselves what should occur in each (novel) work situation to which they might be assigned.

The third managerial step for maximizing staff provision of treatment services involves briefly discussing with staff why therapeutic activities are important and specifying for staff what they will be expected to perform. An in-service meeting should be conducted that provides opportunities for both staff and supervisors to exchange information and ideas in a participative management format (Parsons, Schepis, Reid, McCarn, & Green, 1987). As part of the in-service, supervisors should carefully model (Faw, Reid, Schepis, Fitzgerald, & Welty, 1981) each of the staff roles during several actual activity periods in the living units and then observe staff perform the roles and provide corrective and/or approving feedback (Lattimore, Stephens, Favell, & Risley, 1984) until staff have demonstrated proficiency in performing the designated duties. This latter step of observing staff competently perform their assignments is necessary to ensure that staff are sufficiently knowledgeable regarding their duties.

Once specific activity periods and staff roles have been established and staff have been adequately trained in the various job duties, the fourth managerial step is to institute a behavioral monitoring system (Chapter 4). A good monitoring system allows a manager to systematically and objectively observe staff performance during a portion of the activity period to determine if respective staff members continue to perform adequately or not. A monitoring system is also necessary in order for a supervisor to give objective feedback to each staff member concerning how well he/she is fulfilling his/her role assignment—which represents the fifth step in the management program. While giving feedback, a supervisor can provide suggestions for ways to improve the activities being conducted if necessary. In addition, if specific criteria for staff performance have been established, information resulting from a monitoring system allows a supervisor to provide other (nonfeedback) types of positive consequences (Chapter 4) for those staff who consistently meet or exceed the criterion. In this regard, because direct care staff have typically not been required to exert the effort necessary to provide the level of client activities that are now often expected in congregate care settings, supervisors should be particularly diligent about providing a variety of positive consequences in order to reinforce satisfactory staff performance. If supervisors are indeed consistent in their instructions to staff and frequently provide performance consequences, direct care staff are likely to eventually accept the responsibility of providing therapeutic activities throughout the day as part of the routine job of direct care. It should also be noted, however, that maintaining high levels of staff interactions and therapeutic activities with groups of clients in living areas almost always requires *ongoing* supervisory attention in the form of monitoring and providing performance consequences.

The final step in a recommended behavioral staff management program is to continue to monitor the behavior of the *clients* to ensure that the program engineered to improve staff performance is having the desired effect on the clients' behavior. Such information on client activity provides a manager with a consistent measure of how various schedule adjustments, changes in staff ratios or essentially any major change in a living unit routine affects the level of active treatment provided for clients. Additionally, upper-level supervisors who are responsible for several living areas can use the data collected on client behavior in individual living units to evaluate how well respective managers of individual living units are managing (i.e. how well the latter managers are monitoring staff performance and providing feedback). Data on client behavior can be most conveniently summarized in graphic form so that upper-level managers can quickly assess how a particular living area is functioning over time (see Parsons et al., in press, for elaboration).

Although this chapter has focused on staff management interventions for improving habilitative activities, an issue that is usually of considerable importance in providing therapeutic activities not yet mentioned is the effective management of *materials* used for training clients and prompting leisure activities. In most congregate care environments for dependent clients, the selection and maintenance of materials is quite complex. The complexity is due to several factors, such as securing funds to regularly purchase materials, preventing breakage of materials, and protecting clients from harmful use of materials. Hence, among other things, careful consideration should be taken by managers regarding the kinds of materials purchased for use in the living environments. Included in such consideration should be the purchase of materials that are age-appropriate (Bates et al., 1981; Dyer et al., 1984), where possible. Preventing more fragile materials from being immediately broken or destroyed by various clients' actions also often necessitates restricting certain materials to be used only during those times when there are sufficient staff available to adequately supervise client activity (i.e. when there are adequate staff to fulfill the trainer role mentioned earlier). Other more durable materials may be left in the living area for clients to use with less supervision such as when only one or two staff persons are present. Additionally, maintaining an adequate supply of materials typically requires that a system be developed for continuously inventorying, repairing and replacing training and leisure materials. Such a system frequently involves assigning one staff member in the living area the specific responsibility of ensuring that materials are stored in appropriate places and that broken items are repaired or replaced expeditiously.

REFERENCES

Baer, D.M., Wolf, M.M., & Risley, T.R. (1968). Some current dimensions of applied behavior analysis. *Journal of Applied Behavior Analysis, 1,* 91–97.

Bates, P., Renzaglia, A., & Wehman, P. (1981). Characteristics of an appropriate education for severely and profoundly handicapped students. *Education and Training of the Mentally Retarded, 16,* 142–149.

Brown, K.M., Willis, B.S., & Reid, D.H. (1981). Differential effects of supervisor verbal feedback and feedback plus approval on institutional staff performance. *Journal of Organizational Behavior Management, 3*(1), 57–68.

Burch, M.R., Reiss, M.L., & Bailey, J.S. (1987). A competency-based "hands-on" training package for direct care staff. *Journal of the Association for Persons with Severe Handicaps, 12,* 67–71.

Burg, M.M., Reid, D.H., & Lattimore, J. (1979). Use of a self-recording and supervision program to change institutional staff behavior. *Journal of Applied Behavior Analysis, 12,* 363–375.

Burgio, L.D., Whitman, T.L., & Reid, D.H. (1983). A participative management approach for improving direct-care staff performance in an institutional setting. *Journal of Applied Behavior Analysis, 16,* 37–53.

Christian, W.P., Hannah, G.T., & Glahn, T.J. (Eds.). (1984). *Programming effective human services: Strategies for institutional change and client transition.* New York: Plenum.

Coles, E., & Blunden, R. (1981). Maintaining new procedures using feedback to staff, a hierarchical reporting system, and a multidisciplinary management group. *Journal of Organizational Behavior Management, 3*(2), 19–33.

Dyer, K., Schwartz, I.S., & Luce, S.C. (1984). A supervision program for increasing functional activities for severely handicapped students in a residential setting. *Journal of Applied Behavior Analysis, 17,* 249–259.

Favell, J.E., Favell, J.E., Riddle, J.I., & Risley, T.R. (1984). Promoting change in mental retardation facilities: Getting services from the paper to the people. In W.P. Christian, G.T. Hannah, & T.J. Glahn (Eds.), *Programming effective human services: Strategies for institutional change and client transition* (pp. 15–37). New York: Plenum.

Faw, G.D., Reid, D.H., Schepis, M.M., Fitzgerald, J.R., & Welty, P.A. (1981). Involving institutional staff in the development and maintenance of sign language skills with profoundly retarded persons. *Journal of Applied Behavior Analysis, 14,* 411–423.

Hart, B.M., & Risley, T.R. (1982). *How to use incidental teaching for elaborating language.* Lawrence, KS: H & H Enterprises, Inc.

Kunz, G.G.R., Lutzker, J.R., Cuvo, A.J., Eddleman, J., Lutzker, S.Z., Megson, D., & Gulley, B. (1982). Evaluating strategies to improve careprovider performance on health and developmental tasks in an infant care facility. *Journal of Applied Behavior Analysis, 15,* 521–531.

Lattimore, J., Stephens, T.E., Favell, J.E., & Risley, T.R. (1984). Increasing direct care staff compliance to individualized physical therapy body positioning prescriptions: Prescriptive checklists. *Mental Retardation, 22,* 79–84.

LeLaurin, K., & Risley, T.R. (1972). The organization of day care environments: "Zone" versus "Man-to-Man" staff assignments. *Journal of Applied Behavior Analysis, 5,* 225–232.

Mansell, J., Felce, D., de Kock, U., & Jenkins, J. (1982). Increasing purposeful activity of severely and profoundly mentally-handicapped adults. *Behaviour Research and Therapy, 20,* 593–604.

Martin, R. (1984). The right to effective human service programming. In W.P. Christian, G.T. Hannah, & T.J. Glahn (Eds.), *Programming effective human services: Strategies for institutional change and client transition* (pp. 1–10). New York: Plenum.

Montegar, C.A., Reid, D.H., Madsen, C.H., & Ewell, M.D. (1977). Increasing institutional staff to resident interactions through in-service training and supervisor approval. *Behavior Therapy, 8,* 533–540.

Parsons, M.B., Cash, V.B., & Reid, D.H. (in press). Improving residential treatment services: Implementation and norm-referenced evaluation of a comprehensive management system. *Journal of Applied Behavior Analysis.*

Parsons, M.B., Schepis, M.M., Reid, D.H., McCarn, J.E., & Green, C.W. (1987). Expanding the impact of behavioral staff management: A large-scale, long-term application in schools serving severely handicapped students. *Journal of Applied Behavior Analysis, 20,* 139–150.

Quilitch, H.R., & Gray, J.D. (1974). Purposeful activity for the PMR: A demonstration project. *Mental Retardation, 12,* 28–29.

Reid, D.H., & Favell, J.E. (1984). Group instruction with persons who have severe disabilities: A critical review. *Journal of the Association for Persons with Severe Handicaps, 9,* 167–177.

Reid, D.H., Green, C.W., McCarn, J.E., Parsons, M.B., & Schepis, M.M. (1986). *Purposeful training with severely handicapped persons: A trainer's guidebook.* Morganton, NC: Western Carolina Center.

Reid, D.H., & Whitman, T.L. (1983). Behavioral staff management in institutions: A critical review of effectiveness and acceptability. *Analysis and Intervention in Developmental Disabilities, 3,* 131–149.

Repp, A.C., & Barton, L.E. (1980). Naturalistic observations of institutionalized retarded persons: A comparison of licensure decisions and behavioral observations. *Journal of Applied Behavior Analysis, 13,* 333–341.

Schepis, M.M., Reid, D.H., Fitzgerald, J.R., Faw, G.D., van den Pol, R.A., & Welty, P.A. (1982). A program for increasing manual signing by autistic and profoundly retarded youth within the daily environment. *Journal of Applied Behavior Analysis, 15,* 363–379.

Seys, D.M., & Duker, P.C. (1978). Improving residential care for the retarded by differential reinforcement of high rates of ward-staff behaviour. *Behavioural Analysis and Modification, 2,* 203–210.

Seys, D.M., & Duker, P.C. (1986). Effects of a supervisory treatment package on staff-mentally retarded resident interactions. *American Journal of Mental Deficiency, 90,* 388–394.

Smith, W. (1983). *Active treatment for the developmentally disabled.* Health Care Financing Administration: Baltimore, MD.

Spangler, P.F., & Marshall, A.M. (1983). The unit play manager as a facilitator of purposeful activities among institutionalized profoundly and severely retarded boys. *Journal of Applied Behavior Analysis, 16,* 345–349.

Spreat, S., Piper, T., Deaton, S., Savoy-Paff, D., Brantner, J., Lipinski, D., Dorsey, M., & Baker-Potts, J.C. (1985). The impact of supervisory feedback on staff and client behavior. *Education and Training of the Mentally Retarded, 20,* 196–203.

van den Pol, R.A., Reid, D.H., & Fuqua, R.W. (1983). Peer training of safety-related skills to institutional staff: Benefits for trainers and trainees. *Journal of Applied Behavior Analysis, 16,* 139–156.

Warren, S.A., & Mondy, L.W. (1971). To what behaviors do attending adults respond? *American Journal of Mental Deficiency, 75,* 449–455.

Whitman, T.L., Scibak, J.W., & Reid, D.H. (1983). *Behavior modification with the severely and profoundly retarded: Research and application.* New York: Academic Press.

Zaharia, E.S., & Baumeister, A.A. (1978). Technician turnover and absenteeism in public residential facilities. *American Journal of Mental Deficiency, 82,* 580–593.

Zlomke, L.C., & Benjamin, V.A., Jr. (1983). Staff in-service: Measuring effectiveness through client behavior change. *Education and Training of the Mentally Retarded, 18,* 125–130.

Chapter 6

IMPROVING PARAPROFESSIONAL STAFF PROVISION OF FORMAL TRAINING AND TREATMENT PROGRAMS

As indicated in the preceding chapter, the proficient performance of paraprofessional staff is a vital element in the provision of therapeutic services to dependent clients in congregate care settings. Chapter 5 also emphasized that paraprofessional staff are usually the primary personnel (and often the only personnel) who provide habilitatively related services when residential clients are not involved in formal treatment programming. However, paraprofessional staff can also play a significant role, albeit typically a smaller role, in the provision of *formal, professionally developed programs* with clients. For example, teacher aides are often expected to carry out individualized educational programs developed by teachers or other professional staff in educational settings (e.g. Neef, Shafer, Egel, Cataldo, & Parrish, 1983). Similarly, direct care staff in residential facilities for developmentally disabled persons frequently are assigned formal training or treatment responsibilities by psychologists (e.g. Kissel, Whitman, & Reid, 1983), speech/language pathologists (Ivancic, Reid, Iwata, Faw, & Page, 1981), and/or occupational therapists (Korabek, Reid, & Ivancic, 1981).

An illustration of the variety of types of formal therapy programs that paraprofessional staff have been involved in across different human service settings is presented in Table 6-1. Of course, paraprofessional staff such as nursing home attendants, preschool aides, institutional direct care personnel, etc. generally cannot be expected to have a skill level for conducting the types of therapy regimes exemplified in Table 6-1 that is comparable to the skill level of professional staff; the latter individuals have much more training and educational preparation in their respective professions. Nevertheless, as this chapter will indicate, paraprofessional staff can be effectively involved in implementing formal training and treatment programs with clients under certain conditions.

125

Table 6-1
SAMPLES OF TRAINING AND TREATMENT PROGRAMS
CONDUCTED BY PARAPROFESSIONAL STAFF

General Program Area	*Specific Programs*	*References*
Self-help	feeding, handwashing, dressing, bathing, toileting	Panyan, Boozer, & Morris, 1970
	feeding, dressing, shoe tying, shaving	Patterson, Griffin, & Panyan, 1976
	dressing, feeding, toileting	Pommer & Streedbeck, 1974
	taking off pants — backward chaining	Watson & Uzzell, 1980
	toothbrushing, haircombing, handwashing	Kissel, Whitman, & Reid, 1983
	dining, bathing, dressing	Ford, 1984
	handwashing, haircombing	Realon, Wheeler, Spring & Springer, 1986
Adaptive/Non Self-help	language acquisition, individual/ cooperative play, arts & crafts	Bricker, Morgan, & Grabowski, 1972
	head and neck movement, purposeful reaching, object manipulation	Fabry & Reid, 1978
	ambulation	Greene, Willis, Levy, & Bailey, 1978
	language training	Ivancic, Reid, Iwata, Faw, & Page, 1981
	communication, gross motor	Page, Iwata, & Reid, 1982
Treatment	insight-oriented activities, counseling, assist with client personal needs	Kreitner, Reif, & Morris, 1977
	increase client verbal behavior, encourage clients to read	Stoffelmayr, Lindsay, & Taylor, 1979

In essence, the basic rationale for attempting to involve paraprofessional staff in professional therapy endeavors is straightforward: there simply are not enough professionals to meet all the therapeutic needs of clients served by human service agencies. However, if paraprofessional personnel are to proficiently conduct therapy programs designed by highly trained professionals, then very effective staff training and management procedures are necessary. The reasons for the need for staff training and management systems in this respect are essentially the same as those described in Chapter 5 regarding paraprofessional staff involvement in congregate care services. Specifically, paraprofessional staff usually have no preemployment preparation in conducting technical client treatment or training procedures. In addition, such staff often do not view their roles in human service agencies as involving client treatment or training.

Purpose and Format of Chapter

The purpose of this chapter is to discuss the organizational behavior management research on methods of effectively involving paraprofessional staff in formal training and treatment programs with clients in human service settings. Using the same general format presented in the preceding chapter, a summary of the existing research in this area will be provided followed by a methodological critique of the research. Next, based on information gleaned from the summary and critique, a recommended supervisory strategy will be described for evoking and maintaining proficient paraprofessional staff performance in formal program implementation.

Before summarizing the relevant behavioral research that has been conducted, clarification is in order regarding the differences between the staff performance area addressed here relative to what was discussed in Chapter 5. Essentially, there are two main differences. First, the goal of the two staff performance areas are different, although complimentary. The focus of Chapter 5 was on managing staff performance for engaging dependent clients in activities that either compliment client involvement in formal therapy programs conducted by professional clinicians and/or that prevent client engagement in activities that are counterproductive to the purposes of the therapy programs. In contrast, the emphasis of this chapter is on actually involving staff in the direct provision of the formal therapy programs. The second difference between the staff performance area addressed in Chapter 5 relative to what will be discussed here is that the conditions within which staff are expected to conduct the two types of work duties are noticeably different. In particular, Chapter 5 focused on staff provision of constructive activities to *groups* of clients during traditionally *nonstructured* leisure or nonprogrammatic periods during the day or evening. The staff work responsibilities addressed in this chapter on the other hand involve the provision of highly *structured* program regimes to clients on an *individual* basis (i.e. one staff person working with one client at a time) during formally designated training or treatment sessions. These differing features of the two types of staff job responsibilities result in different work behaviors required of staff and relatedly (as will become more evident throughout this chapter) some different supervisory approaches for ensuring competent staff fulfillment of the responsibilities.

Effectively involving paraprofessional staff in the provision of professionally developed therapy regimes essentially consists of two interrelated components. First, staff must be *trained* in the skills necessary to conduct the therapies. Second, staffs' application of the therapy skills must be *managed* in the routine work environment. Both components almost always have to be incorporated into supervisory programs if staff are going to be consistently proficient in carrying out designated therapy protocols. However, in the majority of cases the most serious obstacles that impede paraprofessional staff performance in this work area occur with the latter component. Consequently, the focus of this chapter is on those investigations that specifically addressed the *day-to-day implementation* of paraprofessional staffs' therapy services, and not on studies that focused solely on staff *acquisition of program-related skills* during a staff training endeavor.

The emphasis on management of staffs' therapy-related work behavior should not be interpreted to mean that the staff training component is of lesser importance. Rather, the emphasis is due to the more serious supervisory problems that have arisen with the management component as just noted. Also, even though most of the studies to be described in this chapter included training components, the staff training procedures employed have already been described in detail in Chapter 3 and to repeat such a description here would be needlessly redundant.

Generally, the organizational behavior management research on paraprofessional staff involvement in professional therapy services has focused on two general areas of staff performance. The first area (and the one that has involved the vast majority of the investigations on staff behavior) involves conducting specific *training programs to teach adaptive skills* to handicapped clients. The second area involves implementing *clinically prescribed treatment programs* of a more varied and general nature with clients in psychiatric settings. Elaboration on the distinction between client *training* and *treatment* programs will be provided in subsequent subsections of this chapter that review the existing research in these respective areas.

Summary of the Research

Managing Paraprofessional Staff Performance in Training Adaptive Skills to Clients

A rather considerable amount of behavioral management research has centered on paraprofessional staff performance in carrying out teaching programs to develop adaptive skills among seriously handicapped individuals such as severely and profoundly mentally retarded persons and chronic psychiatric patients. The emphasis of much of the research has been on teaching *self-help* types of adaptive skills, with the remainder of the investigations addressing more *multi-varied* adaptive behaviors.

Managing staff performance in teaching self-help skills to clients. The attainment of basic self-help skills (e.g. bathing, feeding, dressing) is typically considered a priority training need for those clients in human service organizations who cannot perform self-help skills independently. When clients cannot perform self-care functions for themselves, paraprofessional personnel such as institutional direct care staff are the primary service providers who conduct the basic care for the clients. Because of the involvement in providing personal care for dependent clients, paraprofessional staff are in a rather strategic situation to help the clients develop more independent self-care skills (i.e. by training clients in self-care skills during daily personal care routines). Consequently, these staff are often assigned to conduct self-help training programs developed by professional clinicians as part of their personal care duties with clients. The responsibility of ensuring that staff are adequately trained to carry out the self-help skill teaching programs, as well as ensuring that staff do indeed conduct the programs proficiently once they possess the training competencies, essentially falls on the supervisors of the paraprofessional staff. Hence, a number of organizational behavior management investigations have evaluated supervisory procedures for training and managing proficient staff performance in regard to teaching clients self-help skills.

In an early investigation in this area, Panyan, Boozer, and Morris (1970) focused on the work performance of paraprofessional, direct care staff in a state institution for mentally retarded children. Panyan et al.

attempted to increase staffs' use of behavioral training methods during a variety of self-help routines with the children, including feeding, handwashing, dressing, bathing, and toileting. Each staff member initially attended a four-week, classroom-based inservice in behavior modification. When the staff returned to their regular work stations (client living units) at the conclusion of the formal classroom training, a written feedback procedure (Chapter 4) was initiated in an attempt to reinforce staff for implementing the behavior modification techniques acquired during the inservice. Specifically, the percentage of training sessions conducted by staff in each self-help skill area was recorded on a feedback sheet and presented weekly to individual staff assigned to each of four living units. The percentage of sessions conducted by all staff in respective living units was also publicly posted in order that staff performance across different living units could be compared. Implementation of the privately written and publicly posted feedback was accompanied by noticeable increases in the daily use of the behavioral training methods by the staff in each living unit.

A somewhat unusual set of performance consequences was evaluated in an attempt to increase the amount of daily self-help training sessions conducted by paraprofessional staff in a state retardation facility (Patterson, Griffin, & Panyan, 1976). Initially, the staff received a training booklet containing a memo from the facility director that instructed the staff to conduct a 15-minute self-help training session each day, along with copies of behavioral programs for teaching the self-help skills and data sheets and graph paper for recording client responses to the training endeavors. Three consequence management procedures were then introduced in sequential order: peer competition, bingo money, and peer competition plus money. Peer competition involved public posting of the total number of training sessions conducted by all staff as well as the number of training programs conducted per individual staff member. The latter public posting strategy allowed for comparisons across staff persons (and potential competition) similar to the feedback procedure used by Panyan et al. The staff person who conducted the most training sessions at the end of a designated time period was recognized for his/her training efforts with the temporary title of "Behavioral Engineer." During the bingo money condition, bingo cards were provided once a staff person completed a training session, and then a bingo number was subsequently drawn from a random pool for each training session completed. If the number matched a number on a staff member's bingo card, the latter number was crossed out. When a designated amount of bingo numbers was crossed out, the respective staff person could win a five dollar cash prize. The final management intervention, peer competition plus money, involved the same procedures used in the initial peer competition phase with the addition of a five dollar cash prize awarded to the person chosen as "Behavioral Engineer." Results of the investigation indicated that payment of paraprofessional personnel with relatively small amounts of money contingent on conducting client self-help training was effective in increasing the amount of daily training sessions that were conducted, as was public posting (peer competition) without contingent money, although the increases were somewhat inconsistent.

Monetary consequences were also used as a component in a management program to improve staff performance in a residential child treatment facility (Pommer & Streedbeck, 1974). Antecedent procedures were likewise included via charts that were posted on a bulletin board to delineate each staff member's job (Chapter 4), including responsibilities in self-help training. A second chart was posted that listed idiosyncratic instructional methods that were specific for each of the children. Upon completion of the duties the staff were instructed to fill out a job slip (i.e. self-recording—Chapter 4). The job slips could be exchanged at the end of each month for one dollar per slip. The initial public posting of duties was accompanied by an increase in the amount of staff training conducted with the children, although the increase quickly diminished. When the job slips were introduced in conjunction with the public posting, increased levels of training performance again resulted, with no apparent subsequent reductions in the amount of training conducted.

The studies just described focused primarily on managing staff performance with clients in regard to using job skills (i.e. conducting self-help training) that the staff had previously been trained to use. Watson and Uzzell (1980) were also concerned with the day-to-day management of job performance but concentrated more on thoroughly *training* staff in the appropriate skills relative to *managing* the performance per se. The specific focus of the Watson and Uzzell program was training staff to use a backward chaining technique for teaching self-help skills to mentally retarded clients. Staff from three residential facilities participated in a classroom-based training component which involved a programmed text and slide-tape examples of backward chaining. Staff also participated in a practicum training component that primarily involved modeling and performance practice in the form of role playing (Chapter 3). At the conclusion of the staff training program, staff demonstrated improved skills in teaching self-help behaviors to severely and profoundly mentally retarded persons. Maintenance of the use of the backward chaining strategy to teach self-help skills during the staffs' routine work situation was also noted, reportedly due to the implementation of supervisor monitoring and feedback procedures in the staffs' daily work site. However, no experimental data were presented with which to evaluate the latter report.

In studies that heavily emphasize training staff in the use of a very specific type of client-training technique such as the investigation just noted by Watson and Uzzell, a highly desirable outcome is that not only will staff acquire the client-training skill in the situation addressed by the staff training but also that staff will use, or *generalize,* the skill across other situations (see discussion in Chapter 3 on skill generalization and Whitman, Scibak, & Reid, 1983, chap. 3, for elaboration). To illustrate, if staff are taught a respective behavior modification technique for training a self-care behavior to clients such as dressing, it would be advantageous if staff would generalize the use of the same technique to the training of feeding, handwashing, shaving, shoe-tying, etc. Because of the variety of client teaching responsibilities that paraprofessional staff are often expected to fulfill, it is somewhat unrealistic to assume that supervisors will be able to ensure that staff are trained specifically to address each of the various client training needs. Hence, staff training programs should be designed where possible to help staff learn how to generalize the new skills that they acquire across the different situations in which the skills can be applied.

Kissel et al. (1983) examined the effects of a management program that was specifically designed to teach institutional direct care staff how to generalize use of certain behavior modification procedures across different self-care training regimes with mentally retarded persons. The behavioral procedures trained to staff to in turn use to teach their clients included verbal instruction, physical guidance and contingent reinforcement. Initially, staff were taught to apply the skills in a toothbrushing program with severely and profoundly mentally retarded residents. Staff were simultaneously taught to record, graph, and evaluate resident behavior as well as *their own behavior* in regard to their use of the instructions, guidance, and reinforcement during the toothbrushing teaching sessions. Staffs' recording and evaluating of their own teaching behavior were included to essentially improve staffs' conscious awareness of their training processes such that they would be more likely to intentionally apply those same processes in other training situations. Results indicated that staff successfully acquired and applied the behavior modification skills in the toothbrushing situation, as well as in situations in which staff had not been specifically trained such as haircombing and handwashing training sessions with clients—suggesting that staff did indeed generalize their newly acquired skills in behavior modification.

In essentially all of the investigations described to this point on increasing paraprofessional staff involvement in the provision of professionally designed client training programs, some type of performance feedback procedure was included. Ford (1984) extended the evaluation of feedback procedures by comparing different types of feedback, in this case on staff performance in conducting self-help training programs with severely and profoundly retarded adults. Initially, the staff were videotaped while they conducted a dining, dressing, and bathing self-help training program. Based on staff proficiency during the videotaped sessions, individual verbal feedback, self-recorded feedback (obtained by each staff member viewing and evaluating a videotaped recording of his/her performance) and combined verbal and self-recorded feedback were sequentially implemented with each staff person. Results indicated that the self-recorded feedback using the videotapes in conjunction with supervisor verbal feedback resulted in the greatest and most rapid improvement in work performance.

Realon, Lewallen, and Wheeler (1983) also evaluated the effects of different types of feedback. In the Realon et al. study, verbal feedback in the form of nonevaluative descriptive information (Chapter 4) regarding the proficiency of institutional direct care staffs' training of mentally retarded clients was compared to the same type of verbal feedback paired with specific praise statements. Although both feedback interventions were accompanied by improved quality of training, the feedback that included explicit praise appeared more effective.

In another investigation comparing different management procedures, Realon, Wheeler, Spring, and Springer (1986) evaluated the effects of a monetary group contingency versus individual verbal feedback. Realon et al. compared the two interventions in regard to the relative effects on the quality of self-help training delivered by direct care staff in a mental retardation facility. Staff first participated in an in-service program that included verbal instruction, performance practice and feedback. Next, the proficiency of staffs' application of behavioral training techniques was monitored during various types of client training sessions (e.g. handwashing, haircombing) when staff received individual verbal feedback based on their proficiency in training clients versus when the monetary group contingency was in effect. The latter procedure involved individual feedback and the opportunity for a group of staff to earn money to spend on client-related recreational activities if the performance of the group of staff as a whole met a specified criterion of training proficiency. Results indicated that the feedback alone was accompanied by relatively inconsistent improvements in staff performances in regard to appropriately conducting client training sessions, whereas the monetary group contingency was accompanied by more consistent improvements.

Managing Staff Performance in Teaching Multi-Varied Adaptive Client Skills (Other Than Self-Help Routines). As noted earlier, in addition to self-help training, paraprofessional staff are often required to conduct training sessions with clients that address other areas of adaptive skill development. In this regard, there is a relative variety of instructional skills required of paraprofessional staff that are necessary if staff are going to successfully meet the varied adaptive skill needs of many clients served by human service agencies. However, as will be indicated in this chapter section, the basic supervisory approaches for ensuring proficient staff performance across the different types of client training routines are basically the same as those discussed with client self-help needs: staff typically must be trained in the appropriate instructional skills and then their client-training performance must be consistently managed in the routine work environment.

In an early investigation in this area, staff training performances across a rather wide variety of client adaptive skill needs were addressed (Bricker, Morgan, & Grabowski, 1972). Specifically, staff teaching behaviors were targeted in regard to mentally retarded clients' language acquisition, cooperative individual play, and appropriate participation in arts and crafts activities. Paraprofessional direct care staff in an institutional setting were provided with commercial trading stamps (as reinforcers) for conducting training sessions with clients in each of the skill areas just noted. Staff persons also received on-the-job training to improve their client-teaching skills. The latter management component involved four daily half-hour sessions in which staff were asked to conduct a training session with a client, followed by discussion and feedback regarding the adequacy of the behavioral training techniques demonstrated by the staff. The trading stamp consequences and on-the-job training were accompanied by increases in the amount of time staff spent training clients as well as in the proficiency of their training.

The behavioral management research regarding paraprofessional staff involvement in the provision of professional training services to handicapped clients discussed to this point has involved institutional, direct care personnel. Fabry and Reid (1978) focused on the client-training potential of another group of paraprofessionals: foster grandparents working with institutionalized, severely handicapped persons. The foster grandparents were employed by a federally funded project that was designed to increase employment opportunities for elderly individuals as well as to increase services for mentally retarded youth. Fabry and Reid attempted to train and manage the grandparents' use of behavior modification procedures to enhance mentally and physically handicapped clients' head/neck movement skills, purposeful reaching skills, and object manipulation skills. Management procedures employed with the foster grandparents included verbal instructions, prompts, modeling and verbal feedback—all of which were provided during the foster grandparents daily work routine (i.e. in contrast to a classroom setting). The multifaceted management intervention appeared effective in improving the foster grandparents training performances across each of the different client skill areas.

Greene, Willis, Levy, and Bailey (1978) also focused on staff skills for training motorically impaired, severely handicapped residents of a state institution, although instead of targeting the performance of foster grandparents, Greene et al. focused on the training skills of direct care staff. Greene et al. evaluated the effects of several management interventions on the quality of training that was designed to improve ambulation and other motor skills of the clients. The direct care staff initially participated in an inservice that centered on written instructions and performance practice. The inservice was not very effective in regard to increasing the (appropriate) occurrence of staffs' training activities with clients during their routine workday. Verbal feedback was then provided by a staff supervisor contingent on staff completing assigned training sessions, with relatively small and/or inconsistent increases in staff training performances resulting. In contrast, the use of verbal feedback paired with publicly posted feedback regarding staffs' training performance *and* client responsiveness to the training was accompanied by noticeable and stable increases in staffs' program implementation.

As noted earlier, paraprofessional personnel such as institutional direct care staff are in somewhat of a strategic situation for enhancing the self-help skill development of clients. To reiterate, because direct care staff are routinely expected to carry out self-care procedures for dependent clients who cannot perform their own personal care, the staff have the opportunity to enhance client skill acquisition by conducting self-help skill training simultaneously while providing the personal care. There are also certain clients though whose mental and/or physical handicaps are so debilitating that their development of independent self-care skills is unrealistic. Staff would not be expected to attempt to train self-help skills to such clients while the staff provide for the clients' personal care. However, staff provision of personal care to these types of very seriously mentally and physically handicapped clients may still represent an advantageous situation for teaching other types of adaptive skills. Personal care routines typically involve one staff person working directly with one client and generally occur quite frequently (e.g. at least daily). Such features—one-to-one staff ratio with clients and frequent occurrence—are parameters that often enhance the implementation of effective training regimes.

Ivancic et al. (1981) attempted to capitalize on the features of self-care duties just noted by incorporating language training interactions into institutional self-care routines conducted by direct care staff with young children who had profound mental and physical handicaps. Staff were initially taught to vocalize more while they bathed respective children in an attempt to model appropriate vocal skills for the children. Next, staff were taught to imitate and/or praise child vocalization attempts in an effort to increase the children's vocalizations. Finally, staff were taught to verbally prompt vocalizations. The multifaceted procedures used to teach these language development skills to the staff and subsequently to ensure staff use of the skills while they bathed clients on a routine basis included public posting of instructions and feedback, verbal instruction, modeling and supervisor verbal feedback. Results indicated that staff acquired and used the language training skills during bath routines and that these skills also generalized to another self-care task: dressing.

Somewhat of an indirect method of improving paraprofessional staff provision of client training programs was reported by Page, Iwata, and Reid (1982). Page et al. focused on improving the client-training performance of 45 institutional direct care staff by altering the performance of the staff *supervisors*—that is, in contrast to focusing the management intervention directly on the performance of the staff. The supervisors were first trained by the experimenters to discriminate correct teaching behavior (e.g. appropriate use of prompts and reinforcers) of the direct care staff while the staff conducted communication and gross motor training programs with severely handicapped clients. Supervisors were then taught to instruct, prompt, and praise the occurrence of those staff behaviors while the staff conducted their daily training sessions with clients. Supervisors were trained by experimenter verbal and written instructions, goal-setting regarding their supervisory interactions with staff (Chapter 4) and performance feedback. The latter procedures appeared effective in increasing the targeted supervisory interactions, with subsequent increases in the proficient teaching behavior of the staff.

Managing Paraprofessional Staff Performance in Conducting Treatment Sessions

As noted previously, several investigations have examined the effects of behavioral staff management procedures on paraprofessional staff performance during treatment sessions in settings serving persons with mental illness (i.e. psychiatric hospitals). We have distinguished this type of staff *treatment* work behavior from *training* behavior for two primary reasons. First, the goal of client training regimes as discussed in the preceding section has been rather clearly delineated in terms of helping handicapped persons acquire some type of well-defined adaptive behavior (self-feeding, dressing, etc.). Relatedly, the staff behaviors that were targeted for change generally were carefully articulated. In contrast, the goals of client treatment services and the treatment-related skills targeted with staff in the studies in this section generally are much less well defined. For example, the goals of treatment are generally described as pertaining to the overall well-being of clients, and staff responsibilities are defined simply as conducting treatment sessions. Second, whereas in the preceding section essentially every investigation included a component to teach staff how to train clients, the studies in this section did not include an emphasis on training skills to staff; apparently, the treatment-related skills were assumed to be in the staffs' existing work repertoire.

Each of the studies in the staff treatment area used feedback procedures in an attempt to affect changes in staff performance. Kreitner, Reif, and Morris (1977) used publicly posted feedback via an interoffice memo that listed individual staff names and respective frequencies of conducting treatment sessions to increase the amount of group and/or individual treatment sessions conducted with mental health clients. The treatment sessions were described as involving insight-oriented activities, counseling, and generally assisting with client personal needs. Stoffelmayr, Lindsay, and Taylor (1979) evaluated contingent verbal feedback (as well as verbal prompts) as a means of increasing the frequency with which staff who were working on an institutional ward for schizophrenic patients conducted group treatment sessions. The treatment sessions emphasized increasing client verbal behavior and encouraging clients to read more. The particular focus of Stoffelmayr et al. was staffs' treatment provision on days when supervisory personnel were not present in the work unit, with such treatment services increasing when the supervisor prompts and feedback were provided.

A third study in this area used a more comprehensive, multifaceted management intervention than the investigations just described to increase staffs' frequency of conducting treatment sessions (Prue, Krapfl, Noah, Cannon, & Maley, 1980). The management intervention involved written feedback in the form of summaries of weekly treatment activity, verbal feedback via weekly meetings to discuss the summaries, and public posting of the frequency and general outcome of treatment activity. Increases in general treatment activity accompanied the management procedure, although the staff work behaviors per se that were involved in providing the treatment were not specified.

Critique of the Research

The purpose of this section, as in the preceding chapter, is to critically review the behavioral staff training and management research that was just summarized. The research will be discussed in terms of: (a) the social significance of the staff program-related behaviors targeted for change, (b) the validity of the experimental designs used to evaluate the training and management strategies, (c) the effectiveness of the management procedures that were investigated, and (d) staff acceptance of the training and management strategies.

Social Significance of Staff Program-Implementation Behaviors

In order to carefully evaluate the social importance of respective areas of staff performance, those areas must be clearly described such that a determination can be made regarding exactly *what* staff began doing differently as a result of a particular management intervention. For the most part, the research on staff *training* skills with clients included well-defined descriptions of staff behavior—and especially in the more recent investigations (e.g. Kissel et al, 1983; Page et al., 1982). In contrast, the studies on staff *treatment* services were significantly less well defined such that evaluating the importance of the staff duties is considerably more difficult.

Even if staff work behaviors are not clearly articulated in respective investigations, the importance of those behaviors can be estimated to a degree if measures are included with which to evaluate potential changes in some aspect of client welfare. That is, if a management intervention with staff is accompanied by an apparent improvement in client functioning, then it can generally be concluded that the staff behaviors targeted by the management intervention were indeed important. In this regard though, the majority of studies reviewed did not report data on client performance. Among the relatively few studies that did report measures of client performance, results suggested that the staff behaviors that changed as a result of specific management interventions were socially important, in that corresponding improvements in client welfare were noted. Table 6-2 exemplifies the types of client variables that were beneficially affected as a result of organizational behavior management applications in this area of staff performance (see also Mansdorf & Burstein, 1986, for examples of clinical case studies of behavioral staff management interventions that affected desirable changes in client behavior).

Validity of the Experimental Designs

The confidence with which managers can assume that a management intervention will significantly improve staff performance is of course important in regard to the likelihood that managers will use the supervisory procedure. In turn, the credibility of a management procedure's reported effectiveness is heavily based on the internal validity associated with the experimental design used to evaluate the procedure in a respective investigation. Unfortunately, in this regard, essentially half of the studies discussed in this chapter employed experimental designs with questionable internal validity. For example, replication of the effects of a management intervention was not reported in several cases and pre/post experimental designs were used in other cases with no accompanying control group—factors that seriously detract from internal validity (Barlow & Hersen, 1984; Reid, 1987). Generally, however, more recent investigations

Table 6-2

SAMPLES OF CLIENT BEHAVIORS CHANGED AS
A FUNCTION OF MANAGEMENT INTERVENTIONS
ON PARAPROFESSIONAL STAFF PERFORMANCE

Client Behavior	References
Measurement of range of motion, walking distance within 60 seconds	Greene, Willis, Levy, & Bailey, 1978
Percentage of self-initiated, verbally instructed, and physically guided toothbrushing, haircombing, handwashing behavior	Kissel, Whitman, & Reid, 1983
Percent of client vocalizations	Ivancic, Reid, Iwata, Faw, & Page, 1981
Increases in the number of head and neck skills, purposeful reaching skills, object manipulation skills performed	Fabry & Reid, 1978
Hours of client participation, number of programs that meet criteria	Prue, Krapfl, Noah, Cannon, & Maley, 1980
Percent correct responses in communication and gross motor skills	Page, Iwata, & Reid, 1982
Number of self-help skills taught to clients over 18-month, 2-year periods	Watson & Uzzell, 1980

in this area of staff performance have tended to use more adequate experimental designs (e.g. Ivancic et al., 1981; Kissel et al., 1983; Page et al., 1982).

In regard to external validity, management applications with paraprofessional staff provision of programmatic services have been effective in two major settings in which this type of performance is routinely expected of staff: residential facilities for the mentally retarded (e.g. Ivancic et al., 1981; Greene et al., 1978), and mentally ill (e.g. Kreitner et al., 1977). Such results lend credence to the general effectiveness of behaviorally oriented staff training and management procedures across different types of human service settings (see also Chapter 9 for reports of similar effects with the performance of paraprofessional teaching staff in classroom settings). However, there are also other settings in which the program-related performance of paraprofessional staff can be of considerable importance such as group homes for the mentally retarded and nursing homes for elderly individuals. To date, organizational behavior management research generally has not addressed paraprofessional program services in the latter settings.

Effectiveness of Management Interventions

Basically, all of the investigations described in the preceding section reported improvements in staff performance as a result of a given organizational behavior management application. However, less than one-fourth of the studies included follow-up or maintenance data to evaluate whether the improvements continued over extended time periods. Consequently, the issue of the long-term durability of effects of management interventions in this area of staff performance is relatively unresolved. Encouragement exists in this regard, though, with results of the few studies that did report relatively long-term data. Ivancic et al. (1981), for example, reported maintained improvements in staff program activities throughout a 19-week follow-up period.

Acceptability of Management Interventions

Generally, organizational behavior management researchers have not formally attended to the issue of whether supervisory procedures used to improve paraprofessional staff provision of professionally developed program services are acceptable to staff (or to staff supervisors). There have been two notable exceptions, however. Greene et al. (1978) used a staff questionnaire to assess the perceived likeability of their publicly posted feedback intervention. Results indicated that staff were generally accepting of the public posting procedure. Kissel et al. (1983) used a similar process to evaluate staff acceptance of their multifaceted program, with results also suggesting that behavioral staff management procedures can be well received among staff.

Recommended Strategy for Improving Paraprofessional Staff Provision of Professional Program Services

The basic components of a recommended strategy for improving paraprofessional staff provision of professional program services are essentially the same as the primary steps of the behavioral supervision model described in Chapter 2. However, as will be noted in this section, there are also some variations in methods of implementing the primary steps that are rather specific to this particular area of staff performance.

The first necessary component of an effective management strategy is to clearly *define the work behaviors* expected of staff in regard to implementing formal client training or treatment programs. Actually, though, even before staff performance responsibilities are delineated, *client behaviors* that are likely to be affected by staffs' therapeutic endeavors should be clearly specified (cf. discussion in "Recommendation" section of Chapter 5). Staff persons need to be well aware of what client behavior changes are expected as a result of the staffs' program efforts, because effective client training and treatment regimes entail that staff alter their performance (e.g. the specific training technique used) based on how clients respond to the staffs' efforts. A nice example of the specification of certain client behaviors that staff need to be aware of in order to effectively train clients is provided by Greene et al. (1978).

Once relevant client behaviors have been identified, then the specific staff duties that are intended to alter the client behaviors should be articulated. Where possible, it is advantageous to identify a core component of staff training or treatment skills that can be applied across a variety of client needs. As noted earlier, it is not very realistic to assume that all paraprofessional staff persons will be effectively trained to carry out a large number of different habilitative procedures across every client need. It is more realistic to train a somewhat generic set of staff skills that can be used without serious alterations across individual client programs. A prototypical set of staff skills in this respect that often can be applied across a number of client program areas is basic behavior modification skills such as how to instruct, prompt and reinforce adaptive client behavior (see Kissel et al., 1983, and Page et al., 1982, for exemplification as well as the *multi-varied teaching skill* section in Chapter 9 pertaining to classroom teacher performance). However, in addition to clearly identifying staff training or treatment skills that can be applied across a variety of client service needs, there are almost always at least some client cases for which staff will need to make idiosyncratic adaptations to their basic programmatic approach. Such adaptations also need to be well delineated in terms of specific behaviors expected of staff. A useful approach for assisting staff in making special changes for individual client needs is represented in the system reported by Pommer and Streedbeck (1974). Pommer and Streedbeck initially trained staff in general therapeutic skills and then publicly posted instructions for staff to refer to regarding specific alterations for clients who required more idiosyncratic adaptations.

The second primary supervisory step for improving paraprofessional staff provision of professional program services is to *instruct* staff in the necessary programmatic procedures. Instruction is recommended at this point in the supervisory process in contrast to the usual monitoring step (Chapter 2), because with this particular staff performance area, staff training is essentially always necessary. In other performance situations staff training is not so frequently needed for improving staff performance (e.g. see Chapter 8 on administrative responsibilities). Generally, the recommended instructional approach follows the generic training model described in the conclusion of Chapter 3. To briefly reiterate, staff should be informed via verbal and written instructions regarding what they are expected to do followed by a physical demonstration of the desired client training or treatment program. Staff should then practice implementing the program procedures with subsequent approving or corrective feedback provided to staff. The latter practice and feedback processes should be continued until staff satisfactorily demonstrate implementation of the client program. Additionally, if feasible, given existing time and resources, it can be quite helpful for staff to view a videotaped sample of their training or treatment performance and to critically evaluate their (non)proficiency while a supervisor also evaluates the videotaped sample of performance (see Ford, 1984, and Kissel et al., 1983, for examples). Although this type of self- and supervisor-evaluation process is often time consuming, it nevertheless is frequently warranted because of the relatively intricate nature of many client training and treatment strategies with which staff must become familiar (cf. Watson & Uzzell, 1980).

The third supervisory step is to systematically *monitor* staffs' implementation of the client training or treatment program during their day-to-day work interactions with clients. Usually, it is not very likely that a supervisor will be able to monitor every training or treatment session conducted with each client. Hence, a supervisor needs to establish a schedule to *periodically* monitor staff performance during selected sessions. The monitoring should be as frequent as possible, once a given staff person initially begins implementing program sessions, and involve as comprehensive a sample of different sessions (i.e. across clients or various types of programs) as possible. As respective staff members demonstrate competency in conducting sessions during their ongoing work routine, then the monitoring can be decreased in frequency — although never discontinuing entirely.

In most cases, supervisory monitoring of paraprofessional staff program implementation will necessitate a duration type of observation process (Chapter 2). Duration monitoring in such situations can be facilitated considerably through the use of performance checklists (see Chapter 2). Checklists prompt supervisors regarding precisely what to look for with staff training or treatment performances and subsequently can reduce supervisory time and effort involved in the monitoring.

Another advantage of performance checklists relates to the fourth step in the recommended management strategy: *providing consequences.* Two general types of consequences are typically required to help ensure adequate paraprofessional staff provision of program services. The first type (and the type that is facilitated by the use of checklists) involves specific feedback provided on a systematic, albeit periodic, basis regarding staffs' proficiency in conducting the client training or treatment sessions. Such feedback involves a supervisor verbally informing respective staff persons how well or poorly the designated client program is being implemented (e.g. the adequacy with which appropriate client responses are reinforced by the responsible staff person). This type of criterion-referenced feedback (i.e. referenced to the target staff skills specified in the performance checklist) is necessary to prevent staff performance from gradually drifting away from the specific client training or treatment protocol.

The second type of supervisory administered consequence is needed not so much to ensure proficient staff program implementation per se but to ensure that staff *continue to conduct* the training or treatment sessions over time. Historically, noticeable problems have been reported with staff failing to conduct assigned program sessions with clients over extended time periods as part of their routine job responsibilities (e.g. Ford, 1984; Pommer & Streedbeck, 1974). Although there is no totally clear explanation for the staff performance problems in this regard, one likely reason is that considerable effort is often required of staff to repeatedly carry out program sessions with clients. Hence, rather powerful consequences are often needed to maintain staff work effort in this area. Because of the need for strong consequences, an advantageous supervisory approach is to use a multiple-consequence system (see Ivancic et al., 1981, for elaboration). For example, a variety of verbal (Korabek et al., 1981) and written (Panyan et al., 1970) feedback procedures should be used along with a variety of special recognition consequences (Appendix A). In addition, providing feedback on client progress across the training or treatment sessions conducted by staff can be helpful (Greene et al., 1978).

The final step in the recommended supervisory strategy, *evaluation,* essentially entails continuation of the third step, performance monitoring. That is, staff performance should continue to be periodically monitored to ensure that program implementation and proficiency maintain at a satisfactory level. Further, if staff performance problems develop, then alterations in the ongoing supervisory strategy should be made to regain a satisfactory level of staff performance (e.g. by changing the supervisory consequences that are administered—Pommer & Streedbeck, 1974).

REFERENCES

Barlow, D.H., & Hersen, M. (1984). *Single case experimental designs: Strategies for studying behavior change.* New York: Pergamon Press.

Bricker, W.A., Morgan, D.G., & Grabowski, J.G. (1972). Development and maintenance of a behavior modification repertoire of cottage attendants through TV feedback. *American Journal of Mental Deficiency, 77,* 128–136.

Fabry, P.L., & Reid, D.H. (1978). Teaching foster grandparents to train severely handicapped persons. *Journal of Applied Behavior Analysis, 11,* 111–123.

Ford, J.E. (1984). A comparison of three feedback procedures for improving teaching skills. *Journal of Organizational Behavior Management, 6*(1), 65–77.

Greene, B.F., Willis, B.S., Levy, R., & Bailey, J.S. (1978). Measuring client gains from staff-implemented programs. *Journal of Applied Behavior Analysis, 11,* 395–412.

Ivancic, M.T., Reid, D.H., Iwata, B.A., Faw, G.D., & Page, T.J. (1981). Evaluating a supervision program for developing and maintaining therapeutic staff-resident interactions during institutional care routines. *Journal of Applied Behavior Analysis, 14,* 95–107.

Kissel, R.C., Whitman, T.L., & Reid, D.H. (1983). An institutional staff training and self-management program for developing multiple self-care skills in severely/profoundly retarded individuals. *Journal of Applied Behavior Analysis, 16,* 395–415.

Korabek, C.A., Reid, D.H., & Ivancic, M.T. (1981). Improving needed food intake of profoundly handicapped children through effective supervision of institutional staff performance. *Applied Research in Mental Retardation, 2,* 69–88.

Kreitner, R., Reif, W.E., & Morris, M. (1977). Measuring the impact of feedback on the performance of mental health technicians. *Journal of Organizational Behavior Management, 1*(1), 105–109.

Mansdorf, I.J., & Burstein, Y. (1986). Case manager: A clinical tool for training residential treatment staff. *Behavioral Residential Treatment, 1,* 155–167.

Neef, N.A., Shafer, M.S., Egel, A.L., Cataldo, M.F., & Parrish, J.M. (1983). The class specific effects of compliance training with "do" and "don't" requests: Analogue analysis and classroom application. *Journal of Applied Behavior Analysis, 16,* 81–99.

Page, T.J., Iwata, B.A., & Reid, D.H. (1982). Pyramidal training: A large-scale application with institutional staff. *Journal of Applied Behavior Analysis, 15,* 335–351.

Panyan, M., Boozer, H., & Morris, N. (1970). Feedback to attendants as a reinforcer for applying operant techniques. *Journal of Applied Behavior Analysis, 3,* 1–4.

Patterson, E.T., Griffin, J.C., & Panyan, M.C. (1976). Incentive maintenance of self-help skill training programs for non-professional personnel. *Journal of Behavior Therapy and Experimental Psychiatry, 7,* 249–253.

Pommer, D.A., & Streedbeck, D. (1974). Motivating staff performance in an operant learning program for children. *Journal of Applied Behavior Analysis, 7,* 217–221.

Prue, D.M., Krapfl, J.E., Noah, J.C., Cannon, S., & Maley, R.F. (1980). Managing the treatment activities of state hospital staff. *Journal of Organizational Behavior Management, 2*(3), 165–181.

Realon, R.E., Lewallen, J.D., & Wheeler, A.J. (1983). Verbal feedback vs. verbal feedback plus praise: The effects on direct care staff's training behaviors. *Mental Retardation, 21,* 209–212.

Realon, R.E., Wheeler, A.J., Spring, B., & Springer, M. (1986). Evaluating the quality of training delivered by direct-care staff in a state mental retardation center. *Behavioral Residential Treatment, 1,* 199–212.

Reid, D.H. (1987). *Developing a research program in human service agencies: A practitioner's guidebook.* Springfield, IL: Charles C Thomas.

Stoffelmayr, B.E., Lindsay, W., & Taylor, V. (1979). Maintenance of staff behavior. *Behavior Research and Therapy, 17,* 271–273.

Watson, L.S., Jr., & Uzzell, R. (1980). A program for teaching behavior modification skills to institutional staff. *Applied Research in Mental Retardation, 1,* 41–53.

Whitman, T.L., Scibak, J.W., & Reid, D.H. (1983). *Behavior modification with the severely and profoundly retarded: Research and application.* New York: Academic Press.

Chapter 7

REDUCING STAFF ABSENTEEISM

The two preceding chapters in this section of the text have focused on methods of improving respective areas of staff performance in human service settings. An underlying assumption accompanying the discussions regarding the effective use of behavior management procedures to alter staff work performance is the routine presence of staff in the work place. If staff do not report to work, there is no work activity to improve. When considered in this vein, one of the most serious obstacles to the effective delivery of services to an agency's clients is *staff absenteeism*.

Simply stated, staff absenteeism refers to staff failing to report to work when they are in fact scheduled to work. Of course, some absences from work are expected in any human service agency—most if not all staff persons are likely to be sick from time to time and/or have conflicts that require their presence at places other than the work site. However, staff absenteeism can also occur at a frequency well beyond what would be normally expected. When the latter situation occurs, client services are often detrimentally affected and/or discontinued entirely.

Because of the serious impact of excessive staff absenteeism, as well as the relatively frequent occurrence of high rates of staff absenteeism in a number of human service settings (Zaharia & Baumeister, 1978), effective methods of reducing staff absences warrant the attention of organizational behavior management investigators. It is the purpose of this chapter to discuss the management of staff absenteeism in terms of the research that has been conducted to date and the resulting recommendations that can be made for preventing and/or resolving staff absentee problems.

Format of Chapter

The format of the chapter is similar to that of the preceding chapters, in that a summary of the existing organizational behavior management research will be provided followed by a critique of the research and a recommended management program for resolving absentee problems.

However, because absenteeism is a rather unique type of staff performance problem relative to the other work situations discussed in this text,
several somewhat idiosyncratic aspects of absenteeism will also be discussed.
In addition, because there has been a very considerable amount of
research on absenteeism in nonhuman service business and industry, a
summary of information gleaned from investigations in the latter area
will be provided in light of its potential relevance for the human services.

Special Concerns in Reducing Staff Absenteeism

Defining Absenteeism

When considering the reduction of absenteeism using a behavioral
approach along the lines of the supervisory model discussed in Chapter 2,
the first managerial step is to define what constitutes absenteeism. Earlier
it was noted that the simplest definition in this regard is the absence of
staff from work when those staff are expected to be at work. Although
such a definition suffices from a general perspective, usually more specification is needed in order to successfully implement a management
program to reduce absenteeism. Rather precise delineation is needed,
because there are several different types of absenteeism, and management programs generally have to be developed specifically for a respective type of absentee problem (Shoemaker & Reid, 1980). For example,
one type of absenteeism involves absences that are due to staff persons
(usually a small number of staff members within a given agency) who are
away from work for an extended period(s) of time (e.g. several weeks or
months). Extended absence periods are usually due to serious medical
problems of staff persons such as prolonged illness or physical conditions requiring surgery. To illustrate, back injuries are relatively common among direct care staff who are required to frequently lift and/or
move nonambulatory clients such as certain residents in nursing homes
and institutions for the mentally ill and mentally retarded (Alavosius &
Sulzer-Azaroff, 1986). Back injuries frequently result in extended staff
absences from work for physical recuperation purposes.

Another type of absenteeism that often occurs in many human service
agencies is represented by absences of certain staff that occur for short
durations (e.g. one or two days) yet occur frequently such as every two or
three weeks. For discussion purposes, the latter type of absenteeism can
be referred to as *high frequency absenteeism* in contrast to the *extended*

duration type of absenteeism noted previously. Additionally, absenteeism can be periodic or *predictable* in nature. Periodic absenteeism is exemplified by absences among respective staff persons that occur on a predictable schedule, such as immediately before or after weekends or other routine days off, and by absences that occur during certain seasons (Durand, 1985). Again, each of these different types of absenteeism problems usually requires a different management intervention for resolution.

Regardless of the type of absentee problem that may be plaguing an agency's service provision, there is one important characteristic associated with all absentee problems: the absences are *unplanned* by management or supervisory personnel. In this regard, unplanned or unscheduled absences generally are much more detrimental to an agency's service provision than *planned* absences. Planned absences are a routine part of most service operations and are represented by such events as scheduled vacation time among staff, holiday leave benefits, approved leave for education and training purposes (e.g. for a staff person to obtain an advanced degree), administrative or professional leave (e.g. for a staff member to attend a conference or convention), and approved leave without pay that is scheduled in advance for a staff person to attend to an important nonwork matter that requires his/her presence at some place other than work. Supervisors usually can make various arrangements to compensate for planned absences in order to continue, albeit at times on a partial basis, service delivery in the absence of certain staff. In contrast, it is usually very difficult, if not impossible, to compensate for unplanned absences of the types summarized earlier. It is the latter types of absences that are the focus of this chapter.

Determining (Un)Acceptable Levels of Absenteeism

In addition to defining absenteeism as part of a behavioral management intervention, determining an *acceptable level* of absenteeism is also a necessary step. Because some absenteeism is to be expected in every agency, supervisors must specify for staff what frequency of absences will and will not be tolerated as part of an antecedent (performance delineation) management step (Chapter 4). Unfortunately, it is rare for supervisors to determine and specify for staff what levels of absenteeism are acceptable. Such specification usually does not occur until unplanned absences of given individuals occur at a clearly intolerable level and serious performance problems exist.

Although clearly defining acceptable and unacceptable levels of absenteeism is an important step in the behavioral management of absenteeism, it is a rather difficult process. The difficulty in this regard is due to several factors. Foremost, as noted previously, some absences are expected (and even desired, in that it would be counterproductive to have ill staff persons coming to work instead of taking an unplanned sick leave or day off). Hence, it can be very difficult for a supervisor to determine when staff persons are indeed ill versus when they are misusing designated sick leave because they are not actually sick. Many unexpected events can also occur that affect the absence rates of sincere staff persons who do not routinely (mis)use sick leave, such as nonwork-related injuries, accidents to dependent family members of staff that require staff to miss work, etc. Consequently, any managerial attempt to delineate guidelines regarding acceptable and unacceptable absence rates will need to include the capability of making exceptions for staff when unusual, albeit legitimate, circumstances arise.

A second reason for the difficulty in articulating (un)acceptable levels of absenteeism relates to one of the basic features of human service agencies that has traditionally plagued supervisory approaches: the lack of a bottom-line index to clearly reflect how well or poorly agencies fulfill their human service mission (Chapter 1). When considered in regard to absenteeism, the lack of a bottom-line evaluative index often prohibits an agency's upper-level management from clearly observing the detrimental impact that unplanned staff absences have on client service provision. Without being readily aware of negative effects of absenteeism, executive-level managers are not likely to consistently implement managerial steps to resolve the problem relative to the situation in which managers are astutely aware of a particular problematic issue. On the other hand, however, most direct-line supervisors as well as staff persons themselves are usually very aware of the impact of frequent absences on the work performance within their respective work unit, even if they are not cognizant of the effects of absenteeism on the agency's service provision as a whole.

Another factor relating to the difficulty in determining (un)acceptable levels of staff absenteeism is the varied types of absentee problems described earlier. Guidelines regarding acceptable levels of one type of absenteeism often are not very useful for other types of absenteeism. Establishing a criterion, for example, regarding the frequency of unplanned absent days that is allowable will usually be of little value for reducing absences that are not extremely frequent but are predictably periodic and represent a misuse of sick leave. To illustrate, a person may be absent from work at an overall level well below the established criterion for an acceptable frequency of absences but, nevertheless, consistently misses work the day before and/or after holidays or certain weekends. Hence, guidelines regarding levels of absenteeism generally must be differentially addressed to each of the major types of absenteeism.

A final reason for the difficulty in establishing absentee guidelines is that in many human service agencies, policies exist that subtly promote relatively high rates of absenteeism. For example, civil service systems, under which many human service agencies typically fall, at least tacitly support a rate of absenteeism above that which is generally accepted in nonhuman service business and industry. To illustrate, the entire work year of staff usually includes approximately 260 days (52 weeks multiplied by 5 work days per week). The functional work year is reduced to around 236 days when the typical 12 holidays and 12 vacation days are subtracted. If an employee simply uses his/her normally earned number of sick days for the year (12 or one per month), absenteeism will average 5.08 percent (12 divided by 236). In this manner, staff persons can average above a 5 percent absentee rate and never require more sick days than a governmental civil service system essentially assures them. In business and industry, if absence levels rise above 3–4 percent a problem with absenteeism is considered to exist (cf. Zaharia & Baumeister, 1978). Hence, administrative policies in many human service agencies actually set the occasion for relatively high rates of absenteeism. In this regard, it is common in many agencies to hear the view that if staff persons merely use the number of sick days that agency policies allow on an annual basis, the staff are maintaining an acceptable level of absences—even though that level of absenteeism (i.e. just over 5%) would be unacceptable in the nonhuman service work sector. Consequently, supervisors can be in a quandary regarding at what level an absentee policy should specify (un)acceptable absentee frequencies.

Coordinating Absentee Programs With Traditional Management Practices

A final issue with staff absenteeism that warrants attention pertains to traditional managerial practices designed to correct absentee problems. Most if not all human service agencies have policies that direct supervisors regarding action to take if absentee problems develop. The prototypical managerial approach usually involves a disciplinary action process that becomes sequentially more negative or severe as a given staff person's absenteeism continues (Durand, 1985). For example, a supervisor might informally counsel with a staff person regarding the latter's absentee problems. If the problems do not improve, the supervisor might then issue a formal verbal reprimand followed in turn by a written reprimand, a final written warning and, finally, termination from employment.

Despite the existence of standard policies regarding what managerial action should be taken to resolve absentee problems such as the process just summarized, absenteeism continues to represent a serious issue in many human service settings. High frequencies of unplanned absences continue to occur in this regard due in large part to the failure of supervisors to consistently implement the managerial policies that exist. Also, it is not clear that the recommended action steps that comprise the policies are very effective even if they are conducted consistently, due primarily to the omission of key behavioral management steps from the policies (see later chapter section on recommended strategies for reducing absenteeism). Nevertheless, when considering absentee reduction programs, existing management policies must be taken into consideration. Such policies often originate from large umbrella organizations that govern respective agency practices such as, for example, state personnel offices that dictate certain personnel practices for institutional settings. In these types of situations, individual supervisors are rarely in a position to have the authority to change the managerial policies. Fortunately, however, there are a number of ways that good absentee-reduction programs can be developed that do not contradict traditionally existing managerial policies, and it is incumbent upon supervisors to determine those ways.

Summary of the Research

Similar to the format of the two preceding chapters that focused on specific staff performance problems, the purpose of this section is to summarize the existing organizational behavior management research pertaining to staff absenteeism. In this regard, relative to the research on other staff performance problems in human service agencies, there has been a small number of investigations that specifically addressed absentee problems. To illustrate, during the 18-year period since the first published evaluation of a behavioral staff management strategy for reducing excessive absenteeism (Gardner, 1970), only six studies on this topic have been published—at least based on our review of the literature. The relative lack of behavioral problem-solving research in this area seems somewhat surprising when considering how frequently absenteeism has been identified as a serious problem in human service agencies as noted previously. Nevertheless, as the summary of the research literature will reveal, the existing studies describe several successful staff management procedures for reducing staff absences that can provide useful information for managerial personnel.

Because there has been only a relatively small number of investigations on absenteeism, this research area as a whole does not present as much diversity from an experimental/methodological perspective as do other, more frequently researched areas of staff performance. Hence, for the sake of efficiency, the studies will be reviewed in light of specific methodological features that seem generally noteworthy to the absenteeism area in contrast to focusing on each investigation individually. The investigations will be summarized in regard to the settings and participants with which the research was conducted, the definitions or types of absenteeism targeted, and the management interventions employed to reduce staff absences.

Settings and Participants

The settings in which behavioral research on absenteeism has been conducted as well as the job classification of staff who participated in the studies are quite similar across the investigations in this area. Specifically, all of the investigations occurred in public residential facilities for mentally retarded persons and all involved direct care or paraprofessional personnel. Additionally, the majority of studies focused on staff working in one particular work unit of an agency—usually a residential living unit. The majority of the staff participants in the investigations were women, who typically represent the largest percentage of direct care staff in institutional settings.

Behavior Definitions

As previously discussed, defining absenteeism can be difficult in regard to the types of absences that are of concern and the determination of an acceptable level of absences. Consequently, it is not surprising to find that absenteeism has been defined a number of different ways in organizational behavior management investigations. In the first study in this area, absenteeism was simply defined in very general terms as staff being absent from work (Gardner, 1970). Subsequent investigations have attempted to differentiate between absences due to sick leave versus approved vacation or holiday leave. In essence, the differentiation of most serious concern has been between scheduled (i.e. planned) and unscheduled leave, with most intervention strategies aimed at reducing the amount of unscheduled leave taken by staff (e.g. Durand, 1983; Ford, 1981; Reid, Schuh-Wear, & Brannon, 1978; Shoemaker & Reid, 1980).

Absentee-Reduction Intervention Procedures

Antecedent Interventions. To date, only one study in a human service setting has systematically evaluated an antecedent procedure (Chapter 4) for reducing staff absenteeism. Pierce, Hoffman and Pelletier (1974) compared the effects of a 4-day, 40-hour workweek versus the effects of a 5-day, 40-hour workweek on staffs' use of sick time. Four groups of eight direct care staff participated in the investigation, with two groups assigned to work four 10-hour days each week and two groups assigned to work the traditional five 8-hour days each week. Results indicated no differential effects of the two work schedules on the frequency of staffs' use of sick time.

Consequence Interventions. The organizational behavior management strategies most frequently evaluated in an attempt to reduce staff absenteeism have been consequence procedures (Chapter 4). Five studies were located in which either positive or negative consequences were provided contingent on staff attendance at work or lack thereof, respectively. Two types of positive consequences have been applied in an attempt to reinforce or increase staff attendance at work. One type involved providing staff with the opportunity to rearrange their work schedules if the absences for an entire group of staff remained below a predetermined criterion level (Reid et al., 1978). Work schedules were rearranged such that all staff were allowed more frequent days off on weekends during a four-week period if the absences for the group did not exceed the criterion level during the preceding four-week period. Total staff absences for the four-week period were displayed for each group of staff using a publically posted bar graph. The intervention was implemented in multiple baseline fashion across six groups of staff who worked either the morning or afternoon shift in three institutional living units. Additionally, each group's rate of absenteeism during both the baseline and intervention periods was compared to the same time period during the preceding year when no absentee program was in effect as a control for possible seasonal fluctuations in absenteeism. Reid et al. reported that the group contingency program was effective in reducing the percent of staff absenteeism for five of the six groups of staff.

A second type of positive consequence program was reported by Durand (1983) who evaluated the effects of an absentee-reduction program on the amount of unscheduled leave taken by direct care staff working on a living unit serving highly disruptive mentally retarded clients. The staff participants helped to design the program and selected the positive consequence. Specifically, staff chose eight hours of extra leave time to be awarded to all staff members who did not use any unscheduled leave during a month's time period. The use of unscheduled leave by staff decreased while the (extra leave) consequence program was in effect. However, while unscheduled leave decreased, scheduled leave increased. In fact, overall use of leave (scheduled and unscheduled combined) remained relatively unchanged during the management intervention and across a one-year follow-up period.

In addition to evaluating the effect of the consequence program on scheduled and unscheduled leave time taken by staff, Durand also evaluated the effects on amount of resident disruptive behavior. Results indicated that residents were less disruptive during the time that the staff absenteeism intervention was in effect. That is, reductions in unscheduled staff absences appeared to favorably impact the behavior of the clients even though the *overall* number of absences (scheduled and unscheduled) continued to occur at about the same level. Presumably, resident behavior improved as a result of the supervisor's ability to plan treatment coverage by staff more adequately when leave time was requested and approved in advance.

In regard to the use of negative consequences (i.e. punishment procedures) with staff absenteeism, Ford (1981) evaluated a program in which staff were required to call their immediate supervisor to report their absence. Also, staff were required to report additional information regarding the nature and estimated duration of their illness as well as whether or not they planned to see a physician. When staff reported their absences, they were informed by the supervisor as to the number of staff who had previously scheduled leave during that time period and the number of staff who remained available to provide clients with necessary services. Results indicated that the use of unscheduled sick leave decreased when the punishment procedure was implemented. However, as was the case in the Durand (1983) study, the use of scheduled leave by staff increased. Consequently, the total amount of staff absences remained unchanged, although by the conclusion of the study approximately 80 percent of the absent time was under the scheduling control of management, whereas prior to the intervention only 50 percent of the leave time was scheduled. As in the Durand study, Ford emphasized the benefits of scheduled absent time relative to unscheduled time in terms of allowing for better planning for client care.

A second study investigating the effects of a negative consequence on staff absenteeism was reported by Quilitch (1979). Twenty-three direct care staff working in two client living units were selected to participate in the study, because the rate of absenteeism for each of the two groups of staff exceeded the average level of absenteeism for the entire facility. The intervention consisted of a policy requiring staff who used six or more (unscheduled) sick days since the beginning of the fiscal year to provide a note from a physician to document all subsequent sickness-related absences during the remainder of the year. The policy in effect divided the 23 participating staff into two groups. One group (A) consisted of eight employees who had already used six days of sick leave and were therefore required to provide a doctor's excuse for any subsequent absence. The other group (B) consisted of 15 employees who had used less than six days and were not required to submit a doctor's excuse when subsequently using a sick day. The implementation of the new policy resulted in a drop in the level of absenteeism for Group A from a baseline average of 8.2 percent to an average of 1.5 percent during the 10-week intervention period. The level of absenteeism for Group B changed only slightly from a baseline level of 2.6 percent to a post intervention average of 2.1 percent.

In addition to investigations evaluating positive *or* negative consequences on absenteeism in a human service setting, one study (Gardner, 1970) attempted to evaluate the differential effects of positive *versus* negative consequences. Gardner compared the number of unscheduled absent days taken by two groups of direct care staff when one group received a positive consequence for being present and on time while the second group received a negative consequence for being absent or arriving late. Specifically, four hours of extra time off were awarded to staff members in the first group for every 25 consecutive days during which staff were present and on time. For individuals in the second group, wages were docked for arriving late to work and staff were subjected to dismissal when three or more unscheduled absences were accrued within a month's time period. Gardner reported that during the five months in which the program was in effect, essentially no differences were found between the amount of sick time taken by the two groups. However, because this very early study was conducted with essentially no experimental controls for other variables that may have affected absenteeism, the results of the study should be viewed with considerable caution.

Multifaceted Procedures. Despite the existence of numerous research demonstrations of the rather powerful effects of combinations of antecedent and consequence strategies (i.e. multifaceted interventions—Chapter 4) for improving a number of problem areas of staff performance, these approaches have not been investigated with staff absenteeism very often in organizational behavior management. Specifically, only one study used a large number of procedural components to reduce staffs' use of unscheduled leave time. Shoemaker and Reid (1980) focused on absences of fifteen direct care staff who had been identified as "chronic attendance abusers." The intervention consisted of three basic components. First, staff members received systematic counseling during brief individual meetings at four-week intervals with their supervisors. During the counseling meetings, staff were provided with positive or negative feedback from the supervisor based on their attendance during the preceding four-week time period. Second, staff with perfect attendance during the four-week interval were sent commendation letters which were also placed in each staff member's personnel file. Third, staff with perfect attendance became eligible to participate in a behavioral lottery. The lottery involved randomly drawing four names from the pool of eligible staff following each four-week period. The staff members whose names were selected were allowed to choose one of four privileges or consequences: lunch with the supervisor at the supervisor's expense, the opportunity to rearrange the work schedule (i.e. days off) during the following week, one day with no mealtime duties with residents, and one day with no client training responsibilities. The intervention was implemented in multiple baseline fashion across the participants on the first work shift and then the participants on the second work shift, and resulted in improved attendance for 11 of the 15 staff members.

Critique of the Research

Social Significance of Target Behaviors

Earlier it was noted that essentially all efforts to improve staff performance in terms of providing better services to clients is predicated on the
presence of staff at work to provide those services. When considered in
this context, the social significance of decreasing employee absenteeism
seems obvious. However, because some absences are inevitable in any
work setting as also discussed earlier, determining the significance of
reductions in staff absenteeism can be difficult in regard to identifying
levels of absences that have an unacceptably serious impact on client
service provision. One means of estimating the degree of importance of
reducing levels of absenteeism is by determining the amount of staff
work time saved as absences are decreased. In this regard, in the Reid et
al. (1978) evaluation of a group contingency program, a comparison was
made of the number of work hours lost due to absences prior to the
program versus the number of work hours lost during the management
intervention. Results indicated that some 3,050 work hours were saved
during the intervention relative to baseline; such an amount of time (i.e.
almost 400 work days) would appear to involve a significant representation of service provision.

Although a measure of work time saved as reported by Reid et al. is
one illustration of the social relevance of a change in staff absences
following a management intervention, a measure with potentially increased
utility in this regard would be a more direct index of client welfare.
Durand (1983) attempted to provide such a measure by evaluating the
effects of reduced absenteeism on the level of disruptive behavior exhibited
by clients. Durand's results indicated that as unscheduled staff absences
decreased, client disruptive behavior decreased as well. However, relatively low reliability scores regarding the measurement of client disruptive behavior weakened the conclusions that could be drawn regarding
the relationship between staff's presence at work and client maladaptive
behavior. Regardless, more research on absentee-reduction programs is
needed that includes measures of client welfare to assist managers in
determining what levels of absences cannot be tolerated because of the
resulting (detrimental) impact on client services.

Adequacy of Experimental Designs and Methodologies

Because of the possible effects that small changes in the overall rate or percentage of employee absenteeism can have on an organization's service provision, very thorough and reliable systems for measuring absenteeism are warranted. Unfortunately in this regard, research on management interventions designed to improve attendance has been relatively weak in the area of absentee measurement. In particular, almost half of the studies did not report information regarding the reliability of the absentee measurement systems employed (Ford, 1981; Gardner, 1970; Pierce et al., 1974;). On a more encouraging note, the remaining investigations (i.e. Durand, 1983; Reid et al., 1978; Shoemaker & Reid, 1980; Quilitch, 1979) reported carefully defined target behaviors and generally convincing data on the reliability of the absentee monitoring systems.

In addition to problems with monitoring absenteeism, inadequacies in experimental designs were apparent in several studies, which detracted from the internal validity of the reported effects of given management interventions. As noted repeatedly throughout this text, without assurances that changes in staff behavior were the result of a specified intervention and not extraneous variables occurring simultaneously with the intervention, the potential utility of respective management procedures is questionable. Experimental design problems were most apparent among studies that evaluated the effectiveness of interventions by comparing the frequency of absences between two groups of staff exposed to different experimental conditions. Many of the prerequisite conditions for using such group comparison designs were not met in the reported investigations. To illustrate, in the Gardner (1970) and Pierce et al. (1974) studies involving group comparison designs, the experimental groups were very small, averaging only eight to twelve staff members per group. Also, staff were assigned to the groups based on where staff worked in the facility (i.e. by work shifts in particular living units). Hence, the assignment of staff to experimental groups was not random and the size of the groups diminished the likelihood that the groups were equal in regard to factors that may affect absenteeism rates. The latter problems were compounded in the Gardner study because no premeasure or baseline condition was included. Without measures of absenteeism prior to different interventions being implemented, essentially no conclusions can be made regarding the magnitude of change that may have occurred while either intervention was in effect.

Internal validity was also questionable in the Quilitch (1979) and Ford (1981) investigations of punishment management strategies. Quilitch implemented a management system following baseline without any subsequent reversal or replication of conditions which rendered experimental control questionable. Ford did include a reversal phase to more appropriately establish functional control of the management procedure. However, although use of sick time decreased during the first application of the intervention relative to baseline, the amount of sick time remained at a relatively stable level throughout the second (reversal) baseline and the second application of the procedure. Hence, the factors controlling staff absentee behavior could not be experimentally determined. In contrast to the Quiltich and Ford investigations, as well as the two other investigations just noted, the remaining studies summarized in the preceding section appeared to use adequate experimental methodology such that internal validity did not appear to be problematic (i.e. Reid et al., 1978; Shoemaker & Reid, 1980; Durand, 1983).

Due in large part to the rather small number of organizational behavior management investigations on absenteeism, the *external validity* of reported findings is also relatively weak. The degree of external validation of experimental effects is further weakened, in that, as noted earlier, all of the investigations have been conducted in one type of human service setting: residential facilities serving mentally retarded clients. Although the described management procedures may be applicable for other settings such as mental health centers, day-care centers, nursing homes or school programs, the research to date does not allow any firm conclusions in this regard. Moreover, because the majority of studies involved only a small segment of an agency's staff, it is not clear whether the interventions would result in significant decreases in absenteeism if the procedures were applied to the facility's *entire pool of staff*. The issue of (lack of) external validity is also somewhat unclear when considering that a significant percentage of an agency's staff is likely to be *professional* personnel and, to date, absenteeism research in human service settings has been conducted exclusively with *paraprofessional* staff (i.e. direct care staff persons).

Effectiveness of Management Interventions

Overall, the organizational behavior management research has been relatively effective in reducing staff absenteeism within the human service settings in which the research has occurred. Of the seven studies summarized in this chapter, five reported that the management procedure used to reduce absenteeism was effective (Durand, 1983; Ford, 1981; Quilitch, 1979; Reid et al., 1978; Shoemaker & Reid, 1980). For the most part, absentee-reduction procedures have appeared effective based on changes in the absenteeism of *groups* of staff members. Although information regarding how management programs affect respective agency staff persons as a group is certainly a useful measure of program effectiveness, an additional measure that would be helpful is information on how the absences of *individuals* within the group were affected. Results regarding individual staff behavior is of course important in all areas of staff management research, and such information is particularly relevant in research concerning employee absenteeism. As discussed in the introductory section of this chapter, there are several different types of unacceptable staff absences. Without data on individual staff absenteeism, it is difficult to determine the relative success of management interventions on the different types of absences. Changes in the performance of a group of staff, for example, may have been due to reductions in excessive duration absenteeism of only one or two staff members, whereas the predictable or periodic absences of many staff persons might have been unaffected.

Two of the studies reviewed did report detailed information regarding individual staff members' frequencies of absences (Durand, 1983; Shoemaker & Reid, 1980). Durand's management program involving extra leave time awarded to staff who used no unscheduled leave for a month resulted in reductions in absenteeism for 13 of the 17 staff members who participated in the program. Shoemaker and Reid reported similar effects on individual absences, although a somewhat different approach was taken in regard to the selection of individual staff to participate in the program. Because of the difficulty of determining when staff absences are legitimate (see earlier discussion) and because often only a small portion of an agency's staff exhibit excessive absenteeism (Kempen & Hall, 1977), Shoemaker and Reid focused on employees whose attendance records indicated a *chronic* abuse of unscheduled leave time (i.e. in contrast to involving all staff in a respective work unit). The multifaceted intervention employed by Shoemaker and Reid resulted in reduced absenteeism for 11 of the 15 employees who participated. Simultaneously, the other employees in the work setting continued to maintain a satisfactory attendance record such that overall attendance at the facility was improved rather substantially.

In addition to how absentee-reduction programs affect individual staff members, information is needed regarding the effectiveness of respective interventions over extended time periods. Because rates of absenteeism can tend to fluctuate across certain seasons of the year, at least a one-year period of time is generally needed to accurately evaluate the effects of a management intervention (cf. Durand, 1983). In this regard, several studies involved less than a six-month time period (Gardner, 1970; Pierce et al., 1974) and only one included a follow-up period encompassing a time span of one year (Durand, 1983). The follow-up data in the Durand study indicated that the management intervention remained effective across the one-year time period.

A final issue related to the effectiveness of the staff management procedures described in the investigations on absenteeism concerns the effect that decreasing *unscheduled* leave time has on staff's use of *scheduled* leave time. In the two studies that monitored both scheduled and unscheduled leave (Durand, 1983; Ford, 1981), results indicated that when unscheduled leave decreased, scheduled leave increased. As discussed previously, scheduled absent time of staff typically has much less of a detrimental impact on an agency's services. However, any absent time (including scheduled leave) usually has at least some detrimental effects and, consequently, the overall utility of absentee-reduction programs must be carefully scrutinized in terms of the effects on both types of leave.

Staff Acceptability of Management Procedures

An important variable affecting whether or not a management program designed to reduce staff absenteeism becomes a routine part of an agency's day-to-day operations is the acceptability of the program to both staff members and supervisors. In this regard, supervisory interventions affecting staff use of sick time can easily become a very sensitive issue among staff. Such sensitivity is due in large part to the many different reasons why staff use sick time, and disagreements can often occur between staff and supervisors (as well as among certain staff members themselves) regarding the perceived legitimacy for the sick-time usage. In any case, if staff do not view an absenteeism program as acceptable, serious conflicts between staff and management are likely to result.

One means of promoting staff acceptance of an absenteeism program is to involve staff members in the program's design and/or implementation (Durand, 1985). Two of the reported studies promoted staff involvement in this regard (Durand, 1983; Reid et al., 1978). Durand solicited employee involvement by allowing the participating staff to design the contingency associated with work attendance. Reid et al. involved staff by having them vote every four weeks as to whether or not they wished to continue to participate in the absenteeism program (all staff voted in favor of the program at each opportunity). In both studies, the absentee-reduction program involved the use of positive consequences designed to function as a reward for attendance.

In a study that utilized a negative consequence for unacceptable absences, Quilitch (1979) evaluated the acceptability of the management procedure by asking staff to complete a questionnaire concerning how the staff felt about the program. Sixty-eight percent of the staff members who completed the questionnaire described the management system as *unfair*. In addition, only one of the three supervisors involved in the administration of the procedure recommended that the program continue after the formal investigation was completed.

An approach to reducing absenteeism that may impact the majority of staff members in a more acceptable manner than the Quilitch program is represented by the approach taken by Shoemaker and Reid (1980). As noted previously, rather than including all staff members in a program to reduce absences, only those staff members who had a substantially greater than average use of sick time were involved in the Shoemaker and Reid program. In short, staff members who had used sick time responsibly or legitimately were not subjected to stricter regulations regarding their use of unscheduled leave time. Therefore, the intervention was probably less likely to impact the legitimate use of sick time and, consequently, may have been more acceptable to staff—although Shoemaker and Reid did not measure staff acceptability per se.

In general, measures of staff acceptability have not been routinely included in investigations of management procedures for reducing absenteeism. Based on the limited amount of research that did include at least some indication of acceptability, those programs involving either positive consequences or employee participation in the design and/or implementation of the program seem to be the most promising in regard to staff acceptance of the programs. In contrast, for those programs utilizing negative consequences, the results of the one acceptability measure that was reported indicated serious problems with acceptability.

Absentee Research in Business and Industry

Earlier it was noted that a very considerable amount of research on absenteeism has occurred in business and industrial settings. Although such settings involve many different variables relative to human service work environments (e.g. see discussion in Chapter 1 regarding the profit index), it seems likely that results of research in the former type of settings may be relevant to at least some degree for the latter type of setting. This chapter section provides a brief synopsis of some of the conclusions that can be drawn from absentee research in business and industry that seem especially germane for human service agencies.

A very useful overview of absentee research in business and industrial settings is provided by Durand (1985). Durand succinctly summarizes the research that has occurred and expertly critiques the adequacy of investigations in this area. In essence, the information provided here represents a cryptic reiteration of Durand's review, and the interested reader is referred to his work for elaboration.

Of primary concern for purposes of this text is the conclusions that can be drawn from the business and industry research that are most applicable for *developing and implementing* successful absentee-reduction programs in human service agencies—in contrast to conclusions that have been drawn regarding idiosyncratic staff variables that may affect absenteeism (e.g. family size of staff persons). In this regard, Durand categorizes approaches to absentee reduction into antecedent and consequence procedures, similar to the categorization of strategies for managing routine staff performance used in this text (Chapter 4). Within the antecedent category, numerous variables have been investigated in regard to their potential relationship to staff absenteeism. However, three antecedent variables seem most noteworthy in terms of their likely impact on reducing absenteeism and/or the ability of managers to significantly manipulate the variables in an attempt to reduce absences. First, there is relatively good reason to *believe* (although to date research data do not exist to convincingly *demonstrate*) that staff absenteeism may be reduced by *organizing staff into small work units* relative to structuring all or most of an agency's staff into one or a few large units. Second, *involving staff in the design of an absentee-reduction program* is likely to enhance the efficacy of the program relative to managerial personnel developing the program without staff involvement. Third, providing staff with *flexibility* in regard to the use of scheduled time off from work is likely to deter high frequencies of unscheduled absences.

In considering antecedent components of absenteeism programs of the type just noted, Durand expresses a qualifier similar to that discussed in this text in regard to staff training and management procedures in general: antecedent procedures, even when effective, are likely to have only modest effects on reducing staff absences. More significant reductions are likely to result from the systematic application of *consequences* for absences and/or attendance at work. In this regard, both negative (i.e. punishing) and positive (reinforcing) consequences have been effective in reducing absenteeism in business and industry. Hence, the effectiveness of absentee-reduction programs in human service settings is likely to be enhanced if specific consequences are built into the programs. Durand's review provides a number of examples of the types of consequences that been used in business and industry, although most of the consequences are highly similar to those described earlier in this chapter.

Recommended Management Strategy for Reducing Absenteeism

Before summarizing our recommended strategy for reducing unacceptable levels of staff absenteeism and/or maintaining acceptable levels, a word of caution is in order. Specifically, because only a relatively small amount of organizational behavior management research has been conducted with staff absenteeism, the managerial strategies to be discussed should not be considered as the definitive answer for resolving this type of staff performance problem. Considerably more research is needed to better understand the variables within human service work environments that managers can manipulate to avoid absentee problems. Also, because all of the research to date has been conducted in residential facilities serving mentally retarded persons, particular caution should be exerted in applying the strategies to be recommended here to other types of human service settings. Nevertheless, for managers who must address problems associated with unacceptable levels of absenteeism, results of the research that have been reported do suggest some managerial actions that at least have been tried and tested to some degree.

Similar to the discussions on recommended management programs presented in the two preceding chapters, the basic steps comprising the generic behavioral supervision model (Chapter 2) represent an appropriate framework for developing absentee-reduction programs. However, because of the somewhat idiosyncratic nature of absenteeism as described earlier in this chapter, there are two significant exceptions relative to the general use of the model. First, an initial managerial step should be taken prior to the usual implementation of the model (see discussion in following paragraph). Second, the staff *training* step of the model can generally be eliminated from management programs for reducing absenteeism. Absenteeism typically does not represent a lack of work skills on the part of staff and the only instruction that is usually necessary pertains to informing staff what management's approach to absenteeism involves.

The first recommended step in reducing staff absenteeism is to determine how to *involve staff persons* in the process. Staff involvement in as many aspects of absentee-reduction attempts as possible is likely to increase the probability of the success of the program (see Durand, 1985, for a discussion). Such involvement could include staff participation in designing (and/or altering the continuation) of a program (Reid et al., 1978) as well as the determination of specific performance consequences to be administered based on varying levels of absenteeism (Durand, 1983; Shoemaker & Reid, 1980). Of course, in those human service agencies that are partially or totally unionized, union representation in the design of absentee-reduction programs typically must occur if the programs are to be successfully implemented.

The second step in a recommended management program for reducing staff absenteeism is to *clearly specify levels of absences that are not acceptable*. Although determining appropriate levels in this regard is often difficult due to reasons noted earlier, several guidelines can be helpful. First, separate criteria generally must be specified for each of the extended duration, high frequency, and predictable types of absences. Second, it can be useful to establish an overriding ceiling level of absences regardless of the specific type. For example, a general agency policy could be developed to indicate that absences above a 5 percent level across a designated time period will not be tolerated (cf. Shoemaker & Reid, 1980). However, it should also be noted (and this represents the final guideline to consider) that a supervisor must maintain the ability to be flexible in responding to absences due to unusual or extenuating circumstances.

Maintaining a certain degree of supervisory flexibility in responding to certain absentee problems represents a rather paradoxical situation. On the one hand, flexibility is usually necessary because of the essentially endless variety of reasons, including acceptable reasons, as to why staff might be absent from work. On the other hand, if supervisors respond differently across staff persons in regard to action taken for absences, the occasion is set for staff disgruntlement due to perceptions of favoritism on the part of the supervisor. One potential means of a supervisor avoiding the latter situation, albeit a somewhat cumbersome means, is to maintain a log of all supervisory action taken with each staff person, along with the circumstances of the different absences and the reason for the supervisory action. The supervisor can then review the log as new absentee problems arise to determine action (and rationale) taken with similar cases in the past in order to maintain as much consistency as possible.

Once staff involvement in the development of an absentee-reduction program has been evoked and criteria have been established regarding unacceptable levels of absences, the next managerial step is to systematically *monitor* ongoing absence rates. The monitoring should include attention to levels of absences for specific work units of staff as well as for individual staff persons. Generally, monitoring of staff absenteeism is relatively straightforward, in that monitoring systems already exist in most human service agencies for payroll purposes. In some cases, periodic checks on the accuracy of existing monitoring systems may be needed. The more serious concern in most situations though is to ensure that appropriate supervisors do indeed attend to the results of the monitoring systems that are in place such that absentee problems do not begin to develop without supervisors addressing the problems (see following discussion). As with monitoring of any designated problem area with staff performance (Chapter 2), monitoring of staff absenteeism should continue throughout all aspects of managerial actions taken to reduce staff absences.

The final step in our recommended management approach is to implement a performance *consequence* system. As discussed with consequence systems for paraprofessional staff provision of formal client training and treatment programs in Chapter 6, a multiple-consequence system (Shoemaker & Reid, 1980) is generally recommended as part of absentee-reduction programs. Included in the system would be negative consequences for absentee levels above the established absentee criterion. However, because of some noted problems in regard to lack of staff acceptance of negative consequence systems (Quilitch, 1979) (which is perhaps to be expected with punishment-oriented programs with staff performance), caution should be taken with the use of negative consequences. Hence, we recommend that negative consequences be used only to the degree that the consequences are an integral part of general disciplinary action systems that routinely exist in most human service agencies (verbal warnings, written reprimands, etc.) rather than developing punishment programs beyond what already exists.

Disciplinary action systems that entail progressively more negative consequences as staff performance problems continue to occur can probably suffice as the punishment component of multiple-consequence systems if two criteria are met. First, the systems must be used by supervisors consistently with respective absentee problems. Second, administration of the various disciplinary action steps should be based on specific, predetermined levels of unacceptable absences—with both staff and supervisors being astutely aware of the designated levels.

In regard to the use of positive consequences for acceptable absentee levels, reliance on the simultaneous application of a number of potentially reinforcing processes is more likely to effectively reduce absences relative to reliance on only one specific consequence. A number of possible consequences can be used by managers, depending in large part on creativity, available resources, and/or degree of managerial control of certain variables in the work setting.

Time Off as a Consequence for Acceptable Absentee Levels

In one sense, nonlegitimate staff absences from work involve a powerful consequence for staff: receiving pay (e.g. paid sick leave) for not working. One means of attempting to reverse such a contingency is to provide increased *legitimate* benefits regarding time off from work for maintaining acceptable levels of unplanned absences. Such benefits may be in the form of extra (scheduled) time off from work beyond what is normally granted to staff persons (Durand, 1983), more time off on certain scheduled (desired) days during the workweek (Reid et al., 1978) and/or increased flexibility in determining when to take time off (Shoemaker & Reid, 1980).

Special Work Privileges as a Consequence for Acceptable Absentee Levels

Several types of special work privileges have been used as positive consequences for staff maintaining acceptable levels of absences, such as relief from certain (undesirable) work duties (Shoemaker & Reid, 1980). Of course, if such duties are indeed important, then someone (i.e. another staff member) must perform the job tasks that are relieved of the staff member(s) who demonstrated a commendable absentee level. Hence, what might be reinforcing to one staff person could result in an extra punishing event for another staff person, with the latter person presumably exhibiting a less satisfactory absentee level. The resulting impact of such interrelated contingencies due to special privileges is unclear and represents a potentially important area for future research.

Special Recognition as a Consequence for Acceptable Absentee Levels

Special recognition of commendable staff performance has been used as a positive consequence in a number of organizational behavior management investigations (e.g. see Chapter 6) and could be applied relatively easily to the absentee area. Actually, special recognition such as "Employee of the Month," commendation in an agency newsletter or identification in a local newspaper represents one of the more cost-efficient types of managerial consequence approaches in terms of the time and effort required of managers (see Appendix A for additional examples). However, if these types of consequences are to represent a useful component of a multifaceted absentee-reduction program, then they must be provided more frequently (e.g. once every four to six weeks) relative to what usually occurs in many human service agencies.

REFERENCES

Alavosius, M.P., & Sulzer-Azaroff, B. (1986). The effects of performance feedback on the safety of client lifting and transfer. *Journal of Applied Behavior Analysis, 19,* 261–267.

Durand, V.M. (1983). Behavioral ecology of a staff incentive program: Effects on absenteeism and resident disruptive behavior. *Behavior Modification, 7,* 165–181.

Durand, V.M. (1985). Employee absenteeism: A selective review of antecedents and consequences. *Journal of Organizational Behavior Management, 7*(1/2), 135–167.

Ford, J.E. (1981). A simple punishment procedure for controlling employee absenteeism. *Journal of Organizational Behavior Management, 3*(2), 71–79.

Gardner, J.M. (1970). Effects of reinforcement conditions on lateness and absence among institutional personnel. *Ohio Research Quarterly, 3,* 315–316.

Kempen, R.W. & Hall, R.V. (1977). Reduction of industrial absenteeism: Results of a behavioral approach. *Journal of Organizational Behavior Management, 1*(1), 1–21.

Pierce, P.S., Hoffman, J.L., & Pelletier, L.P. (1974). The 4-day workweek versus the 5-day workweek: Comparative use of sick time and overtime by direct care personnel in an institutional facility for the severely and profoundly retarded. *Mental Retardation, 12,* 22–24.

Quilitch, H.R. (1979). Applied behavior analysis studies for institutional management. In L.A. Hamerlynck (Ed.), *Behavioral systems for the developmentally disabled: II. Institutional, clinic and community environments* (pp. 70–102). New York: Brunner/ Mazel.

Reid, D.H., Schuh-Wear, C.L., & Brannon, M.E. (1978). Use of a group contingency to decrease staff absenteeism in a state institution. *Behavior Modification, 2,* 251–266.

Shoemaker, J., & Reid, D.H. (1980). Decreasing chronic absenteeism among institutional staff: Effects of a low-cost attendance program. *Journal of Organizational Behavior Management, 2*(4), 317–328.

Zaharia, E.S., & Baumeister, A.A. (1978). Technician turnover and absenteeism in public residential facilities. *American Journal of Mental Deficiency, 82,* 580–593.

Chapter 8

IMPROVING ADMINISTRATIVE PERFORMANCE

Throughout the preceding chapters in this text, the focus has been on changing and/or maintaining staff work behavior in order to improve client welfare. The rationale underlying the behavioral research reviewed to this point has been that by improving the proficiency with which human service staff conduct their caregiving and/or habilitative duties, as well as the frequency with which staff report to work, the quality of life of dependent clients will be enhanced. It has been repeatedly emphasized that management interventions designed to improve the proficiency of staff performance cannot be considered as truly successful unless staff performance *and* well-delineated indices of client welfare are shown to be enhanced. However, it has likewise been noted (Chapters 2 and 3), albeit briefly, that there are also important areas of staff performance that do not, in and of themselves, directly affect client welfare.

Staff duties that do not result in an immediate and/or readily apparent impact on client welfare are actually quite numerous in many human service agencies. For example, considerable amounts of staff time and effort are often necessary to maintain the aesthetic quality and cleanliness of the physical plant of a human service setting. Although most persons would agree that it is important for human service agencies to look nice and be clean, such features of an agency typically do not have a direct impact on client functioning per se. Similarly, determining, securing and maintaining adequate materials, equipment and supplies — ranging from bed sheets and pillows in residential settings to ditto machines in public schools — also require staff fulfillment of a variety of nonclient-related work responsibilities. Ensuring timely and accurate payment of agency staff along with the appropriate processing of various insurance and retirement benefits represent another set of work responsibilities required of human service staff that are not directly related to observable indices of client welfare, yet are nevertheless important.

One of the largest areas of staff responsibilities that generally does not have a clearly visible impact on client welfare is administrative duties. In

171

many ways, referring to staff work responsibilities under the domain of *administration* represents a rather nebulous reference to work behavior. That is, it is often difficult to determine exactly what agency staff persons mean when they report that they perform administrative functions. Because of the difficulty frequently encountered when attempting to specify what administration involves, administrative personnel are frequently viewed by direct client-service staff (i.e. caregivers and clinicians) as fulfilling a relatively unnecessary or even wasteful role. Upon closer scrutiny, however, it becomes apparent that without the effective fulfillment of certain administrative duties, direct client services would often be impossible to provide.

Generally, administrative operations within human service agencies can be grouped into several general types of responsibilities. First, *establishing the overall mission* of the agency as well as the week-by-week or month-by-month agency goals that relate to fulfillment of the primary mission is in part an administrative function. Second, *communicating* to agency staff regarding the established mission and/or ongoing changes in related agency goals is a major administrative responsibility. Third, *developing and initiating procedures* for carrying out the agency's mission and goals represents an administrative function. The latter area of administration involves a wide variety of procedural operations, ranging from maintaining a means of hiring, paying, and firing staff to securing payment from clients (or client representatives) for agency services.

The description of what administration refers to as just presented is of course very general. The generality in this regard seems to be traditionally inherent in typical references made to administrative duties in human service settings—*administration* frequently seems to include essentially all work activity beyond those jobs that result in a change in client welfare (e.g. a client learning a new skill or a client being bathed) or an alteration of the physical environment (e.g. a classroom wall being painted, the grass being mowed, or a meal being prepared). The former type of (nonadministrative) duties are typically referred to as clinical, medical, or direct service responsibilities, whereas the latter represent maintenance, housekeeping and dietary types of functions. In essence, administrative duties are often defined by exclusion: whatever is not included in the kinds of responsibilities just noted is considered to be administrative in nature. However, there are also several characteristics that tend to differentiate administrative duties rather uniquely from other types of agency work responsibilities.

One of the most common characteristics of administrative roles is an abundance of *paperwork:* writing, preparing charts or reports, etc. As with administration in general, paperwork is frequently viewed by non-administrative personnel as representing a work activity that essentially is not very important. Again, upon closer scrutiny though, several significant reasons become apparent for the existence of paper-related duties as part of human service operations. The most important reason in this regard relates to a fundamental characteristic of human service agencies: there is usually no clearly visible index of how well or poorly a human service agency fulfills its caregiving and/or habilitative mission (Chapter 1). Because of the common lack of such an index, emphases are often placed on other means of attempting to determine that a human service agency is fulfilling its mission, with the most common means being paper-related *documentation.* That is, (paper) records are maintained on numerous work activities in an attempt to document that the intended activities (i.e. the means by which an agency attempts to fulfill its mission) did indeed occur, and occurred with sufficient quality.

A second reason for the importance placed on administrative paperwork that stems from the lack of a clear evaluative index within human service agencies just noted is the abundance of *external regulations* with which many agencies must comply—and the fact that the primary method by which an agency is judged to adhere to external regulations is through the (paper) documentation that the agency maintains. External regulatory guidelines generally are imposed on human service agencies from two main sources. First, state and federal governments legally mandate that respective agencies function in accordance with certain standards in an attempt to ensure that: (a) agency clients are protected from harm or inhumane practices, and (b) an agency is providing the type of service that it is intended and/or funded to provide. Second, various professional groups impose operating standards on respective human service agencies in an attempt to ensure that the quality of treatment provision provided by an agency represents professionally acceptable and/or state-of-the-art treatment services.

Generally, the larger the human service agency and/or the more diverse types of services offered by an agency, the more external regulations are imposed on the agency (and, consequently, the more administrative, paper-related documentation required of an agency). Often, an agency must comply with the external guidelines in order to ensure the obtainment of a very significant part of the agency's operating funds.

Such funding and related regulatory guidelines may stem from insurance companies that pay for certain client services, state and federal laws enacted to ensure treatment services to special subgroups of handicapped persons, and private philanthropic foundations. An illustration of the relatively pervasive influence external funding and regulatory guidelines can have on a human service agency, as well as the resulting paper-related documentation required, is presented in Table 8-1. Table 8-1 summarizes a sample—albeit a very small sample—of the types of external regulations, the sources of the regulations, and the resulting paper documentation that can be required of a public residential facility serving mentally retarded persons.

In addition to a focus on paperwork, a common characteristic of administrative activities is *meetings*. Administrators are frequently known for spending a considerable amount of time in meetings with other agency staff. Although meetings occur on a seemingly infinite variety of topics, the fundamental purpose of meetings is for a given staff person(s) to obtain information from other staff members and/or to disseminate information to staff persons. Such meetings may involve several agency staff persons representing one specific work unit within an agency, representatives from all or most of an agency's work units, or just two agency staff members.

Purpose and Format of Chapter

Earlier it was noted that preceding chapters have not focused on administrative performances. The lack of attention to administrative work behavior is due to the fact that the vast majority of organizational behavior management research and applications have not targeted this area of human service provision. Rather, the organizational behavior management field has been more concerned with staff performance areas that clearly and directly impact the welfare of clients. However, due in part to the reasons for administrative responsibilities in human service provision as just discussed, as well as the noted existence of performance problems in this area, there have been some important behavioral investigations on administrative functions. The purpose of this chapter is to discuss the research that has occurred.

Two general performance areas within the domain of administration will be reviewed based on the focus of the organizational behavior management research that has been reported. The first area involves

Table 8-1
EXAMPLES OF DOCUMENTATION REQUIRED BY REGULATORY AGENCIES FOR
RESIDENTIAL PROGRAMS FOR CLIENTS WITH DEVELOPMENTAL DISABILITIES

Regulatory Agency	*Sample of Documentation*
Federal Health Care Finance Administration	• client evaluations • interdisciplinary program plans • client performance data • monthly program plan review • client activity schedules
Accreditation Council on Services for People with Developmental Disabilities	• client personal histories • agency organizational table • committee reports and minutes • individual resident financial accounts • alleged violations of client rights and actions taken to intervene
U.S. Department of Labor Federal Wage and Hour Division	• client work records • client job time studies • individual client disability information • evidence of comparable community wages
U.S. Congress, Public Law 94-142 (for public education)	• record of staff with access to student information • permission to evaluate • annual individual educational plans • documentation of efforts to involve parents in educational planning • parental notice of placement decisions
Joint Commission Accreditation for Hospitals	• monthly records of drug inspections • documentation of quarterly implementation of fire plans

Note: The samples of required documention represent only a very small subset of all documentation required by each regulatory body.

documentation responsibilities regarding the development, implementation and evaluation of client treatment plans. The second area pertains to staff adherence to agency policies that are designed to ensure that respective agencies operate in a manner consistent with the fulfillment of the agency's designated mission.

Following the format used throughout the other chapters in this section of the text, a summary of the available research in the areas just mentioned will be provided, followed by a critique of the research.

Within the critique section, special attention will be directed to the *social significance* of the administrative work behaviors targeted for change by management interventions. Emphasis will be placed on social significance because of the frequently unclear relation noted earlier between certain administrative duties and client welfare. In essence, if managerial time and attention are directed toward improving specific administrative work functions, then scrutiny is warranted to ensure that those functions are truly important and that they warrant the effort invested in their improvement.

Summary of the Research

Organizational Behavior Management Procedures Used to Improve Client Treatment Documentation

Organizational behavior management research focusing on improving staff proficiency in documenting client treatment services has occurred in a variety of human service settings. Such research has also addressed a number of different types of documentation responsibilities. The varied kinds of documentation-related job duties that have been addressed, as well as administrative tasks in general, are exemplified in Table 8-2. This chapter section reviews the staff research in performance areas related to documentation duties according to the types of management procedures used to improve staff fulfillment of such responsibilities.

Antecedent Management Procedures. Several investigations have relied mainly on antecedent procedures (Chapter 4) to improve staff proficiency in client treatment documentation. In one such study, Page et al. (1981) evaluated a classroom-based training program as a means of improving the proficiency with which professional staff developed appropriate goal statements and behavioral objectives as part of treatment plans for developmentally disabled residents in a state institution. Page et al. reported that after receiving classroom instruction, which included repeated opportunities to practice writing goal statements and behavioral objectives, staff successfully acquired the skills needed to write treatment goal statements and behavioral objectives in an appropriate format. Somewhat unexpectedly—at least based on results of other research with antecedent interventions (Chapter 4)—the goal and objective writing skills acquired by staff during training were maintained throughout a six-month follow-up period after completion of the training program

Table 8-2
ADMINISTRATIVE WORK BEHAVIOR TARGETED
IN STAFF MANAGEMENT INVESTIGATIONS

Investigation	Setting	Staff Behavior
Quilitch (1978)	MR institution	submitting suggestions to management
Shook, Johnson & Uhlman (1978)	school	maintaining client progress graphs
Epstein & Wolfe (1978)	juvenile delinquent center	writing information in client records
Andrasik, McNamara & Abbott (1978)	psychiatric center	documenting staff responses to client work absences
Repp & Deitz (1979)	MR institution	writing client progress notes, submitting completed time records
Ford (1980)	MR institution	writing client treatment goals
Hutchison, Jarman & Bailey (1980)	MR institution	attending meetings
Page, Christian, Iwata, Reid, Crow, & Dorsey (1981)	MR institution	writing client treatment goals
Christian, Norris, Anderson, & Blew (1983)	private residential program for autistic youth	maintaining client case records
Lovett, Bosmajian, Frederiksen, & Elder (1983)	mental health center	writing client intake summaries, treatment plans, and progress notes
Barrowclough & Fleming (1986)	nursing home	writing client treatment goals
Jones, Morris, & Barnard (1986)	psychiatric emergency room	completing civil commitment forms

without any additional experimenter-controlled performance contingencies in the daily work routine. Page et al. discussed the latter results in light of the fact that all of the staff participating in the study were professionals and that perhaps the advanced educational background or related self-imposed contingencies the professionals placed on their own performance contributed to the durability of the effects of inservice training.

Barrowclough and Fleming (1986) also evaluated the effects of in-service training, although the focus of their training program was on increasing the active involvement of paraprofessional staff in planning habilitative strategies for elderly clients in day treatment and residential programs. The effectiveness of the training was evaluated by rating staff performance on a simulated written exercise immediately following the inservice. Subsequent measures of staff attendance at routinely occurring goal planning meetings, and of client progress toward specified treatment goals, were used to further evaluate the impact of the staff training program. After participating in the training all staff members were rated as at least "fair" in regard to their performance in completing the simulated goal planning exercise, and the majority of staff subsequently increased their involvement (i.e. attendance) at goal planning meetings. However, in somewhat of a contrast to the Page et al. results, when client progress toward the newly developed treatment goals was reviewed it was found that over half of the goal plans initiated as a function of the staff training program were abandoned after the inservice training was completed.

In a third study evaluating an antecedent intervention on staffs' completion of client treatment-related documentation duties, Epstein and Wolff (1978) used in-service training in combination with a prompting procedure to improve written entries made by staff in clients' medical records. Staff at a residential facility for juvenile delinquents were trained in the use of the *Problem-Oriented Medical Record* (POMR). Specifically, direct care staff were provided with instructions and written models of record entries that included three essential components of the POMR: a statement of a client's problem behavior, the action(s) staff took to remedy the problem and an evaluative statement regarding the effectiveness of the intervention toward resolving the client's problem behavior. In addition to providing staff with instructions and a model of appropriate record entries, the experimenters verbally prompted staff three times each week to enter the designated information in the clients' records. The instructions, written model and prompting procedures resulted in increases in the number of appropriate POMR entries, although the increases appeared less than maximal in regard to the number of written record entries that were expected of staff.

Consequence Management Procedures. In addition to the studies utilizing exclusively antecedent strategies, there have been two behavioral staff management investigations that focused on client-related documentation duties that relied primarily on consequence procedures (Chapter 4) to improve staff performance. Repp and Deitz (1979) evaluated the effects of privately written feedback on the timeliness and comprehensiveness of client progress reports prepared by staff in a residential facility for mentally retarded persons. Initially, each of 87 staff members, both professional and paraprofessional, received an individualized memorandum indicating the percentage of progress reports that had been entered into client records on time. The written feedback was accompanied by an increase in the percentage of progress notes punctually entered from a baseline average of 0 percent to a post-intervention average of 46 percent. However, only 30 percent of the progress notes contained all of the information that was suppose to be in each note based on administrative policy. The feedback intervention was then expanded to reflect the percentage of progress notes entered on time *and* that contained all the required information. Following this latter management action, the average percentage of progress notes entered on time was 80 percent, and of that number, 65 percent contained all the needed information. The improvement in staffs' completion of client progress notes was maintained across a four-month time period. Subsequently, the same feedback format was used to improve staffs' timely completion of other types of client progress reports.

Egan, Luce and Hall (1988) also used privately written feedback as a consequence procedure for staffs' documentation of client treatment activities (see Christain, Norris, Anderson & Blew, 1983, later in this chapter for a description of the staff performance responsibilities). As in the Repp and Deitz study just noted, the privately written feedback was accompanied by improved documentation performances of staff — improvement that also maintained across a six-month period.

Multifaceted Management Investigations. Three investigations utilized multifaceted combinations of antecedent and consequence procedures (Chapter 4) to remediate staff performance problems relating to client treatment documentation. In an investigation conducted in a rural mental health center, a multifaceted management approach was used to increase staffs' completion of client records that involved client-intake summaries, treatment plans and progress notes (Lovett, Bosmajian, Frederiksen & Elder, 1983). The target staff at the mental health center included 40 outpatient counselors who were coordinating services for approximately 1,200 clients. In order to improve staffs' completion of the necessary components of the documentation responsibilities, a three-part intervention system was implemented. First, the recording procedures that staff were expected to perform were simplified. Specific forms were redesigned with preprinted information in order to prompt staff to record all necessary components, as well as to reduce the amount of writing required of staff to complete each form. Relatedly, assessment instruments for identifying clients' strengths and weaknesses, along with instructions for using the instruments, were collected and placed conveniently in specified locations in the agency to facilitate staffs' obtainment of the instruments when needed. Second, staff began receiving feedback regarding the completeness of their client records. Supervisors met on a regular basis with each of the outpatient counselors and provided corrective feedback and/or social praise based on the supervisor's review of a sample of the counselor's charts. Third, the staff were informed that results of the chart reviews were being reported to a senior administrative officer. The three-part intervention package appeared to result in increases in the percentage of client records that contained the required information.

The second study utilizing a multifaceted management approach to improve staffs' client treatment documentation was conducted with personnel in the emergency room of a state psychiatric hospital (Jones, Morris, & Barnard, 1986). The purpose of the study was to evaluate the effects of instruction and feedback on staffs' proficiency in completing three forms that were required to legally commit clients to the psychiatric facility. The requirements included notice of rights forms, imminent harm applications and witness lists. Beginning with one of the forms, training on the correct completion of the form was provided either individually or to a small group of the emergency room staff. During training, the employees—who were all professional staff—were provided with verbal and written instructions to assist the staff in filling out the form correctly when on duty in the emergency room. Following training, staff began receiving weekly graphs depicting the percentage of forms that were correctly completed by all staff during the previous week. The instruction and feedback package was subsequently implemented with the two other forms and resulted in improvements in the number of correctly completed forms each time the management program was implemented.

In a third application of a multificeted procedure, Christian et al. (1983) attempted to improve the recordkeeping performance of case managers in a private residential program for autistic children. Each of the case managers, who also functioned as direct service staff, was responsible for maintaining all appropriate service documentation in one designated client record. Prior to implementing the management program, a checklist was developed to indicate the appropriate content and organization of the case records. Staff were instructed to use the checklist for conducting quarterly reviews of their respective records. A three-part intervention was then implemented sequentially with three groups of staff. Initially, a written memorandum was posted in the work area reminding staff of their responsibility for record reviews. The written instructions appeared to have an insignificant effect on staffs' completion of the client records. Next, each case manager was provided with a written summary of the deficiencies found in his/her assigned case record. The case managers were asked to correct the record deficiencies and were instructed that a follow-up review would occur within two to three weeks. The written feedback also did not appear to substantially improve staffs' record keeping. Consequently, individual feedback sessions were held during which each case manager was individually assisted in conducting a review of his/her record and in correcting documentation deficiencies. The individual (verbal) feedback was accompanied by increases in the average percent of cases that were correctly completed by each of the three groups of staff members.

Differential Effects of Intervention Components on Staffs' Client-Related Documentation. The studies described to this point regarding the improvement of staffs' documentation related to client treatment activities have generally focused on the effects of one management intervention, be it an antecedent, consequence or multifaceted approach. In contrast, two studies have more directly evaluated the *relative* effects of different management interventions on staffs' completion of client habilitation-related documentation. One such investigation evaluated the effects of several different antecedent and consequence applications on the number of client progress graphs maintained by staff working in a day treatment facility for mentally retarded individuals (Shook et al., 1978). The study consisted of two experiments. The first experiment evaluated the effects of the antecedent procedures of instructions and response cost reduction (i.e. reducing the work involved in maintaining the graphs) on the number of graphs maintained on a daily basis. The staff who participated in the study were students at a nearby university who worked in the agency on a part-time basis. The provision of bulletin board space on which blank graphs were posted (to reduce staff effort in locating and preparing the format of the graphs) resulted in a slight increase in the percentage of client graphs that were appropriately completed in a timely fashion. Posting written instructions to complete the graphs along with the graphing materials resulted in a more substantial increase. However, the effect of providing the materials and posting written instructions diminished over time. Hence, a consequence component was implemented by publicly posting each day the percentage of all graphs that were kept up to date. The latter intervention (i.e. group feedback) did not result in significant improvements. Subsequently, in a second experiment, the combined effects of providing materials, posting written instructions and providing publicly posted *individual* feedback (i.e. in contrast to *group* feedback) were evaluated, with a substantial increase resulting in terms of the percentage of client graphs that were updated daily. Adding social praise consisting of written commendation memos and public recognition of individuals who were graphing client data on a regular basis resulted in an additional, albeit slight, improvement.

In a second study that compared different management components, the relative effects of the *frequency* of feedback provided to staff were investigated (Ford, 1980). The investigation was conducted in a residential facility for mentally retarded persons and compared the effects of no feedback, weekly feedback and monthly feedback on the correct completion of client goal statements by staff after the staff had been trained in the appropriate preparation of the treatment goals. Individuals who received no feedback following training tended to decrease their goal writing performance over time, whereas staff who received monthly feedback performed slightly better—and continued to perform better over a six-month period. Weekly feedback resulted in levels of staff performance that were very similar to the performance levels of the staff who received monthly feedback. Because monthly feedback was less costly than weekly feedback in terms of the supervisor's time, it appeared that providing feedback to staff on a monthly basis was the more desirable management approach.

Organizational Behavior Management Procedures Used to Improve Adherence to Administrative Policies

As indicated earlier, several investigations in the administrative area were not directly related to client treatment documentation but, rather, involved behavioral staff management procedures designed to enhance the likelihood that staff would adhere to other types of administrative policies. An example of one such study was conducted by Repp and Deitz (1979) who focused on improving the timeliness of staffs' completion of their time and attendance work records. The intervention consisted basically of withholding staffs' pay for any time worked that was not reported on the time and attendance work sheets. Prior to implementation of the policy, 69 percent of the staff were either not completing time sheets or were not submitting the time sheets to management by the designated deadline. Following implementation of the pay-withholding policy, less than 1 percent of the employees failed to promptly submit a completed timesheet. During the eight weeks following the removal of the pay-withholding policy, only one employee failed to turn in a completed attendance sheet on time.

In another study involving staff compliance with administrative policy, the effects of applying consequences for staff adherence (or lack thereof) to a policy regarding unexcused client absences from a sheltered work program were evaluated in a forensic psychiatric center (Andrasik, McNamara, & Abbott, 1978). The policy required that a client's supervisor document an unexcused client absence from work and deduct points from the client's earnings that were used by the client to qualify for specific privileges—a policy with which staff rarely complied. To increase the percentage of incidences of unexcused client absences for which staff took appropriate action, the staff were required to complete a form indicating the action taken as a result of each unexcused absence for individual clients. Staff compliance with the documentation requirement was compiled into a report that was forwarded to the agency's superintendent. The report indicated the action taken by staff members relative to the action that should have been taken according to the policy. The report was also made available for individual staff to review. Following the management intervention, the percentage of client absences for which staff reported that they took the correct disciplinary action increased noticeably and maintained throughout the thirteen-week management intervention period. However, data were not reported to verify that what staff *reported* they did in regard to action taken with clients coincided with what the staff *actually did.* Perhaps relatedly, the reported improvement in staffs' compliance with the policy of documenting consequences provided for client work absences was not accompanied by a significant reduction in actual client absences from work.

Earler it was noted that a characteristic of administrative work responsibilities is a rather abundance of meeting-related functions. Despite the frequency of meeting-related activities in this regard though, to date behavioral staff management investigations generally have not focused on this area of staff performance. In one rare study on staff meeting behavior, Hutchison et al. (1980) used a public posting procedure to improve staff attendance at meetings in a residential center serving mentally retarded clients. Focusing on an interdisciplinary team of professional staff, attendance at team meetings pertaining to client treatment and evaluation was publicly posted via a graph that displayed the presence or absence of staff at the meetings as well as the late arrival of staff persons. The graphs were posted on the wall in the meeting area for staff to view. The public posting appeared effective in reducing staff absences at team meetings but was ineffective in reducing the frequency of staff arriving late for meetings. Hutchison et al. also monitored the percentage of agenda items that were completed during the meetings as a function of when public posting of attendance and tardiness was and was not in effect. More agenda items were successfully addressed in each team meeting during the public posting phase (i.e. when more interdisciplinary team members attended the meetings). Hence, improving attendance at team meetings appeared to coincide with business being conducted more efficiently, even though staff received no feedback or other consequences relative to the number of agenda items completed.

In another relatively unique investigation involving administrative responsibilities, Quilitch (1978) increased staffs' submission of suggestions to management regarding various agency operations in a residential facility for the mentally retarded. Initially, a suggestion box and bulletin board were installed near the main entry to the facility followed by an instructional memorandum to staff informing them how to use the suggestion system. One of the facility's administrators was designated to review all suggestions submitted by staff and to post both the suggestion and a written response (i.e. feedback) to the suggestion on the bulletin board within two days after receiving the suggestion. After seven weeks, public posting of suggestions was replaced by a procedure whereby a privately written response was delivered to the individual staff member who submitted the suggestion. After six weeks of privately written feedback, public posting of management responses was reinstituted. Results indicated that public posting of feedback was accompanied by more than twice as many suggestion submissions from staff than was privately written feedback. Based on a questionnaire survey of staff opinion regarding the acceptability of the management procedures it appeared that staff preferred public posting relative to privately written responses. A measure of the cost of the management intervention was also reported in terms of the time required of the manager who was responsible for maintaining the public posting system, with only approximately six minutes of the manager's time required per each staff suggestion that was submitted.

Critique of the Research

As in preceding chapters, the purpose of the critique section in this chapter is to provide a critical review of the behavioral staff management research that has just been summarized. Also similar to preceding chapters, the organizational behavior management research involving investigations on staff proficiency in regard to client treatment documentation and adherence to (other) facility administrative policies will be discussed in regard to: (a) the social significance of the administrative behaviors targeted for change, (b) the validity of the experimental designs used to evaluate the management interventions, (c) the effectiveness of the management strategies, and (d) the acceptability of the management practices.

Social Significance of Administrative Behaviors

In many ways administrative duties represent a unique set of job responsibilities. On the one hand, as noted previously there are some administrative functions that are integral to a human service agency's operating existence—such as completing documentation requirements that are necessary to ensure an agency's funding. On the other hand, as exemplified by staff concerns over the (non)importance of certain administrative tasks as also noted earlier, in some cases it is not readily apparent that administrative duties contribute in any meaningful way to the actual services provided to clients. Because of the uncertainty associated with respective administrative functions, managers need to be particularly careful in terms of the effort exerted in ensuring that staff consistently fulfill administrative responsibilities—effort should be extended only on performance areas that clearly are important. Similarly, organizational behavior management researchers should attend closely to the significance of the administrative behaviors that are being targeted for change in respective investigations. To date, such attentiveness has not been the case in the management research; relatively little formal research attention has been directed to the social validity of administrative duties.

Only three of the investigations summarized in the preceding section included formal measures relating to the social significance of the administrative duties that were addressed by the management interventions. Two of the three studies failed to provide support for the notion that improving the proficiency of certain administrative duties results in improved client services. In the Andrasik et al. (1978) investigation that evaluated the impact of staff adherence to a policy mandating specific staff actions when clients were absent from work, there was no significant decrease in actual client absences when staff compliance with the facility's policy improved. Similarly, in the Barrowclough and Fleming (1986) study that investigated the effects of a somewhat extensive staff training program regarding client goal planning on the progress of elderly clients toward specified treatment goals, the majority of the goal plans that were initiated by staff immediately following training were subsequently discontinued before the clients reached the goals. On a more encouraging note, Hutchison et al. (1980) demonstrated that improved staff attendance at meetings was accompanied by more agenda items being successfully addressed at treatment planning meetings. However, an even *more* encouraging outcome of the Hutchison et al. investigation would have been the presentation of data to indicate that improvements in completing the agenda items resulted in improved client treatment.

Due to a relative lack of social significance components in research on administrative responsibilities, as well as the results just summarized that did not provide support for the service-related utility of certain administrative functions, questions remain as to which administrative duties warrant the most serious attention in regard to ensuring proficient staff fulfillment of such duties. Research is needed to more clearly indicate which administrative tasks have the most (if any) impact on client welfare, be it directly or indirectly, and/or on the overall day-to-day operation of an agency. The importance of establishing the relationship between administrative duties and a relevant index of client welfare is well illustrated in research on the effects of different frequencies of data collection on client responsiveness to training programs. In one investigation (Holvoet, O'Neil, Chazdon, Carr, & Warner, 1983), it appeared that staff members who were training mentally retarded clients to perform a skill made better training decisions when the staff recorded client performance data during *each* training session relative to when they recorded data on a less frequent basis. However, the quality of training decisions was essentially based on clinical opinion of professional trainers, not on client responsiveness to the training per se. In a subsequent study reported in a similar setting (McCarn & Reid, in press) it was demonstrated that the progress of mentally retarded clients in daily training programs did not differ whether staff were recording daily training data or were recording less frequent, weekly measures of progress. In essence, the more rigorous and administratively time-consuming schedule of (daily) data collection did not appear to positively affect client progress— progress which, for a residential training facility, should be the *bottom-line* measure of the utility of this type of administratively related staff performance. Such results again indicate that researchers and supervisors need to be well assured that the effort required to systematically improve staff fulfillment of respective administrative duties will indeed enhance an agency's services in some meaningful way.

Validity of the Experimental Designs

As noted repeatedly in preceding chapters, a critical component in the evaluation of information resulting from applied research is the degree of confidence a manager can have that management interventions in respective investigations were responsible for the reported improvement in staff behavior (internal validity), and that the interventions can be successfully implemented in other service settings (external validity). In regard to the former issue, four of the investigations discussed in this chapter used rather weak experimental designs, rendering conclusions about internal validity somewhat tentative (see also Andrasik & McNamara, 1977, for a case study in the administrative area). Specifically, Barrowclough and Fleming (1986) reported only post-intervention data in their investigation on the effect of intensive staff training on staffs' ability to write goal plans for clients. Because no data were reported on the goal planning skills of staff prior to training, a thorough evaluation of the effects of the training is not possible. Two other studies used relatively weak AB experimental designs (Hersen & Barlow, 1977, chap. 9) in an attempt to demonstrate functional control of management interventions on administrative staff performance (Andrasik et al., 1978; Repp & Deitz, 1979, Experiment III). Both studies reported only one application of the management intervention and did not include an experimental control group to rule out other coincidental factors that may have been responsible for changes in staff behavior. Another design weakness was apparent in the Ford (1980) study that compared the effects of various schedules of feedback on the maintenence of staff skills in writing client goal statements. Results of the Ford study were difficult to evaluate, because the effects of the staff training program were not reported prior to introducing the various schedules of feedback—disallowing a thorough comparison of the effects of the respective feedback schedules across the different groups of staff. In contrast to these investigations, however, essentially all of the other studies reviewed used experimental designs that allowed for convincing demonstrations of the internal validity of the reported effects of given management interventions.

In regard to external validity, the behavioral management research on administrative performance has been relatively strong. Staff management procedures have been evaluated and demonstrated as effective for improving the administrative proficiency of staff in a variety of work settings, including residential facilities for the mentally retarded (Repp & Deitz, Experiment I, 1979), autistic (Christian et al., 1983) and mentally ill (Jones et al., 1986) as well as outpatient mental health clinics (Lovett et al., 1983) and a center for juvenile delinquents (Epstein & Wolff, 1978). Research on administrative performance has also been conducted in a setting serving elderly clients (Barrowclough & Fleming, 1986), a type of environment in which organizational behavior management research in general has been infrequently conducted.

As a further indication of strong external validity, the majority of management investigations in the administrative area have targeted relatively large numbers of staff. For example, six studies summarized previously (Andrasik et al., 1978; Barrowclough & Fleming, 1986; Jones et al., 1986; Lovett et al., 1983; Quilitch, 1978; Repp & Deitz, Experiments I and III, 1979) included 30 or more staff members as experimental participants—a large number for applied behavioral research. Moreover, several of the investigations (e.g. Ford, 1980; Hutchison et al., 1980; Jones et al., 1986; Lovett et al., 1983; Page et al., 1981; Quilitch, 1978; Repp & Deitz, 1979) addressed the performance of professional staff. In this regard, the administrative area represents one of the few staff performance areas in which organizational behavior management research has focused on the work activities of personnel other than paraprofessional staff (see also Chapter 9 on classroom teacher performance).

One outcome of the research in the administrative area with professional staff is that more investigations seem needed on the (potential) differential effects of management interventions involving professional versus paraprofessional staff. To illustrate, results of the Page et al. (1981) study indicated that inservice training alone may be an effective intervention in some areas of performance with professional staff, even though inservice has been repeatedly shown to be an insufficient intervention for substantially changing the day-to-day performance of paraprofessional staff (Chapters 3 and 4). There may be other procedures that are more (or less) effective when used with professional versus paraprofessional staff members that could be identified through management research (see previous discussion by Page et al. on possible factors affecting professional staff performance).

Although the settings in which investigations on administrative performance have been conducted have been relatively varied, the focus of the research in terms of the specific staff performance areas targeted has been somewhat restricted. The vast majority of the studies reviewed were concerned with improving some aspect of client treatment documentation. As discussed earlier, *administration* refers to a much broader range of job duties than just client treatment documentation. Sound management research on methods of improving (as well as validating the importance of) the myriad of other types of administrative duties required of many human service staff is seriously needed.

Effectiveness of Management Interventions

Regardless of whether or not investigations have addressed administrative staff behaviors that are truly relevant to an agency's service provision and/or have used adequate experimental designs to demonstrate the effects of a management intervention, if staff work performance did not substantially improve following the intervention, then the management strategy is of limited or no benefit to managers. In this regard, three studies reported relatively minimal or no changes in administratively related staff performance following a management intervention. In the Epstein and Wolff study (1978) which utilized *antecedent* management procedures including a staff inservice and verbal prompts, relatively small improvements were reported with staffs' documentation performance. Barrowclough and Fleming (1986) also reported small (and short-lived) effects of an antecedent, staff inservice program—in this case, in respect to staffs' active involvement in treatment planning activities. In regard to the relative ineffectiveness of *consequence* management strategies, Hutchison et al. (1980) found public posting to be effective in reducing staff absences at habilitation team meetings but not for reducing staff tardiness at the meetings.

In contrast to the three investigations just noted, all other studies reviewed that focused on administrative performance reported rather substantial changes in staff behavior following management interventions.

Such results, involving primarily consequence and multifaceted managerial approaches, provide strong support for the utility of organizational behavior management procedures for improving administrative performance. However, with few exceptions (e.g. Page et al., 1981; Ford, 1980), data on managerial effectiveness have been provided only in regard to the average performance of a *group* of staff persons. More information about the responsiveness of *individual* staff members to various management interventions along with the general group response would allow a better analysis of the effectiveness of respective management procedures.

In evaluating the overall effectiveness of management procedures designed to improve administrative staff performance, special concern is warranted regarding the *long-term* effects on staff behavior. The durability of the efficacy of management procedures is important in this regard, because administrative responsibilities often involve repetitive duties with seemingly little intrinsic reinforcement for staff persons—a characteristic that frequently results in staff dislike of a work activity. In addition, as referred to earlier, some staff often wonder about the importance of certain administrative duties. These two features (i.e. staff dislike and uncertainty regarding the utility of a job task) tend to detract from the likelihood of staff performing a task for very long. Among the investigations reviewed in this chapter, several reported follow-up or maintenance periods of greater than four months (e.g. Christian et al., 1983; Egan et al., 1988; Ford et al., 1980; Jones et al., 1986; Lovett et al., 1983; Page et al., 1981). Although results of these studies suggested that the effects of the management procedures were durable over time, considerably more research is still needed to better build a management technology for maintaining staff performance of administrative duties.

In addition to the characteristics of a work task as just noted that affect consistent completion of the task by staff, a factor that may affect the durability of the effects of a management procedure is the amount of managerial effort required to implement the management strategy with staff. In short, a management procedure will not have a significant impact on staff performance if *managers* do not routinely use the procedure. Generally in this regard, the more effortful a management intervention is to apply, the less likely it is that the procedure will be used consistently by managers over time. Two studies in the administrative area reported specific information pertaining to the amount of supervisory effort required to implement management strategies. Shook et al. (1978) reported that monitoring client graphs and providing publicly posted, individual feedback to staff required about ten minutes of a supervisor's time each day. Quilitch (1978) reported that maintaining a public posting system for responding to staff suggestions involved an approximate average of six minutes of a manager's time for each submitted suggestion. These results suggest that inordinate amounts of managerial time were not necessary in order to implement effective behavioral management procedures. It would be helpful for future investigations to expand on these types of supervisory response cost measures to allow for a more thorough evaluation of the utility of respective management strategies. Relatedly, more comparison research would be useful along the lines of the Ford (1980) study that compared two management procedures and found that a less time-consuming strategy (i.e. monthly feedback to staff) was as effective in maintaining certain administrative performances as a more time-consuming approach (weekly feedback).

Staff Acceptability

Related to the efficiency of implementation of a management strategy, a somewhat salient variable that can affect the long-term effectiveness of a management intervention is the acceptability of the procedure among staff and supervisors. In this regard, Quilitch (1978) evaluated staff opinions concerning the public posting of management responses to staff suggestions by asking staff to complete a questionnaire indicating how they felt about the management program. Results indicated that 98 percent of the staff thought the system should be continued. The favorable staff response, in conjunction with the small amount of management time required to operate the system as just noted, suggests that public posting of managerial responses to staff suggestions is a very acceptable means of promoting communication between line staff and management. Unfortunately, other than a few anecdotal reports of staff responses to various management interventions (Andrasik et al., 1978; Repp & Deitz, 1979), the Quilitch (1978) investigation represents the only study we located in the administrative area that formally addressed the acceptability issue. Consequently, additional research on procedural acceptability in this area is warranted.

Management Procedures Most Likely to Improve
Administrative Staff Performance

As implied in the preceding section, the technology for managing staff documentation and other administrative duties is far from complete. Nevertheless, based on the number of management interventions that have been successful as represented earlier in this chapter, there are also some behavioral management procedures that could be quite useful for human service managers. The purpose of this section is to describe a set of procedures gleaned from the organizational behavior management research that is likely to be both an effective and efficient supervisory strategy for resolving problems with administrative staff performance.

The first step in the process is to *evaluate the significance of the administrative task* being addressed by considering whether the targeted staff behaviors are likely to impact important aspects of the day-to-day operation of the facility and/or in some way enhance services to clients. Such an evaluative step is necessary for several reasons. First, as noted previously the ultimate importance of many administrative duties is not always readily apparent. Second, there has been a lack of applied research addressing the social significance of administrative tasks, and some research suggests that certain administrative requirements in fact have not been very important (e.g. Andrasik et al., 1978). Third, our experience has been that administrative duties in human service settings are among those staff activities that are most likely to continue to be required of staff after the need for the task has passed. To illustrate, a situation that frequently occurs in residential training centers for mentally retarded persons during the summer months is that many of the clients' routine training sessions are cancelled due to staff vacations or client recreational activities. As a result of the cancellations, management personnel require client treatment staff to prepare monthly cancellation reports as a means of monitoring (and subsequently reducing or preventing) excessive treatment cancellations. After the summer months have passed and service cancellation is no longer a significant problem, the treatment staff continue to be required to prepare the cancellation report, even though the managerial personnel who initially requested the report no longer attend to, or act on, the information in the report. In essence, at times administrative duties appear to be required of staff simply because "that's the way it has always been done" rather than because the tasks serve any real role in improving an agency's services.

Once a supervisor is convinced of the significance of the targeted administrative task, then the next step for improving staff completion of the task is for *the task to be clearly defined* (Chapter 2). Defining the task may be as simple as, for example, verbally instructing that a completed travel request must be submitted to a supervisor three days before a planned outing or as complex as carefully delineating all the required components of a comprehensive client treatment plan. Even though defining some areas of administrative performance can be somewhat difficult because administrative roles are often quite nebulous, such duties must be clearly articulated before any behavioral management steps can be effectively taken.

After the target administrative task has been clearly defined, the next recommended managerial step is to systematically *monitor* (Chapter 2) staff performance regarding the identified task. Fortunately in this regard, monitoring of administrative tasks is often rather easy for supervisors relative to monitoring other types of staff performance—particularly if the tasks entail documentation. Documentation involves producing a permanent product (e.g. a client progress note, a signed attendance sheet) that can be reviewed essentially at a supervisor's convenience, in contrast to a supervisor having to be present in a staff work unit precisely when the staff are working on a designated task. Also, a supervisor's job of monitoring documentation responsibilities in terms of ensuring that the documents contain all the appropriate information can be facilitated through the use of checklists (see Chapters 2, 3, and 6 for elaboration and exemplification). Checklists can be developed for many types of documentation responsibilities that clearly delineate the necessary components of the documents that a supervisor should monitor.

Subsequent to validating, defining, and monitoring staff performance, it is frequently advantageous for a manager to consider ways of simplifying the administrative task expected of staff in order to reduce staff effort that is required to complete the task (cf. Lovett et al., 1983; Shook et al., 1978). For example, forms can be prepared for staff who have to complete periodic, standard types of reports. The forms may include preprinted subheadings and other standard information with spaces for staff to fill in idiosyncratic information, thereby eliminating much of the writing required of staff (i.e. staff do not have to repeatedly write the standard, repetitious information). Similarly, lengthy narrative reports on client progress required in many service settings as exemplified in most of the studies on documentation described earlier can sometimes be replaced by graphic progress reports that only require trainers to plot client performance data at regular intervals. Usually, updating a graph requires considerably less staff time than writing a report. Relatedly, ensuring that needed materials to complete an administrative task are readily available in the staffs' work environment may also be helpful by reducing staff time and effort involved in securing necessary materials (Lovett et al., 1983). Another means of simplifying some documentation tasks is through the use of microcomputers. Smith and Wells (1983), for example, demonstrated that trainers' appropriate preparation of reports on client progress in a residential program for the mentally retarded was enhanced if the reports were prepared with computer assistance relative to if the reports were prepared totally by hand. In short, in a number of cases reducing staff effort required to complete an administrative task—be it by simplifying the task or by arranging the environment to make completing the task more convenient—can improve staff proficiency in performing the task. Although reducing staff effort in this regard cannot be considered a totally sufficient step for improving administrative performance, even in those cases where performance is not immediately impacted this managerial step can enhance the effectiveness of subsequent managerial actions.

As previously discussed (Chapters 3 and 4), supervisory verbal instructions provided to staff are probably the most commonly used staff management procedure in human service settings. Instructions should also be a common part of a strategy (i.e. the fourth step in the overall managerial process) to improve administrative performance. If a supervisor is confident that staff have the needed skills to perform an administrative task (which is often the case with administrative duties), then the purpose of instructions is essentially to direct or remind staff to complete a particular job. When instructions are intended to serve as a reminder, the format of the instructions in terms of being written or verbal is not as important as is the assurance that some instructions are indeed provided. If, however, staff do not have the skills required to perform a given administrative task, then instructions should be designed to teach staff how to perform the task. When instructing staff how to perform administrative duties, an *individual* or *small group* instructional format is usually most effective (i.e. in contrast to instructions presented in a *large group* utilizing a didactic training format), with opportunities for staff to practice completing the task. As emphasized in preceding chapters, however, instructions alone (although often necessary) will probably not sufficiently ensure that staff will perform the designated administrative task over time in the routine work situation.

The final step in managing employees' performance of administrative duties involves the systematic delivery of consequences contingent on staffs' performance of the specified work behaviors. *Performance feedback* has been the consequence procedure most widely used in organizational behavior management research on improving staff performance in the administrative area. A number of formats for providing feedback to staff have been successful in remediating administratively related problems, including publicly posting feedback on group and/or individual performance, privately presenting verbal feedback to individual staff and providing individual feedback in writing. None of these formats for delivering feedback have been used more predominately than any other in the research to date, and any of the formats is likely to help improve administrative behavior of staff (the interested reader is referred to Chapter 4 for additional information regarding the relative merits and limitations of respective performance feedback procedures).

REFERENCES

Andrasik, F., & McNamara, J.R. (1977). Optimizing staff performance in an institutional behavior change system. *Behavior Modification, 1,* 235–248.

Andrasik, F., McNamara, J.R., & Abbott, D.M. (1978). Policy control: A low resource intervention for improving staff behavior. *Journal of Organizational Behavior Management, 1* (2), 125–133.

Barrowclough, C., & Fleming, I. (1986). Training direct care staff in goal planning with elderly people. *Behavioural Psychotherapy, 14,* 192–209.

Christian, W.P., Norris, M.B., Anderson, S.R., & Blew, P.A. (1983). Improving the record-keeping performance of direct service personnel. *Journal of Mental Health Administration, 11(2),* 4–7.

Egan, P., Luce, S.C., & Hall, R.V. (1988). Use of a concurrent treatment design to analyze the effects of a peer review system in a residential setting. *Behavior Modification, 12,* 35–56.

Epstein, L.H., & Wolff, E. (1978). A multiple baseline analysis of implementing components of the problem-oriented medical record. *Behavior Therapy, 9,* 83–88.

Ford, J.E. (1980). A classification system for feedback procedures. *Journal of Organizational Behavior Management, 2(3),* 183–191.

Hersen, M., & Barlow, D.H. (1977). *Single case experimental designs: Strategies for studying behavior change.* New York: Pergamon.

Holvoet, J., O'Neil, C., Chazdon, L., Carr, D., & Warner, J. (1983). Hey, do we really have to take data? *Journal of the Association for Persons with Severe Handicaps, 8,* 56–69.

Hutchison, J.M., Jarman, P.H., & Bailey, J.S. (1980). Public posting with a habilitation team: Effects on attendance and performance. *Behavior Modification, 4,* 57–70.

Jones, H.H., Morris, E.K., & Barnard, J.D. (1986). Increasing staff completion of civil commitment forms through instructions and graphed group performance feedback. *Journal of Organizational Behavior Management, 7*(3/4), 29–43.

Lovett, S.B., Bosmajian, C.P., Frederiksen, L.W., & Elder, J.P. (1983). Monitoring professional service delivery: An organizational level intervention. *Behavior Therapy, 14,* 170–177.

McCarn, J.E., & Reid, D.H. (in press). Comparing data collection frequencies for severely handicapped students: Effects on training, efficiency and progress. *Education and Treatment of Children.*

Page, T.J., Christian, J.G., Iwata, B.A., Reid, D.H., Crow, R.E., & Dorsey, M.F. (1981). Evaluating and training interdisciplinary teams in writing IPP goals and objectives. *Mental Retardation, 19,* 25–27.

Quilitch, H.R. (1978). Using a simple feedback procedure to reinforce the submission of written suggestions by mental health employees. *Journal of Organizational Behavior Management, 1*(2), 155–163.

Repp, A.C., & Deitz, D.E.D. (1979). Improving administrative-related staff behaviors at a state institution. *Mental Retardation, 17,* 185–192.

Shook, G.L., Johnson, C.M., & Uhlman, W.F. (1978). The effect of response effort reduction, instructions, group and individual feedback, and reinforcement on staff performance. *Journal of Organizational Behavior Management, 1*(3), 206–215.

Smith, D.W., & Wells, M.E. (1983). Use of a microcomputer to assist staff in documenting resident progress. *Mental Retardation, 21,* 111–115.

Chapter 9

IMPROVING TEACHER PERFORMANCE
IN THE CLASSROOM

Throughout the preceding chapters in this section of the text the focus has been on organizational behavior management research and application in regard to improving specific work performances of human service staff. The behavioral research that has been discussed is perhaps best characterized by its general *problem-solving* orientation (Reid, 1987, chap. 1) and, in particular, its focus on demonstrating effective means of solving problems with staff work performance. The emphasis of this chapter is also problem-solving in nature. In contrast to previous chapters though, the focus is not on solving one type of problem with staff work performance per se. Rather, this chapter addresses problems related to a variety of staff job duties, all of which are performed by professional personnel in one type of human service setting: teachers working in school classrooms.

The change in focus of this chapter from one specific performance-related problem to varied work behaviors of one group of staff (teachers) in one setting (school classrooms) is due to several factors. However, there is also one primary reason for the somewhat circumscribed focus on the work performance of teachers. Specifically, teacher performance in school classrooms represents the most pervasive provision of human services that affects the most people in our society for the longest period of time. Almost every person in this country spends at least several years of his/her life receiving educational services from school teachers, and the vast majority of individuals spend a rather substantial portion of their lives in school classrooms. Given the scope of this sector of human services, the (non)proficiency with which teachers provide educational services warrants close scrutiny within the staff training and management field.

A second reason for the focus on teacher performance stems from the fact that school classrooms represent one of the first human service

197

settings in which applied behavioral research was conducted in a problem-solving format. The focus of the initial applied behavioral research in educational settings was on demonstrating means of improving problematic student behavior in the classroom (see O'Leary & O'Leary, 1972, for a summary of the early behavioral research in this area). However, it soon became apparent that in order to bring about significant changes in student performance, the classroom behavior of teachers warranted as much attention from applied behavioral researchers as did the behavior of the students (e.g. Hall, Lund, & Jackson, 1968). Consequently, a considerable amount of behavioral research has been conducted on methods of training and managing teacher behavior in the classroom. Actually, there has been more organizational behavior management research involving teachers than any other group of human service professionals.

Another reason for focusing on the work performance of teachers as a distinct class of (professional) job duties is that problems have been repeatedly identified in regard to the effectiveness of educational services provided in school classrooms. Such problems have been publicized in both the popular media (e.g. see cover story of *Time Magazine*, February 1, 1988) and professional literature (see O'Leary & O'Leary, 1972, for examples). Somewhat relatedly, classroom teacher performance often warrants attention from a training and management standpoint, because job expectations placed on teachers are frequently changing. That is, new methods of teaching students are continuously being developed and/or refined, and teachers need assistance to periodically upgrade and maintain their skills in accordance with state-of-the-art educational technology. It is incumbent upon managerial personnel to help provide that assistance through effective training and management practices.

Format of Chapter

The format of this chapter is similar to that of preceding chapters. However, because several areas of work performance will be addressed in contrast to focusing on just one problematic performance area, the literature review section of the chapter will be somewhat different from the corresponding section in previous chapters. Specifically, the review section will be organized according to each of two primary types of teacher performance areas that have been addressed in organizational behavior management research. It should also be noted that because of the large amount of attention given to classroom teacher performance in the professional literature, a totally exhaustive review of the literature in this area will not be provided. Rather, the focus will be on those aspects of teacher performance that have received the most research attention in organizational behavior management. Also, emphasis will be on those investigations that targeted actual performance in the classroom in contrast to teacher training research that did not include direct measures of day-to-day teacher work behavior.

Summary of the Research

The types of work responsibilities expected of teachers vary immensely across the diverse kinds of classroom environments that exist in school settings. Teachers as a professional group are charged with meeting a wide variety of student educational needs, including, for example, overcoming illiteracy among legally incarcerated juveniles, providing creative academic challenges for intellectualy gifted adolescents, teaching social interaction skills to young first graders, fulfilling personal care needs of severely handicapped students, and teaching the gamut of academic curricular material. Consequently, the amount, diversity and complexity of skills required of teachers are enormous.

In an attempt to impose a degree of organization to the varied types of skills required of teachers, behavioral researchers and practitioners have often categorized teaching skills into two general groups: *classroom management* skills and *academic instructional* skills. The former set of skills pertains to enhancing the classroom social behavior of students. That is, generally before effective teaching can occur in a classroom in terms of helping students acquire academic knowledge, teachers must ensure that students display a certain degree of classroom etiquette. Teachers must be able, for example, to manage student behavior in regard to ensuring that students stay in their designated seats and attend to assigned work, that students comply with teacher directives, and that students do not disrupt and/or harm other students. The second set of skills required of teachers relates more directly to the academic development of students and involves the effective application of instructional methods across all kinds of formal educational curricula (mathematics, health sciences, social studies, humanities, etc.).

Most of the organizational behavior management research involving teachers can be categorized based on its (primary) focus on one of the two types of skills as just exemplified. Hence, the existing research will be summarized in accordance with these two general categories of classroom teacher performance.

Improving Classroom Management Skills of Teachers

When classroom management problems exist, be they student disruptive behavior, general inattentiveness or even outright hostility between students and teachers, classroom environments typically become nonconducive for educational service provision. As a result of problems in this regard, the learning potential of students as well as the opportunity for teachers to actually teach become seriously hampered. In addition, the overall classroom atmosphere can become quite unpleasant. One of the most effective means for a teacher to address these types of classroom problems is through the use of *behavior management* strategies with students. As alluded to previously, behavior management procedures have been effectively used to resolve a wide variety of student behavior problems in numerous classroom settings (O'Leary & O'Leary, 1972). Unfortunately, though, many teachers cannot and/or do not implement behavior management or modification practices very effectively.

In many cases, teachers as well as other educational personnel have some understanding of the theoretical underpinnings of behavior management; however, they often do not *apply* such knowledge to routine practices in the classroom. Consequently, a considerable amount of organizational behavior management research has occurred on methods of *training and managing teacher skills in using behavior modification techniques* to improve the classroom management of student behavior. The applied research in this area generally has focused on either training staff to use *one specific* behavioral intervention strategy to manage a relatively circumscribed type of student social behavior, or training staff to use *a variety* of behavioral interventions for more general classroom management purposes.

Training teachers to use one specific behavioral intervention to manage student behavior. Probably the singular most effective behavior management strategy for altering inappropriate student behavior (at least based on research to date) is the systematic presentation of teacher *praise* and/or *attention* contingent on appropriate student performance (see O'Leary & O'Leary, 1972, for examples of the effective use of teacher praise). Hence, a number of organizational behavior management studies have focused specifically on training teachers how to contingently attend to desirable student behavior in the classroom. Frequently, teacher training programs designed to improve teachers' use of contingent attention have involved multifaceted training programs (Chapter 3) that included a number of instructional strategies. To illustrate, a prototypical approach to teacher training in this area is exemplified in a comprehensive program reported by Speidel and Tharp (1978). The inservice program described by Speidel and Tharp consisted of multiple training procedures, including lectures on the principles and effects of reinforcement (i.e. positive teacher attention), videotaped examples of contingent reinforcement application, practice in observing and recording student behavior, performance feedback, modeling of attention-giving practices, and performance practice by the teacher trainees. The latter component, performance practice, also involved videotaped feedback and group discussion. Results of the Speidel and Tharp investigation indicated that this type of intensive, multifaceted training program can be quite effective for increasing teachers' use of contingent attention with appropriate student behavior.

Although the multifaceted type of program just exemplified is a somewhat common training approach used in organizational behavior management research with teachers, there have also been a number of investigations in which one or a small number of staff training and/or management procedures were evaluated. Hence, for the sake of organization, the classroom research will be described in regard to the specific type of management procedure that was evaluated singularly (or as a predominant part of an intervention) to improve teacher performance in regard to attending to appropriate student behavior.

Providing contingent positive attention basically involves a teacher's timely engagement (i.e. when a student is behaving appropriately) in a discrete type of behavior, be it a praise statement, a smile, a pat on the back, etc. These features of providing contingent positive attention — discrete teacher behaviors emitted only at certain times — lend modification of this type of teacher performance nicely to the application of *antecedent* staff training and management procedures (Chapters 3 and 4). One type of antecedent procedure that generally has not been applied to other areas of staff performance discussed in this text yet has been used in a number of applications with teacher attention-giving skills is *audio-cueing*. A good illustration of an audio-cueing procedure is described by Bowles and Nelson (1976) who taught teachers to wear a radio earpiece through which instruction (i.e. an audio cue) from an experimenter via a wireless FM microphone was presented. The instruction prompted the teachers regarding precisely when they should attend to, or praise, student behavior. The audio-cueing procedure was accompanied by increases in teachers' effective application of contingent praise.

Another form of antecedent cueing was described by Hall et al. (1968). Hall et al. used *visual* cueing in which a small square of colored paper was held up by an experimenter in the classroom to indicate to a teacher when to praise a student for appropriate behavior. This type of cueing also appeared helpful in increasing teacher praise rates. Somewhat similarly, visual cueing was used to help teach a teacher's aide how to appropriately reinforce (i.e. praise) student compliance with staff requests (Neef, Shafer, Egel, Cataldo & Parrish, 1983). Neef et al. used hand signals delivered by an experimenter in the classroom to represent the visual cues. Electromechanically presented visual cueing has likewise been used to train systematic use of teacher attention and praise via an experimenter-controlled signal light that was placed on a student's desk (Ward & Baker, 1968). The light was activated when the student engaged in task-relevant behavior to cue the teacher to praise the student at that time. The light-cueing procedure was implemented in conjunction with weekly discussions with the teacher, with the procedures being accompanied by increases in teacher praise behavior.

A more traditional type of antecedent procedure, *verbal instruction,* was evaluated as one component of a program designed to increase the effective use of teacher attention (Cossairt, Hall & Hopkins, 1973). However, in this case verbal instruction in the form of information regarding the importance of teacher praise did not result in consistent increases in teacher praise rates (nor student attending rates). In contrast, feedback plus social praise from the experimenter contingent on teacher attention-giving did result in consistent increases in teacher praise behavior as well as increases in appropriate student performance.

Another antecedent procedure used in a teacher training program centering on skills for reinforcing appropriate student behavior has been *performance modeling* (Ringer, 1973). Ringer focused on teaching a teacher to administer token reinforcement as well as verbal praise. An experimental "token helper" demonstrated the reinforcement procedures in the classroom while the teacher was simultaneously encouraged to praise appropriate student behavior. The "token helper" gradually faded out of the classroom while meeting with the teacher outside of the classroom to discuss the teacher's application of the reinforcement procedures. The modeling and feedback sessions were accompanied by improvements in the teacher's contingent use of token reinforcement but not in the use of praise statements.

Although results of antecedent management procedures as just described have been somewhat inconsistent in regard to increasing teachers' use of contingent attention to improve student behavior, overall there has been more support for the effectiveness of these types of management procedures with this area of teacher performance than with antecedent procedures in staff training and management in general (Chapters 3 and 4). The greater effectiveness of antecedent procedures with teacher attention-giving behavior is due primarily to the effective use of antecedent cueing strategies as discussed earlier. The relative efficacy of antecedent cueing procedures in this regard is perhaps best indicated in an investigation reported by Van Houten and Sullivan (1975) who compared an antecedent cueing procedure with a *consequence* strategy for increasing teacher praise rates. Specifically, audio-cueing was compared to *self-recording* (Chapter 4). During the first phase of the study, teachers in two classrooms were requested to count, using a wrist counter, each time they praised a student for his/her appropriate behavior. The teachers then calculated and graphed their praise rates. The teachers were instructed to try to maintain a praise rate of two praise statements per minute. No feedback or evaluative comments regarding the teachers' frequency of praise were provided by the experimenters. During the second phase of the study, the same teachers as well as another teacher in a third classroom were instructed by the experimenter to praise a student for appropriate classroom behavior every time the teachers heard a "beep" over the school intercom system (the audio cues were presented every two minutes). The auditory cues were accompanied by marked increases in teacher praise rates, whereas the self-recording process was not accompanied by significant increases.

In somewhat of a contrast to the results of the Van Houten and Sullivan investigation, Horton (1975) reported that the consequence procedure of self-recording was effective for increasing rates of teacher praise. In this case the teachers wore a small wireless microphone which transmitted the teachers' verbal behavior to an FM receiver connected to a tape recorder. The teachers subsequently recorded and graphed their rates of praise (for appropriate student behavior) as determined from their review of the tape recordings.

The investigations on classroom teacher performance discussed to this point have relied on observers entering respective classrooms to collect data on teacher behavior. As discussed in Chapter 2, a methodological concern when overtly observing staff performance is the reactive effect of staff to the observer's presence—and particularly when the observations are obtrusive. In this regard, an observer(s) entering a self-contained classroom specifically for the intended purpose of collecting data on teacher behavior can represent a rather obtrusive process. In order to evaluate a management program to improve teacher attention-giving performance *without* obtrusively observing teacher behavior, Gross and Ekstrand (1983) monitored teacher praise by using 30-minute cassette recordings of classroom activity. The recordings were conducted randomly during the day without the teachers being aware of the specific times the recordings were activated. Initially, the experimenter met with the staff to explain the importance of teacher praise on student behavior and to provide examples of how to appropriately praise such behavior. The experimenter also *publicly posted* graphs of the rate of teacher praise each day in the classroom. The public posting was accompanied by increases in the frequency of teacher praise based on an analysis of the (unobtrusive) tape recordings. Subsequently, the public posting was discontinued and the increased rate of praise maintained while the experimenter provided verbal feedback to the teacher one to two times per week.

Graphic data on teacher behavior has also been used to provide *privately written* feedback regarding teacher praise (Wasik, Senn, Welch & Cooper, 1969). Wasik et al. graphed daily rates of the type, duration, and frequency of teachers' verbal interactions with students as well as information on specified student performance. The data were provided individually to teachers and allowed a comparison of changes in teacher behavior with changes in student performance, as well as an examination of teacher consistency and immediacy of interactions with students. In a similar study using privately written feedback, elementary school teachers received information on a daily basis regarding student on-task rates and teacher attention-giving rates for the on-task behavior (Hall, Panyan, Rabon, & Broden, 1968). The privately written feedback in both the Wasik et al. and Hall et al. investigations appeared effective in increasing teacher attention-giving behavior.

In addition to written feedback, *verbal feedback* has been used in a number of programs focusing on teachers' use of contingent attention to improve the classroom management of student performance. For example, verbal feedback has been used in preschool programs and elementary schools in an attempt to help teachers increase their contingent attending behavior (Cooper, Thomson, & Baer, 1970; Kazdin & Klock, 1973). As with the use of verbal feedback in other areas of staff work activity in human service settings (Chapter 4), this management strategy has generally been effective in improving teacher attention-giving behavior.

In summary, a number of organizational behavior management procedures have been employed to increase teachers' use of attending or approval behavior to improve various aspects of student behavior in the classroom. However, there has also been a certain degree of inconsistency regarding the effectiveness of the various staff training and management procedures that have been evaluated. A brief summarization of the (in)effectiveness of the different antecedent and consequence procedures is presented in Table 9-1.

Training Teachers to Use Multi-Varied Behavioral Interventions to Manage Student Behavior. In contrast to the focus of the preceding section on training and managing teacher skills in using one particular type of classroom management procedure (i.e. contingent attention), this section addresses organizational behavior management research that centered on the development of staff competencies in using multi-varied classroom management strategies. In essence, the purpose of the latter set of investigations has been to evaluate methods of providing teachers with a broad repertoire of skills with which to address a variety of classroom management problems (Anderson, Kratochwill, & Bergan, 1986). In many ways, the intent has been to teach teachers a rather generic set of skills in order to conduct a behavior analysis of classroom problems and to alter their behavior management interventions based on the nature of the problems that are being addressed.

A variety of staff training and management procedures have frequently been incorporated into respective programs to improve teachers' use of multi-varied classroom management strategies. To illustrate, Templeman, Fredericks, Bunse, and Moses (1983) used a multifaceted management intervention to improve a number of teacher competencies, including use of: (a) a common behavioral vocabulary, (b) a task-analyzed curriculum, (c) systematic data-collection procedures to record individualized and group data on instructional programs, and (d) behavioral instructional and classroom management strategies. Templeman et al. initially sent teachers to a demonstration site where they received instruction on the application of behavioral techniques and theory. While at the

Table 9-1

STAFF TRAINING AND MANAGEMENT PROCEDURES USED IN INVESTIGATIONS
ON INCREASING TEACHER PRAISE

Procedure	Classroom Setting	Behavior Change	Reference
self-recording	special education/elementary	no	Van Houton & Sullivan, 1975
self-recording	elementary	yes	Horton, 1975
audio-cueing	special education/elementary	yes	Van Houton & Sullivan, 1975
audio cueing	elementary	yes	Bowles & Nelson, 1976
visual-cueing	elementary	yes	Hall, Lund, & Jackson, 1968
visual-cueing	special education	yes	Neef, Shafer, Egel, Cataldo, & Parrish, 1983
performance demonstration	elementary	no	Ringer, 1973
public posting	preschool handicapped	yes	Gross & Ekstrand, 1983
verbal feedback	elementary	yes	Cossairt, Hall & Hopkins, 1973
verbal feedback	preschool	yes	Cooper, Thomson, & Baer, 1970
verbal feedback	special education	yes	Kazdin & Klock, 1973
written feedback	elementary	yes	Hall, Lund, & Jackson, 1968
written feedback	demonstration/low-income	yes	Wasik, Senn, Welch, & Cooper, 1969
written feedback	elementary	yes	Hall, Panyan, Rabon, & Broden, 1968
multifaceted	elementary	yes	Speidel & Tharp, 1978

demonstration site, the teacher trainees also observed experienced staff in the demonstration classroom implementing the competencies being trained. Next, trainees practiced specified skills with students whose educational needs closely approximated the needs of the students in the teachers' own classrooms. Periodic videotaping and direct observation were used to monitor the teachers' performance in the demonstration classroom and to provide a basis for feedback on their performance proficiency. Upon completion of the performance-based training program, follow-up visits at the teachers' regular classrooms were conducted to monitor maintenance of the classroom management skills acquired during the demonstration-based training.

Teacher performance objectives similar to those in the Templeman et al. study were also addressed in a comparative analysis of the effects of different teacher training procedures (McKeown, Adams, & Forehand, 1975). McKeown et al. compared the effects of group instruction using a multifaceted training approach (written materials, lecture, discussion, and performance practice) with instruction based solely on written material. Results indicated that increased knowledge of general behavior management principles and procedures, as well as decreases in levels of classroom disruptive behavior among students, occurred only for those teachers who participated in the multifaceted training program.

A rather unique type of comprehensive training program designed to improve general classroom management skills involved the use of computer-assisted video instruction (Singer, Sowers, & Irvin, 1986). The computer-based program was evaluated with a teacher's aide in an attempt to train behavior modification skills for application with a deaf-blind child who was severely mentally retarded. Each of five lessons presented via the computer included a description of what the lesson would cover, a rationale for why the targeted skill (e.g. task analysis) was important, a description of performance components, a demonstration of the specified skill and questions and feedback related to the trainee's understanding of the content presentation. Results indicated that the trainee acquired and began using the majority of the classroom management techniques that were addressed by the training program.

Among the multifaceted training and management programs designed to improve teacher use of a variety of behavior modification procedures with students, a common component has been performance practice (e.g. Templeman et al., 1983; McKeown et al., 1975). Performance practice has also been used singularly or in conjunction with only a few other procedures to improve teacher performance in this area (Burka & Jones, 1979; Cowen, Jones, & Bellack, 1979; Jones & Eimers, 1975; Jones, Fremouw, & Carples, 1977). Typically, the performance practice or role playing (Chapter 3) occurred in a mock classroom in which trainees alternated playing the role of teacher and student. The performance practice was usually paired with positive and negative feedback and generally appeared successful in enhancing teacher use of a broad range of classroom management skills.

As noted earlier, a primary reason for the organizational behavior management attention given to teacher performance is an attempt to help teachers maintain state-of-the-art skills in classroom instruction and management. Leach and Dolan (1985) evaluated an interesting means of essentially teaching teachers to help themselves in this regard. Specifically, teachers were briefed on, and provided with, written summaries of research literature concerning classroom management strategies that could enhance student on-task levels. No specific recommendations were provided to the teachers in terms of which strategies the teachers should adopt. Observational data were then collected on student on-task levels, and this information was presented to the teachers in a nonevaluative manner following the teachers' review of the various research reports. Results suggested that the written information in conjunction with feedback concerning student performance effectively increased student on-task behavior. Although no formal data were collected, teachers were incidentally observed to increase their rates of contingent praise and attention, to modify task difficulty levels of assignments given to students, to minimize external distractions, and to give more direct instruction — changes in teacher behavior that at least in part were probably responsible for the improved student performance.

Improving Academic Instructional Skills of Teachers

To date, the vast majority of organizational behavior management investigations on methods of improving teacher performance have focused on classroom management skills as reflected in the preceding section. Although several of the studies just summarized attended to (albeit usually indirectly) the impact of improved classroom management of teachers on student academic achievement, the latter area typically received relatively minimal attention. In short, few studies have focused on improving teacher work skills that *directly* result in enhanced academic development of students. There have been two studies, however, that represent notable exceptions to the general inattention given to this area (Koegel, Russo, & Rincover, 1977; Langone, Koorland, & Oseroff, 1987). In each of these investigations, teacher instructional skills were carefully defined to reflect teachers' appropriate presentation of directions to students, use of prompting procedures to maximize the probability of evoking correct academic responses from students, and effective delivery of consequences immediately upon completion of student responses. Training procedures used in both studies to improve these types of teacher instructional methods included written materials, video and/or experimenter demonstration of the methods and performance practice paired with feedback. In each investigation these training procedures resulted in improvements in the teachers' use of the targeted teaching skills, with some subsequent improvements in student academic-related performance.

The Koegel et al. and Langone et al. investigations just noted represent rather rare but nevertheless effective use of behavioral staff training and management procedures for helping teachers become proficient in the application of behavior modification procedures for teaching basic academic skills to students. A related area of research that has also received minimal investigatory attention yet is of considerable importance is training and management procedures for helping teachers *design* behavior management programs. One investigation in the latter area was reported by Hundert (1982), who developed a training package to instruct teachers of multihandicapped deaf students to use a general problem-solving strategy for writing behavior modification programs. In the first phase of the study, teachers were taught how to develop student behavior change objectives and to measure student performance. In the second phase, teachers were trained how to write behavior modification programs to help the students master the designated objectives. The teacher training procedures for both phases centered on written instructions and verbal feedback. After training, teachers improved their program development skills as well as their proficient use of behavior modification instructional procedures, with resulting improvements in student skill acquisition.

Critique of the Literature

The purpose of this section is to critically review the teacher training and management research methodology in order to objectively evaluate the effectiveness of the organizational behavior management procedures that have been evaluated. Due in essence to the large number of investigations on teacher performance, a critique of each study will not be provided. Rather, the focus will be on general strengths and weaknesses in the research area as a whole.

Social Significance of Target Behaviors

Because the focus of behavioral teacher training and management procedures has been on improving teacher performance in the classroom in order to enhance student social behavior and/or academic skill acquisition, the social significance of the targeted teacher performances (and changes therein) should ultimately be determined based on improvements in student functioning. In this regard, approximately two-thirds of the studies reviewed in this chapter included a measure of student functioning. Examples of types of student behaviors that were monitored, and subsequently affected by changes in teacher behavior that accompanied a respective management intervention, are presented in Table 9-2. Results such as those exemplified in Table 9-2 suggest that the targeted teacher behaviors were indeed socially important. In regard to the studies that did not report student performance data, the social significance of the reported changes in teacher behavior cannot be definitively determined.

Table 9-2
SAMPLES OF CLASSROOM STUDENT BEHAVIORS
CHANGED AS A FUNCTION OF
MANAGEMENT INTERVENTIONS ON TEACHER PERFORMANCE

Student Behavior	Reference
Inappropriate/disruptive classroom behavior (e.g. out of seat, talking to other pupils, fighting, aggression)	Burka & Jones, 1979
	McKeown, Adams, & Forehand, 1975
	Cowen, Jones, & Bellack, 1979
	Jones, Fremouw, & Carples, 1977
	Jones & Eimers, 1975
Appropriate classroom behavior (e.g. begin work immediately, answering teacher questions, raising hand, writing in workbook)	Thomas, Becker & Armstrong, 1968
	Ringer, 1973
	Kazdin & Klock, 1973
	Burka & Jones, 1979
Compliance to requests	Neef, Shafer, Egel, Cataldo, & Parrish, 1983
Percent correct child responses	Koegel, Russo, & Rincover, 1977
Rate of productivity (arithmetic)	Jones, Fremouw, & Carples, 1977
	Jones & Eimers, 1975
Skill acquisition (e.g. social skills, reading, writing, spelling, math)	Hundert, 1982
	Cossiart, Hall, & Hopkins, 1973
Academic engagement rate	Leach & Dolan, 1985

Thoroughness and Reliability of Observation Systems

The majority of the studies reviewed included generally clear definitions of staff and/or student performance which allowed for a good understanding of the specific behaviors that were altered. Additionally, the observations of the targeted behaviors generally occurred with an acceptable level of interobserver agreement presented, which enhanced the credibility of the reported changes in classroom behavior. However, the sample of teacher and/or student behavior that was monitored in most investigations was quite small. The average duration of experimental sessions across the studies that systematically monitored staff and/or student behavior was only approximately 30 minutes. Consequently, it is not clear that reported changes in behavior during these (brief) sessions would be representative of changes throughout the approximate six-hour classroom day that occurs in most school programs (see Chapter 1 for elaboration on problems related to experimental sessions of short duration).

Validity of Experimental Designs

Approximately half of the studies reviewed used experimental designs that allowed for an experimentally sound demonstration that the training and/or management procedures employed were responsible for the reported changes in teacher behavior. The remaining studies used a variety of pre/post designs or AB designs, making it difficult to draw definitive conclusions as to whether respective management interventions were responsible for the behavior change noted.

Effectiveness of Management Interventions

From a rigid methodological standpoint, few studies experimentally assessed the effectiveness of one training procedure exclusively. Even in those cases in which one procedure such as feedback was the focus of an investigation, the procedure was typically paired with at least one other procedure such as verbal instruction. Hence, it is difficult to discern specifically which of the procedures employed in many of the investigations had the greatest impact on teacher behavior. However, essentially all studies reported some change in teacher behavior such that even though the efficacy of a procedure used in isolation was often unclear, respective behavioral management packages as a whole appeared quite effective. On a practical level, the lack of precise evaluation of singular management procedures is not especially problematic, because rarely would a given procedure be used totally in isolation (e.g. at least some verbal instruction typically accompanies most management interventions). The primary concern is for managers to know which procedures accompanied the use of a primary procedure in an investigation in order for managers to be able to implement the same overall management approach to improve teacher performance. Of course, as discussed in preceding chapters, from a time-efficiency standpoint it would be helpful to be able to delineate the specific components of interventions that are effective in order to eliminate (time-consuming) components that are not necessary.

The general efficacy of behavioral management interventions as reflected in the research as just summarized pertains to *short-term* changes in teacher behavior. In regard to *long-term* changes, the teacher training and management research has not provided a very substantial amount of information—less than one-third of the studies included any follow-up data. However, among the investigations that did report information on the durability of changes in teacher behavior that initially accompanied a management intervention, the results were rather encouraging in regard to maintenance of behavior change.

Staff Acceptability

As noted repeatedly in preceding chapters, a key variable affecting the ultimate outcome of a staff training or management program is staff acceptance of the program. Unfortunately, in this regard, few organizational behavior management investigations on teacher performance evaluated teacher acceptability, and only one investigation formally evaluated an aspect of acceptability (Singer et al., 1986). Consequently, minimal conclusions from the research can be drawn regarding teacher opinions of behavioral staff management procedures.

Recommended Management Approach for Improving Classroom Teacher Performance

Unlike the corresponding sections in preceding chapters regarding recommended management programs, this section will not describe a stepwise procedure for improving teacher performance. A detailed supervisory strategy for changing the types of teacher behaviors addressed by the investigations summarized in this chapter cannot be adequately described because of the *variety* of performance areas that have been targeted (e.g. teacher attention-giving skills for student social behavior, program development and writing skills, academic instructional skills). In essence, recommended managerial strategies would differ according to the type of teacher performance that is desired to be changed. However, there is a common nucleus of various supervisory approaches that are likely to be effective. Specifically, the managerial actions comprising the basic behavioral supervision model as described in Chapter 2 should represent the foundation of any organizational behavior management application with teacher performance (the interested reader is encouraged to review the information in Chapter 2 as well as recommended applications of the model in the "Recommendation" sections of preceding chapters).

As just alluded to, in order to effectively resolve respective problems with teacher performance, implementation of the components of the behavioral supervision model will most likely need to be altered based on the particular teacher behaviors of concern. In a general sense, improving comprehensive performance areas such as generic classroom management skills that are applicable across different types of student behavior problems will require a more diversified management approach (e.g. a multifaceted intervention) than improving more circumscribed performance areas such as teacher provision of contingent attention. The latter type of teacher performance can often be improved through the application of one or a few management strategies such as self-recording and verbal feedback.

Another general consideration in using the behavioral supervision model with teacher performance is to incorporate more of a reliance on antecedent management procedures relative to the usual application of the model. Antecedent procedures (e.g. audio-cueing)—which usually require less managerial time than consequence procedures—have been used more successfully in research on teacher performance than in research on other types of staff performance in other human service settings. As noted in Chapter 8 on administrative duties, there is some indication that antecedent management strategies are more effective with professional staff performance than with the work behavior of paraprofessional personnel. The fact that teachers receive considerably more formal educational preparation for their profession relative to paraprofessional staff in other human service settings may account for the increased efficacy of antecedent procedures (see the discussion concerning the Page et al., 1981, study in Chapter 8 as well as the Page et al. paper itself as referenced in Chapter 8 for elaboration on this issue).

Regardless of the specific antecedent and/or consequence management procedures used when implementing the behavioral supervision model, special concern should be directed to maintaining any improvements that are initially brought about with teacher behavior. As noted in the preceding section, organizational behavior management researchers have given relatively little attention to supervisory procedures for maintaining desired teacher performances. We recommend that efforts be directed at implementing systematic management programs for maintaining teacher behaviors of concern along the lines of some of the monitoring and feedback systems discussed in Chapter 5 for maintaining appropriate treatment provision in congregate care settings for dependent clients (see also Parsons, Schepis, Reid, McCarn, & Green, 1987). In essence, if managerial time and effort is directed to improving certain aspects of classroom teacher performance, then some additional time and effort seems warranted to periodically monitor the continuance of the improvements and to take responsive remedial steps if the improvements begin to diminish.

REFERENCES

Anderson, T.K., Kratochwill, T.R., & Bergan, J.R. (1986). Training teachers in behavioral consultation and training: An analysis of verbal behaviors. *Journal of School Psychology, 24,* 229–241.

Bowles, P.E. Jr., & Nelson, R.O. (1976). Training teachers as mediators: Efficacy of a workshop versus the bug-in-the-ear technique. *Journal of School Psychology, 14,* 15–26.

Burka, A.A., & Jones, F.H. (1979). Procedures for increasing appropriate verbal participation in special elementary classrooms. *Behavior Modification, 3,* 27–48.

Cooper, M.L., Thomson, C.L., & Baer, D.M. (1970). The experimental modification of teacher attending behavior. *Journal of Applied Behavior Analysis, 3,* 153–157.

Cossairt, A., Hall, R.V., & Hopkins, B.L. (1973). The effects of experimenter's instructions, feedback, and praise on teacher praise and student attending behavior. *Journal of Applied Behavior Analysis, 6,* 89–100.

Cowen, R.J., Jones, F.H., & Bellack, A.S. (1979). Grandma's rule with group contingencies—A cost-efficient means of classroom management. *Behavior Modification, 3,* 397–418.

Gross, A.M., & Ekstrand, M. (1983). Increasing and maintaining rates of teacher praise: A study using public posting and feedback fading. *Behavior Modification, 7,* 126–135.

Hall, R.V., Lund, D., & Jackson, D. (1968). Effects of teacher attention on study behavior. *Journal of Applied Behavior Analysis, 1,* 1–12.

Hall, R.V., Panyan, M., Rabon, D., & Broden, M. (1968). Instructing beginning teachers in reinforcement procedures which improve classroom control. *Journal of Applied Behavior Analysis, 1,* 315–322.

Horton, G.O. (1975). Generalization of teacher behavior as a function of subject matter specific discrimination training. *Journal of Applied Behavior Analysis, 8,* 311–319.

Hundert, J. (1982). Training teachers in generalized writing of behavior modification programs for multihandicapped deaf children. *Journal of Applied Behavior Analysis, 15,* 111–122.

Jones, F.H., & Eimers, R.C. (1975). Role playing to train elementary teachers to use a classroom management "skill package." *Journal of Applied Behavior Analysis, 8,* 421–433.

Jones, F.H., Fremouw, W., & Carples, S. (1977). Pyramid training of elementary school teachers to use a classroom management "skill package." *Journal of Applied Behavior Analysis, 10,* 239–253.

Kazdin, A.E., & Klock, J. (1973). The effect of nonverbal teacher approval on student attentive behavior. *Journal of Applied Behavior Analysis, 6,* 643–654.

Koegel, R.L., Russo, D.C., & Rincover, A. (1977). Assessing and training teachers in the generalized use of behavior modification with autistic children. *Journal of Applied Behavior Analysis, 10,* 197–205.

Langone, J., Koorland, M., & Oseroff, A. (1987). Producing changes in the instructional behavior of teachers of the mentally handicapped through inservice education. *Education and Treatment of Children, 10,* 146–164.

Leach, D.J., & Dolan, N.K. (1985). Helping teachers increase student academic engagement rate: The evaluation of a minimal feedback procedure. *Behavior Modification, 9,* 55–71.

McKeown, D. Jr., Adams, H.E., & Forehand, R. (1975). Generalization to the classroom of principles of behavior modification taught to teachers. *Behavior Research and Therapy, 13,* 85–92.

Neef, N.A., Shafer, M.S., Egel, A.L., Cataldo, M.F., & Parrish, J.M. (1983). The class specific effects of compliance training with "do" and "don't" requests: Analogue analysis and classroom application. *Journal of Applied Behavior Analysis, 16,* 81–99.

O'Leary, K.D., & O'Leary, S.G. (1972). *Classroom management: The successful use of behavior modification.* New York: Pergamon Press.

Parsons, M.B., Schepis, M.M., Reid, D.H., McCarn, J.E., & Green, C.W. (1987). Expanding the impact of behavioral staff management: A large-scale, long-term application in schools serving severely handicapped students. *Journal of Applied Behavior Analysis, 20,* 139–150.

Reid, D.H. (1987). *Developing a research program in human service agencies: A practitioner's guidebook.* Springfield, IL: Charles C Thomas.

Ringer, V.M.J. (1973). The use of a "token helper" in the management of classroom behavior problems and in teacher training. *Journal of Applied Behavior Analysis, 6,* 671–677.

Singer, G., Sowers, J., & Irvin, L.K. (1986). Computer-assisted video instruction for training paraprofessionals in rural special education. *Journal of Special Education Technology, 3*(8), 27–34.

Speidel, G.E., & Tharp, R.G. (1978). Teacher-training workshop strategy: Instructions, discrimination training, modeling, guided practice, and video feedback. *Behavior Therapy, 9,* 735–739.

Templeman, T.P., Fredericks, H.D.B., Bunse, C., & Moses, C. (1983). Teaching research in-service training model. *Education and Training of the Mentally Retarded, 18,* 245–252.

Thomas, D.R., Becker, W.C., & Armstrong, M. (1968). Production and elimination of disruptive classroom behavior by systematically varying teacher's behavior. *Journal of Applied Behavior Analysis, 1,* 35–45.

Van Houton, R., & Sullivan, K. (1975). Effects of an audio-cueing system on the rate of teacher praise. *Journal of Applied Behavior Analysis, 8,* 197–201.

Ward, M.H., & Baker, B.L. (1968). Reinforcement therapy in the classroom. *Journal of Applied Behavior Analysis, 1,* 323–328.

Wasik, B.H., Senn, K., Welch, R.H., & Cooper, B.R. (1969). Behavior modification with culturally deprived school children: Two case studies. *Journal of Applied Behavior Analysis, 2,* 181–194.

Chapter 10

SUMMARY AND KEY FUTURE DIRECTIONS

The research discussed in preceding chapters provides strong support for the viability of organizational behavior management as a means of effectively supervising staff performance in human service settings. Over 120 investigations have been reviewed that demonstrated a training and/or management strategy for improving some aspect of staff work behavior in a human service agency. In this regard, the fact that organizational behavior management has focused on applied research in human service agencies to empirically demonstrate the effectiveness of supervisory procedures is a feature that noticeably distinguishes organizational behavior management from other approaches to staff supervision (see introductory comments to this text).

The utility of behavioral strategies for training and managing the work behavior of human service staff has been best represented in the research on resolving the five major types of staff performance problems discussed in Chapters 5 to 9, respectively. These performance areas (i.e. ensuring active treatment in congregate care situations, conducting client training and treatment programs, maintaining acceptable absentee levels, fulfilling administrative responsibilities and providing classroom educational services) have received the major amount of attention from applied behavioral researchers, albeit at different levels of attention across the five areas. Additionally, there have been other performance areas that have been investigated to a degree by researchers in organizational behavior management that have not been addressed in-depth in this text. In particular, several investigators have focused on methods of improving direct care staffs' provision of personal care to institutionalized persons (Edwards & Bergman, 1982; Iwata, Bailey, Brown, Foshee, & Alpern, 1976; Korabek, Reid, & Ivancic, 1981; Lattimore, Stephens, Favell, & Risley, 1984) and/or such staffs' fulfillment of safety-related caregiving responsibilities (Alavosius & Sulzer-Azaroff, 1986; van den Pol, Reid, & Fuqua, 1983). Other behavioral researchers have evaluated methods of assisting classroom teachers in anxiety management (Forman, 1982; Sharp

& Forman, 1985) and helping preschool teachers to be more affectionate with their clients (Shreve, Twardosz, & Weddle, 1983).

Undoubtedly, there are other areas of human service staff performance that have been investigated at least somewhat within an organizational behavior management framework that we have not noted. Generally, however, an insufficient amount of research has been reported on performance areas other than what has already been discussed in this text to warrant research-based conclusions at this point. In this regard, although major advances in training and managing human service staff performance have occurred as a result of organizational behavior management research and application, the work is by no means complete; a comprehensive technology for supervising human service staff performance really does not yet exist. Rather, continued research in human service agencies is needed to continue progress toward the eventual development of such a technology. The purpose of this chapter is to discuss several key directions that we believe research should take in order that a practical and effective technology for managing the work performance of human service staff will indeed become a reality.

Future Directions

Essentially, the most productive venture for eventually developing a comprehensive technology for supervising staff performance would be for organizational behavior management researchers to continue working along the lines that began with the initial research in the early 1970s. Specifically, the research area as a whole should continue to address *additional types of staff performance problems* and to *refine existing managerial procedures* for better resolving respective problems with staff work activity (cf. Whitman, Scibak, & Reid, 1983, chap. 11). The latter direction— that of refining existing supervisory strategies for improving specific areas of staff performance—is likely to occur as a rather natural result of the continued growth of organizational behavior management as a problem-solving, epistemological process (Reid, 1987, chap. 1). The former direction—applying behavioral supervisory strategies to additional performance areas—is perhaps not such a natural result. Hence, this chapter section attempts to delineate some of the areas of human service staff performance that would be most advantageous to address from an organizational behavior management framework (the reader is also referred to the "Research Critique" sections of preceding chapters for reference to staff performance areas in need of research attention).

Using Behavioral Supervisory Procedures to Improve Staff Morale

One of the most frequently occurring problems affecting human service staff and supervisors alike is poor staff morale. Discussions of morale problems are commonplace in many human service agencies as well as in the professional literature (e.g. Horner & Hannah, 1984; Schinke, 1979). However, experimentally valid and/or empirically substantiated reports of specific supervisory procedures for resolving morale problems are essentially nonexistent. Because of the frequency of morale problems, as well as the lack of well-delineated and experimentally validated management procedures for resolving such problems, this area of staff performance warrants serious attention among organizational behavior management investigators.

Organizational behavior management strategies may be particularly advantageous for addressing staff morale problems relative to other types of managerial approaches for a variety of reasons. The first reason pertains to the somewhat ambiguous nature of "poor morale." Although individuals in human service fields may agree as to what poor morale refers to on a very general basis, rarely is the phenonemon defined to the degree that individuals agree as to specifically what staff are doing that indicates poor (or good) morale. Poor morale is usually described quite generally in regard to, for example, staff being dissatisfied with work or simply being "burned out." Although such descriptors are helpful for general communication purposes, they are not very useful for assisting a supervisor in identifying (and subsequently resolving) problems with staff morale. An organizational behavior management approach to problems with staff morale can assist a supervisor in delineating the area of staff activity that the supervisor should specifically address, and with which the supervisor should take subsequent corrective action.

Part of the reason that poor morale represents an ambiguous phenomenon as just noted is that usually there is no single staff behavior that represents a consistent indicator of poor morale. Rather, poor morale is typically assumed to exist when staff engage in a variety of activities such as, for example, frequent complaining, infrequent initiation of new work tasks, increased absenteeism and/or decreased intensity of work effort. Consequently, from a behavioral point of view, poor morale is perhaps best viewed as an interrelated *response class* of staff work activity. That is, the various staff work indices of poor morale as just exemplified should be targeted as a whole with a management intervention in contrast to the usual behavioral approach of intervening with each particular type of behavior (although each type of activity should still be clearly delineated as the first step in a behavioral supervisory strategy).

The second reason why an organizational behavior management approach can be relatively advantageous for resolving morale problems is the focus on positive means of changing staff work activity. The vast majority of supervisory procedures for changing and/or maintaining staff performance discussed in preceding chapters utilized positive consequences as the performance-change intervention (i.e. approving feedback, increased staff flexibility in arranging work schedules, special recognition, etc.). Generally, a reliance on positive managerial approaches has a beneficial impact on staff morale, at least relative to those supervisory approaches that focus on punishment-oriented, disciplinary action strategies for changing staff performance. In this respect, even though organizational behavior management investigations on specific areas of staff performance generally have not attended consistently to staff acceptance of managerial actions (see previous "Research Critique" chapter sections), across all investigations in all performance areas there have been numerous evaluations of staff acceptability. The overwhelming majority of the reported studies that evaluated staff acceptability indicated that staff have reacted quite favorably to behavioral managerial strategies (see in particular Green, Canipe, Way, & Reid, 1986; Greene, Willis, Levy, & Bailey, 1978; Korabek et al., 1981; Parsons, Schepis, Reid, McCarn, & Green, 1987).

The favorable reactions of staff to behavioral management procedures have generally been reported in respect to studies that evaluated the frequent provision of positive consequences that were clearly contingent on well-delineated staff work behaviors. Positive consequences can also be used in another way to beneficially impact staff morale. Specifically, supervisors can use a myriad of positive consequences as exemplified in Appendix A that are not necessarily provided on a frequent and clearly contingent basis in regard to specified staff behaviors. That is, positive consequences such as special recognition or commendation can be provided on a periodic basis for a general response class of overall satisfactory performance among certain staff persons—performance that involves many different aspects of acceptable work activity. The intent in the latter cases is not really to reinforce specific work behavior per se but, rather, to program a staff person's work environment in order to involve a number of desirable events.

In essence, the more desirable events in a staff member's work routine, the less likely it is that the staff person will dislike the work situation and develop morale problems. Supervisors can impact the staff work environment in such a manner by routinely—albeit on a relatively infrequent basis such as every few weeks—providing positive consequences for staff who are essentially exhibiting no apparent performance problems. In fact, it can be most helpful for supervisors to consider it a *routine part of the supervisory job* to periodically provide positive consequences (e.g., Employee of the Month recognition, a desired change in work duties, a detailed commendation memorandum) for overall satisfactory performance as a means of enhancing morale. Providing intermittent positive consequences for acceptable work performance on a general basis can be *independent* of the implementation of the specific component steps of the behavioral supervision model. As discussed in-depth in Chapter 2, systematic application of the entire behavioral supervisory model can be reserved for certain staff performance areas that are most crucial to any agency's service provision and/or are the most problematic at any given point in time. Less systematic and time-consuming applications of certain steps of the model (and particularly the provision of positive consequences in the manner as just noted) can then be used periodically to compliment the model for morale purposes.

Training and Managing Effective Supervisory Performance

Given the repeated demonstrations of effective applications of organizational behavior management procedures for improving the work activity of human service staff, an important direction for future research is training and managing *supervisor* performance in regard to competently using behavioral managerial procedures. As noted repeatedly in preceding chapters, effective behavior change and/or maintenance procedures are of little utility unless appropriate managerial personnel actually use the procedures. To date, behavioral investigators have only begun to address the issue of training and managing supervisory skills in using the types of management procedures discussed in this text (e.g. Conrin, 1983; Hanel, Martin, & Koop, 1983; Page, Iwata, & Reid, 1982). It seems likely that the same types of training and management procedures used with staff work behavior could also be effective with supervisory performance. However, given some differential effects of certain organizational behavior management procedures with different populations of human service personnel as noted in Chapters 5 and 9, it is also likely that some variations in managerial practices with supervisors will be necessary. The exact degree to which such variations are warranted can really only be determined through increased research efforts on improving supervisory performance.

Expanding the Impact of Organizational Behavior Management

A direction for future research that is related to training and managing supervisor performance is expanding the scope of the impact of organizational behavior management in the human services (cf. Reid & Whitman, 1983). The vast majority of behavioral management investigations to date have generally been restricted to relatively small-scale demonstration projects (Frederiksen, 1984; Mayhew, Enyart & Cone, 1979). Studies have typically addressed only a small portion of an agency's staff and/or client population for relatively brief samples of an agency's routine service provision (Christian, 1983). In order to more significantly impact human services, investigations are needed to demonstrate that organizational behavior management approaches can be effectively applied in a comprehensive fashion across large domains of respective agencies' service responsibilities. Such comprehensive, and effective, applications of behavioral supervisory approaches are beginning to be reported in several different types of human service agencies, including residential settings for developmentally disabled persons (Dyer, Schwartz, & Luce, 1984; Parsons, Cash, & Reid, in press), schools (Parsons et al., 1987) and psychiatric hospitals (Prue, Krapfl, Noal, Cannon, & Maley, 1980). The successful results of these applications, albeit small in number at this point, should provide serious optimism for the continued and expanded utility of organizational behavior management for significantly improving the human services. It is hoped that this text will serve the function of assisting, and perhaps encouraging, specific research efforts to continue the development and application of managerial practices for enhancing human service provision.

REFERENCES

Alavosius, M.P., & Sulzer-Azaroff, B. (1986). The effects of performance feedback on the safety of client lifting and transfer. *Journal of Applied Behavior Analysis, 19,* 261–267.

Christian, W.P. (1983). A case study in the programming and maintenance of institutional change. *Journal of Organizational Behavior Management, 5*(3/4), 99–153.

Conrin, J. (1983). A comparison of two types of antecedent control over supervisory behavior. *Journal of Organizational Behavior Management, 4*(3/4), 37–47.

Dyer, K., Schwartz, I.S., & Luce, S.C. (1984). A supervision program for increasing functional activities for severely handicapped students in a residential setting. *Journal of Applied Behavior Analysis, 17,* 249–259.

Edwards, G., & Bergman, J.S. (1982). Evaluation of a feeding training program for caregivers of individuals who are severely physically handicapped. *Journal of the Association for the Severely Handicapped, 7,* 93–101.

Forman, S.G. (1982). Stress management for teachers: A cognitive-behavioral program. *Journal of School Psychology, 20,* 180–187.

Frederiksen, L.W. (1984). Discussion – "If it's not implemented, it can't work." *Journal of Organizational Behavior Management, 6*(2), 45–52.

Green, C.W., Canipe, V.S., Way, P.J., & Reid, D.H. (1986). Improving the functional utility and effectiveness of classroom services for students with profound multiple handicaps. *The Journal of the Association for Persons with Severe Handicaps, 11,* 162–170.

Greene, B.F., Willis, B.S., Levy, R., & Bailey, J.S. (1978). Measuring client gains from staff-implemented programs. *Journal of Applied Behavior Analysis, 11,* 395–412.

Hanel, F., Martin, G., & Koop, S. (1983). Field testing of a self-instructional time management manual with managerial staff in an institutional setting. *Journal of Organizational Behavior Management, 4*(3/4), 81–96.

Horner, R.D., & Hannah, G.T. (1984). State level coordination of the transition from institution-based to community-based services. In W.P. Christian, G.T. Hannah, & T.J. Glahn (Eds.), *Programming effective human services: Strategies for institutional change and client transition* (pp. 267–288). New York: Plenum Press.

Iwata, B.A., Bailey, J.S., Brown, K.M., Foshee, T.J., & Alpern, M. (1976). A performance-based lottery to improve residential care and training by institutional staff. *Journal of Applied Behavior Analysis, 9,* 417–431.

Korabek, C.A., Reid, D.H., & Ivancic, M.T. (1981). Improving needed food intake of profoundly handicapped children through effective supervision of institutional staff performance. *Applied Research in Mental Retardation, 2,* 69–88.

Lattimore, J., Stephens, T.E., Favell, J.E., & Risley, T.R. (1984). Increasing direct care staff compliance to individualized physical therapy body positioning prescriptions: Prescriptive checklists. *Mental Retardation, 22,* 79–84.

Mayhew, G.L., Enyart, P., & Cone, J.D. (1979). Approaches to employee management: Policies and preferences. *Journal of Organizational Behavior Management, 2*(2), 103–111.

Page, T.J., Iwata, B.A., & Reid, D.H. (1982). Pyramidal training: A large-scale application with institutional staff. *Journal of Applied Behavior Analysis, 15,* 335–351.

Parsons, M.B., Cash, V.B., & Reid, D.H. (in press). Improving residential treatment services: Implementation and norm-referenced evaluation of a comprehensive management system. *Journal of Applied Behavior Analysis.*

Parsons, M.B., Schepis, M.M., Reid, D.H., McCarn, J.E., & Green, C.W. (1987).

Expanding the impact of behavioral staff management: A large-scale, long-term application in schools serving severely handicapped students. *Journal of Applied Behavior Analysis, 20,* 139–150.

Prue, D.M., Krapfl, J.E., Noah, J.C., Cannon, S., & Maley, R.F. (1980). Managing the treatment activities of state hospital staff. *Journal of Organizational Behavior Management, 2*(3), 165–181.

Reid, D.H. (1987). *Developing a research program in human service agencies: A practitioner's guidebook.* Springfield, IL: Charles C Thomas.

Reid, D.H., & Whitman, T.L. (1983). Behavioral staff management in institutions: A critical review of effectiveness and acceptability. *Analysis and Intervention in Developmental Disabilities, 3,* 131–149.

Schinke, S.P. (1979). Staff training in group homes: A family approach. In L.A. Hamerlynck (Ed.), *Behavioral systems for the developmentally disabled: II. Institutional, clinic, and community environments* (pp. 222–238). New York: Brunner/Mazel.

Sharp, J.J., & Forman, S.G. (1985). A comparison of two approaches to anxiety management for teachers. *Behavior Therapy, 16,* 370–383.

Shreve, C., Twardosz, S., & Weddle, K. (1983). Development and evaluation of procedures to encourage teacher affectionate behavior in day care centers. *Behavior Therapy, 14,* 706–713.

van den Pol, R.A., Reid, D.H., & Fuqua, R.W. (1983). Peer training of safety-related skills to institutional staff: Benefits for trainers and trainees. *Journal of Applied Behavior Analysis, 16,* 139–156.

Whitman, T.L., Scibak, J.W., & Reid, D.H. (1983). *Behavior modification with the severely and profoundly retarded: Research and application.* New York: Academic Press.

POPULAR PERFORMANCE CONSEQUENCES FOR MOTIVATING HUMAN SERVICE STAFF PERFORMANCE

The information presented in this appendix is based on a national survey of managers in public residential facilities for the mentally retarded (Green & Reid, 1988). Over 460 managers (Directors of Residential Programs and Directors of Psychology) responded to a mailed questionnaire regarding performance consequences they used to motivate or reinforce the work performance of direct care staff. The responses of the managers are grouped into six categories of types of performance consequences (or motivators): feedback, tangible items, special privileges, special recognition, organizational involvement, and general miscellaneous. The following listings present the consequences reported by managers within each category. The performance consequences that were used by five or more managers in different facilities around the United States are indicated by an asterisk (*).

FEEDBACK

* • written feedback: short notes, memos
* • feedback based on formal work plans, evaluations using pre-established performance objectives
* • publicly posted feedback
* • general verbal feedback
* • self-posting of information on work behavior
* • videotaped feedback
* • information on client progress
* • peer/professional verbal feedback
* • quality assurance information

TANGIBLES ITEMS

These are items that have some monetary value.

* • free meals
* • gift certificates
* • lottery tickets for prize drawing
* • recognition gifts (pins, shirts, baseball caps)
  • savings bonds
  • award of professional books
  • "We Care" pins
  • birthday cards
  • discount coupons

PRIVILEGES

These have been classified as idiosyncratic opportunities to do something desirable at work that would normally not be available.

* • attendance at conferences, workshops
* • opportunity to work on special projects
* • flexible work schedules
* • individualized parking space
  • tuition paid for attending school classes
  • choice of holiday time
  • time granted for research projects
  • time granted for physical fitness programs
  • organize own work day
  • group trips
  • every other weekend off
  • consultation opportunities

SPECIAL RECOGNITION AND AWARDS

Consequences designed to provide highly noticeable commendation that have no monetary value.

* • employee of the month/year
* • recognition in newsletter, local newspaper
* • formal recognition certificate
  • peer-selected "high performer"
  • work group selected as unit of month or quarter
  • telephone contact from senior administrator

- special ceremony for attendance
- recognition on "grounds" signs

ORGANIZATIONAL

These are privileges that are intended to impact the management operation of a facility.

* • increased staff involvement in manageral decisions
* • supervisor "hands-on" activity with staff
* • supervisor sharing work-related information
* • obtaining higher organizational status
* • increasing clarity of job expectations
* • participating in quality circles
- job rotation
- stable work teams
- seniority for shift assignment

MISCELLANEOUS

- on-campus day care
- on-campus housing

Overall, the most frequently reported means of reinforcing staff performance (63 respondents) in response to the open-ended question regarding consequences used to motivate staff performance was increasing staff involvement in management decision making.

REFERENCE

Green, C.W., & Reid, D.H. (1988). *Reinforcing staff performance in residential facilities: A survey of common and effective managerial practices.* Manuscript submitted for publication.

AUTHOR INDEX

229

SUBJECT INDEX

A

Absenteeism, 4, 10, 31, 84, 147–170, 217
  acceptable vs. unacceptable, 149–151,
    166–167
  chronic, 157, 161–162
  definition, 148–149, 153–154
  duration absenteeism, 149, 151
  high-frequency absenteeism, 148
  predictable absenteeism, 149, 161
  reduction procedures, 154–157
  scheduled vs. unscheduled, 149, 155–156,
    162
Academic instructional skills, 199, 208–209
Acceptability (of supervisory practices),
    15–16, 60–61, 114, 107–109, 141,
    162–164, 168, 184–185, 191, 212,
    220–221
Accreditation Council on Services for People
    with Developmental Disabilities, 175
Administrative performance, 4, 10, 55–56,
    171–196
  definition, 172
  characteristics, 172–174, 190–191, 192
Affectionate behavior, 218
Age appropriate activities (for clients), 108
Antecedent supervisory procedures (see also
    *audio cueing, differentiated prompting, goal
    setting, instructional supervisory procedures,
    modeling, prompting, training, visual
    cueing*), 11, 19, 57, 70–76, 105, 112, 131,
    149, 154, 164–165, 176–178, 181–182,
    189–191, 201–203, 213
Anxiety management, 217–218
Applied behavioral research, 46
  characteristics, 9
  criteria, 12–16
  problem-solving, 197
Audio cueing, 201–202, 203, 206, 213

B

Business (nonhuman service), 5–6, 164–165
Behavior management (see *behavior
    modification*)
Behavior modification, 53–55, 132–133, 142,
    200–209

C

Checklists, 24–25, 181, 193
Classroom-based training, 58–59, 130, 131–132,
    176–177 ·
Classroom management, 199–208
Client behavior (as index of staff
    performance), 5, 13, 32, 39–40, 86,
    101–102, 110, 115–116, 119, 139–140, 142,
    155, 158, 178, 183, 186–187, 208–209, 210
Consequence supervisory procedures (see also
    *feedback, monetary consequences,
    punishment, reinforcement, self-recording*),
    11, 19, 57, 70, 73, 76–89, 105, 109,
    130–131, 134–135, 144, 154–157, 165,
    167–169, 178–179, 181–182, 189–191,
    203–205, 213, 225–227
Computer-assisted instruction, 194, 207

D

Differentiated prompting, 75–76, 93
Documentation performance (see also
    administrative performance), 173–174, 175,
    176–182, 193

E

Evaluation (see also *monitoring*), 27, 145, 150,
    192

235